FOOD IN THE CIVIL WAR ERA

Books in the American Food in History Series

FOOD
IN THE CIVIL WAR ERA

THE NORTH

Edited by Helen Zoe Veit

Michigan State University Press

EAST LANSING

♾ The paper used in this publication meets the minimum requirements
of ANSI/NISO Z39.48-1992 (R 1997) (Permanence of Paper).

Michigan State University Press
East Lansing, Michigan 48823-5245

Printed and bound in the United States of America.

20   19   18   17   16   15   14   1   2   3   4   5   6   7   8   9   10

Library of Congress Cataloging-in-Publication Data
Food in the Civil War era : the North / edited by Helen Zoe Veit.
pages cm.— (American food in history)
Includes bibliographical references and index.
ISBN 978-1-61186-122-8 (cloth : alkaline paper)—ISBN 978-1-60917-412-5 (ebook)
1. Cooking, American—History—19th century. 2. Cooking, American—History—19th
century—Sources. 3. Cookbooks—United States—History—19th century. 4. United States—
History—Civil War, 1861–1865—Social aspects. 5. Food—United States—History—
19th century. 6. Food—Social aspects—United States—History—19th century.
7. Food habits—United States—History—19th century. I. Veit, Helen Zoe.
TX715.F684 2014
641.5973—dc23
2013025306

Cover and book design by Erin Kirk New
Cover illustration is from N. K. M. Lee, *The Cook's Own Book: An American Family Cook Book*
(New York: James Miller, 1864), front matter, MSUSC.

Michigan State University Press is a member of the Green Press Initiative and
is committed to developing and encouraging ecologically responsible publishing practices.
For more information about the Green Press Initiative and the use of recycled paper
in book publishing, please visit www.greenpressinitiative.org.

Visit Michigan State University Press at www.msupress.org.

CONTENTS

ACKNOWLEDGMENTS

I gathered many debts as the editor of a new series on historical cooking. The idea for the series came from Gabriel Dotto at the Michigan State University Press, and he has been an unflagging supporter of the project for years now. I am extremely grateful for his enthusiasm and his many excellent ideas. This book would not exist without him. I am also grateful to the other good people at the press who made this book a reality, especially Kristine M. Blakeslee, Travis Kimbel, and Annette Tanner. The authors of the introduction, Kelly Sisson Lessens and Adam Arenson, were both wonderful to work with, and I am grateful to have their excellent article as the introduction to the book. I am also very thankful for the help of Jan Longone and JJ Jacobson at the Janice Bluestein Longone Culinary Archive at the University of Michigan.

Lastly, I owe an enormous debt of gratitude to the staff of Michigan State University's Special Collections, especially Leslie Behm and Peter Berg. Leslie's help was indispensable. She spent hours converting cribbed printed texts to readable modern type, and she tirelessly digitized dozens of images. I can't thank her enough for her time and hard work. Peter was enthusiastic about the series from the start, and he very generously put Special Collections' vast cookery resources at my disposal. I'm not sure he realized how fully I would take advantage of his generosity, but I know he is as delighted as I am to be able to make some of the collection's holdings more widely available through this book.

FOOD IN THE CIVIL WAR ERA

Feeding the North

KELLY J. SISSON LESSENS AND ADAM ARENSON

Before dawn on April 12, 1861, cannons opened fire on Fort Sumter, the federal installation in Charleston Harbor, South Carolina. With this act, the newly formed Confederacy put force behind its objections to President Abraham Lincoln and moved to make the secession of seven states—soon to be joined by four more—a permanent separation from the United States.

The firing on Fort Sumter involved military strategy, political bluster, and martial enthusiasm. But it was also about food. While supporters of the new Confederate government simply seized many federal arsenals throughout the South, Fort Sumter was one of the military installations that held out in the face of a blockade from Southern forces. Yet its commander, Major Robert Anderson, knew that he could only maintain Fort Sumter as a Union bulwark as long he had ammunition, firewood, and food. Anticipating both the arrival of these supplies and the protracted federal occupation that they would enable, Major Anderson refused to surrender. His Confederate opponents knew from the outset that regional systems of agriculture, transportation, markets, and consumption would likely favor the North, and the confrontation at Fort Sumter was an early example of the Confederate need to overcome this advantage. It was the chance to attack before food arrived in a Union flotilla that led to the cannon's blare that April morning.[1]

As the Civil War began, each side had to consider anew the questions central to the human experience: What will we eat? Where will we get it? How can we cook it? And can we preserve it for another day? The answers to these questions had changed dramatically in the previous generation. In the areas of the country that coalesced into what we call the Civil War North, patterns of urbanization, immigration, and industrialization transformed the rituals and tasks associated with food production and consumption. The mobilization of the massive Union army and the provisioning for its needs required products that could be produced in large volumes and with less labor, stored for long periods, and distributed to soldiers in far-flung

"Halt of a Wagon Train" depicted Union soldiers cooking over an open fire. *Harper's Weekly*, February 6, 1864, 88–89, Michigan State University Special Collections.

locations. As individuals and institutions responded to wartime needs, they also permanently altered the manners in which Northern civilians procured and prepared their meals. By the end of the Civil War, therefore, Northerners would confront a host of new food products and adopt novel culinary practices. The new conception of the rest of the North as the Union home front continued and ramified these changes in the ways these cookbooks make evident.

This essay starts with the most general view, gazing down on the nation's farms, and then we work our way through the fields, on the canals and trains, into the markets, and then finally onto the tables of Northerners

before and during the Civil War. Along the way, it will go west with the wagons on the overland trails, stow away with Americans traveling at sea, and peek into the packs of Union soldiers on the march. After all, as a journalist declared in 1857, "Everywhere, people *will* eat."[2] By exploring how these trends transformed the material, economic, and cultural landscapes of the North before and during the Civil War, this essay will provide insight into the dramatic changes—and fascinating continuities—that shaped Americans and the foods they ate.

To understand food in the Civil War era, it's necessary to understand the many changes that had taken place in food, farming, and transportation in the previous decades. It all begins on the farms. In 1815, the United States was largely a nation of farms, and no regions more closely matched Thomas Jefferson's vision of a nation of yeoman farmers—grounding their governing philosophies in their experience with the land—than the states of New England, the mid-Atlantic, and the emerging Middle West. More than 90 percent of all Americans lived on farms, and these individuals worked most of the time just to produce the food and goods that would sustain them throughout each year, in seasons of plenty and in seasons of want. Farm families were always engaged with larger markets; indeed, they could not have purchased coffee, tea, spices, molasses, or any number of manufactured goods without having produced items such as butter, homespun, or wheat to sell in larger regional or international markets. But, by and large, they produced most of the food that they expected to consume.[3]

Seasonal changes had long ruled these farm families' cycles of food production. Energy available from the sun, wind, and water as well as farm animals' own reproduction patterns had direct bearing on a family's food supplies. For farmers and their children, springtime meant plowing furrows in the ground, sowing seeds, and cultivating fields to prevent weeds from overtaking young crops. Nearly all northern farms raised maize (corn), a highly adaptable plant that could be eaten fresh in the summer or, after being dried on the stalk during the fall, ground into meal. Depending on their location, which influenced soil type, weather patterns, and access to

regional markets, farm families would also usually grow some combination of hay, potatoes, oats, wheat, rye, or buckwheat, each of which had its own set of planting rituals and cultivation requirements. Domesticated animals and cultivated plants would themselves do part of the work to transform the local environment to better serve their needs.[4] The seasons also dictated which foods would be available, a reality reflected in all the cookbooks excerpted here.

While men performed the bulk of field work, women and children provided crucial labor during time-sensitive planting and harvesting seasons. In spring women returned to the garden, where—in addition to maintaining their daily milking duties, tending poultry, preparing family meals, and raising children—they produced the family's vegetable stores, including cabbages, carrots, and turnips. Spring was the time that cows, pigs, and sheep bore their young, while chickens also laid the bulk of their eggs during this season of renewal. During the late spring and early summer, excess male calves and chicks—animals that would not contribute to food stores as rapidly as cows' and hens' female offspring, which provided milk and eggs—frequently provided meat for the family table or extra cash after sale. Meanwhile, women scrambled to churn butter and preserve eggs during these weeks of bounty.

In the late fall and early winter, families harvested crops and slaughtered more animals, especially hogs. Come November and December, the onset of cold weather enabled farm families to preserve meat. After the hogs had been killed, bled, and their carcasses scalded and left to cool, women would brine slabs of pork in one-hundred-pound barrels of salt, vinegar, and spices to preserve the meat for the coming months. They would also render the animals' fat into soap for household laundering, or lard for frying, baking, and emulsifying. "Fritters" of all kinds, fried oysters and fried fish, staples such as cornmeal "slapjacks" and pie "pastes," and treats such as gingerbread all depended on the supply of rendered animal fat.[5]

Although these practices were far from unchanging, northern farm families and urban dwellers alike faced new choices as the nation's increasingly integrated economy cycled through booms and busts, and as the first sustained wave of industrialization coupled with new patterns of immigration. After the Panic of 1819, the first major financial crisis of the nineteenth century, market prices and land values alike dropped. Meanwhile, the soil on many older farmsteads was becoming worn out to the point that raising crops was no longer financially sustainable. The new generation on the farms therefore had two options: either leave in pursuit of opportunities elsewhere, or improve the quality of their soils.

While many, as we shall see, looked west to newly opened lands in places such as Illinois and Indiana, or emigrated to cities to obtain nonagricultural jobs, a cadre of farmers began to promote soil "improvement," a practice of rotating crops and proactively applying manure to worn-out soils in hopes of enriching the land and rescuing established communities from emigration-caused population losses. James Pemberton Morris, of Bucks County, Pennsylvania, was one such "improver." Between 1823 and 1824, Morris grew and raised root vegetables and cover crops in addition to his wheat, hay, and garden vegetables, so he could create productive meadows for the merino sheep he bred for wool and the cattle he selected for his dairy. Morris also planted oats in the fruit orchards, to ensure that grazing cattle would manure the land. Writing in proceedings of the Philadelphia Society for Promoting Agriculture, Morris advocated soil conservation by way of capital-intensive improvements as the best means to maintain his community and his investments in local land.[6]

Morris was an elite farmer and a prosperous man. But for farm families without his financial or labor resources—or for those unconvinced of the merits of his improvement schemes—the best option was often to move on. Ongoing developments within northern states' transportation networks were increasing the connections between eastern cities and western lands.

The nation's "internal improvements"—canals, better roads and waterways, and finally railroads—proved crucial to the task of creating new opportunities for farmers and immigrants alike. They would also make new kinds and quantities of foods available to growing numbers and concentrations of city dwellers.

The completion of the Erie Canal was the signature transportation accomplishment of the era. Constructed between 1817 and 1825, the canal relied on a system of locks that connected the Great Lakes to the Atlantic

Ocean by linking Buffalo to New York City, via the Hudson River. Because floating goods on water was easier and faster than hauling heavy items overland—especially through the Appalachian mountain passes—the canal radically reduced the cost of transporting grain and other products from the fertile western valleys to the bulk of northeastern consumers, and to markets across the Atlantic. These changes led to a new economic environment and enabled greater specialization: by the 1830s, as the historian Ann Vileisis writes, "even frugal Yankee farmers" were purchasing "mass produced flour . . . from afar instead of growing [wheat] for themselves."[7]

Soon railroads joined canals in creating new points of access between food-producing regions and burgeoning urban markets. In New York City, for example, "distillery dairies" had long produced milk for urban consumers by feeding the cows the mash left over from the whiskey-production process. The milk they produced, however, was often so foul it was dangerous. But soon after the opening of the Erie Railroad in 1841, milk produced in Orange County, New York, could arrive in New York City four and a half hours later. In less than a decade, eight million gallons of milk were being delivered each year along that route.[8]

For those who moved west, new farms not only had unexhausted soils and better transportation options, but they also had more efficient shapes. Historically, the boundaries of eastern farms had followed streams or hills, or had been delineated by particular natural markers enhanced by wooden fences.[9] But in 1785, Thomas Jefferson changed those patterns with the Northwest Land Ordinance. Although Jefferson intended that the act promote orderly settlement, it also had the effect of creating a checkerboard system for surveying and distributing western lands. Because these new parcels did not follow natural contours or wander around obstacles but instead conformed to a surveyor's marks, settlers could purchase square swaths of land to plow in long, straight, efficient lines. As a result, western farmers began to enjoy new economies of scale that were unheard-of in more densely populated eastern farm communities.[10]

Who were the new midwestern farmers? The earliest white settlers to the best agricultural regions west of the Appalachians—Ohio's Miami and Scioto valleys—were actually upland southerners.[11] Though they were largely of English, Scotch-Irish, and German descent, these upland southerners had brought the descendants of the hogs and cattle that those Spanish explorers such as Hernando De Soto had, centuries earlier, carried to the Americas from Europe. They also brought with them a particular kind of corn that Spaniards had brought from Mexico to what became the southeastern United States during the sixteenth century. It was a soft variety known as "Dent," notable for the ease with which cattle and hogs could chew it, and supposedly named for the dent that appeared in the kernel when it dried. And because these upland southerners had long practiced meat production by feeding animals with corn, they also continued regional traditions of building corncribs and smokehouses on their farms.[12]

Though the natural attributes of the Miami and Scioto valleys varied, their appeal can be attributed to two longer historical trajectories. First, these regions had received rich glacial deposits, making their soil deep, dark, and fertile. Second, Native Americans had long improved those lands by means of prairie burning and tree girdling to further their own agricultural practices. These tracts thus already comprised prime agricultural landscapes when white scouts and settlers initially encountered them.[13] Scioto Valley settlers drove corn-fed cattle to sale in eastern markets; Miami Valley farmers took advantage of that region's river system to ship slaughtered and barreled animals to southern markets.[14] In Ohio, it was these up-country southerners—not later Yankee migrants—who brought the practices that structured what became known as "Corn Belt" agricultural production: large corn crops fattening stock.[15]

During the 1820s and 1830s, these emigration patterns spread north and west, as settlers from Kentucky, Tennessee, and Virginia joined the children of the first white Miami and Scioto Valley settlers on fertile Illinois prairies.[16] Sangamon County, Illinois, became home to one such settlement of farmers. Within a decade, Sangamon County farmers with southern roots were leading all of Illinois in corn production, and they disposed of their 1.4 million bushels by feeding the crop to their 90,000 cows and hogs. One emigrant family, the Lincolns, moved from Ken-

tucky to Indiana and into Sangamon County, Illinois, thereby shaping the worldview of their son, the future president.[17] This is another way, however remote, that the food-production patterns of the evolving North shaped the course of the Civil War.

After 1830, interior regions filled with newcomers, including emigrants not only from the upland South but also from the Northeast and overseas. Many of these settlers moved west as family units, selling eastern farms to avoid facing family separation, as sons and daughters sought plots large enough and fertile enough to provide for future generations.[18] Meanwhile, the United States' population quadrupled between 1820 and 1850—not as much through natural increase as through the greatest period of immigration in the nation's history. Increasing numbers of German and Irish immigrants fleeing political strife and famine joined British and Scottish immigrants seeking better opportunities.[19]

Many of these newcomers settled in the river valleys of America's interior, often lured by the boasts of land speculators.[20] There they balanced old foodways and agricultural traditions with new opportunities and resources. Many German peasants settled into life in America as "gardener-farmers," regularly producing familiar foods including sausages and sauerkraut on their holdings in Pennsylvania and places farther west. Sauerkraut, a fermented cabbage dish, was a "cold-weather food" eaten with different accompaniments during the year: fresh pork during the fall, turkey at Christmas, pork on New

Year's Day for good luck, salt pork in late winter, and fish during Lent.[21]

As settlers moved onto apparently endless tracts of "virgin" land, they exchanged the intensive, closed-nutrient, manure-saving methods of eastern farms for new tools and implements with which they sought to "tame" western soil.[22] In turn, they transformed what and how they—and the rest of the nation—ate. On farms throughout western states and territories, tools such as the mechanical reaper, invented in 1831, dramatically increased harvesting speed, and by extension, the total acreage that one farmer might cultivate.

Because wheat is so sensitive to the vagaries of weather—if gathered wet, for instance, it can rot, sprout, or spoil—growing large quantities of wheat at a given time had long been untenable. But the McCormick Company's reaper, introduced in 1845, surmounted this problem and enabled farmers to engage in extensive wheat production in western states and territories.[23] This machine decreased the hours needed to harvest wheat, made wheat flour available at much more affordable prices, and prompted widespread dietary shifts among antebellum Americans. The reaper's effects became especially clear during the Civil War. By one estimate, every reaper enabled two or three men to leave the farm and enlist in the army.[24] Massive volumes of cheap wheat, moreover, would not only be processed into "hardtack" (flour and water mixtures baked slowly into durable crackers) for soldiers on the move, but, as an integral item of wartime trade, would disincline

A guide to pig carving. Miss Eliza Acton, *Modern Cookery in All its Branches* (Philadelphia: John Potter, 1861), 186, Michigan State University Special Collections.

Great Britain—which needed American grain to feed its citizens—from formally recognizing the Confederacy.[25]

Like the reaper, John Deere's "singing plow," made of curved steel (which hummed as it broke through dense soil) and patented in 1837, became another vital tool of extensive western agriculture and a key factor in the engine of food production that supported the North during the war.[26] The thick root systems anchoring ancient prairie grasses to the land were so dense that they stymied emigrant farmers' efforts to use traditional wooden plows, or even rough iron ones, to turn over the soil. But starting in the 1850s, Deere's company began to make plows of cast steel, which were able to cut through those roots with comparable ease.[27]

As the war turned more decisively in favor of the North by
early 1864, this illustration from *Harper's Weekly* contrasted the
abundance of food and able-bodied men in the North with the
scarcity of both in the South. *Harper's Weekly*, January 2, 1864, 8–9,
Michigan State University Special Collections.

Collectively, tools such as reapers, plows, threshers, and mowers allowed farmers to replace tall-grass prairies with wheat, corn, cattle, and hogs and permitted agricultural production to soar. Between 1849 and 1859, for example, the nation's corn production increased more than 40 percent, while wheat production shot up by 70 percent.[28] In 1850, the Corn Belt states of Illinois, Indiana, Ohio, and Iowa had more than 20 million acres in agricultural production. A decade later, that number had climbed to nearly 38 million.[29] Because southerners increasingly relied on cotton production and its profits to finance their society before the war, instead of diversifying their agricultural output, the tremendous growth in antebellum northern grain production would offer a clear advantage for the North after secession.

This surplus benefitted the North in other ways. Because midwestern farmers were able to fatten more cattle and hogs on greater amounts of grain, the country's major meat-processing centers became increasingly centered in northern states. Many of the foodstuffs that farm families produced moved downstream to interior cities, which were the hubs of processing and distribution, and from there to eastern and southern consumers. In urban centers such as Cincinnati and Chicago, packers mastered the art of the "disassembly line," butchering large numbers of hogs or cattle with terrific efficiency. Because their expenses were so low, they could afford to pay the region's farmers higher prices and to create mutually beneficial networks of trade in food products.[30]

These midwestern hubs grew in direct proportion both to the economies of scale achieved in their surrounding rural areas and to the numbers of urban dwellers. In 1800, only 6 percent of Americans lived in cities; by 1860, nearly 20 percent of the people who lived in the United States made their home in settlements of more than twenty-five hundred people—what those at the time could readily recognize as an urban environment.[31]

Although some urban households had enough space for their own gardens and even livestock, the majority of clerks, salesmen, politicians, teachers, ministers, "factory girls," and others employed in the businesses of the city needed to purchase their meals or foodstuffs. These urban eaters' demands were strong enough to influence many northeastern farmers to produce items such as fruit, vegetables, milk, butter, and poultry products for sale in regional markets, rather than focus solely on their own subsistence or on hardy export crops such as wheat.

Beyond that, the vast new networks of production and distribution brought urban eaters their flour, their (salted, later refrigerated) meat, and their fish. Indeed, northern food networks benefited from the technological advances in steam locomotives, the new forms of organization, and the increase in freight traffic that characterized the rapidly changing railroad industry between the 1840s and 1860s. As their speeds and carrying capacities improved, railroads began to capture the passenger and cargo traffic that canals had so recently commanded. This is because railroads were cheaper to maintain, could operate in a broader range of weather conditions, and permitted more intensive use. They also provided more direct routes than canals. Shipping foodstuffs and other products by rail, therefore, became

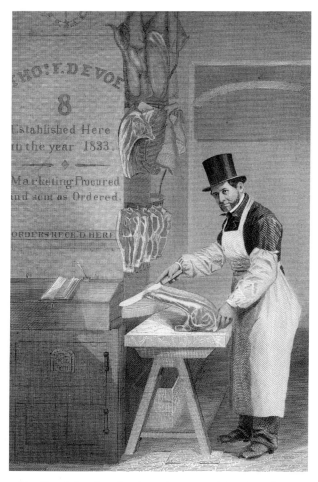

Small-scale butchers faced growing competition throughout the Civil War era from large meatpacking companies. Engraving of Thomas De Voe by Robert Hinshelwood, in Thomas Farrington De Voe, *The Market Assistant, Containing a Brief Description of Every Article of Human Food Sold in the Public Markets of the Cities of New York, Boston, Philadelphia, and Brooklyn* (New York: Hurd and Houghton, 1867), frontispiece, Michigan State University Special Collections.

faster and cheaper than doing so by canal. In turn, rail construction outpaced canal building by some 5,600 miles during the 1840s, while the next decade saw an additional 21,000 miles of track laid.[32]

By 1860, it took the same amount of time for a wagonload of goods to travel 150 miles as it did for a railroad to carry the same quantity 1,000 miles.[33] The "iron horse" enabled hunters and trappers to send increasing quantities of wild animals to eastern food markets. Oysters, wild birds, and even bears came to eastern markets in such abundance that urban shoppers thought nothing of the deteriorating or disappearing supplies in these animals' actual points of origin. During the 1860s, for example, the famed "blue point" oysters that had originally been sourced in New York waters disappeared. Intrepid oystermen, however, would supplant those bivalves with lesser imitators from other locations.[34] Toward the end of the century, railroads would continue to haul iced barrels of freshly killed passenger pigeons from ever-more-remote locales to New York restaurants, obscuring the fact that the birds were going extinct.[35]

We can glimpse the diversity of foods that many Americans would have encountered in an account coming from a time of cholera: one Massachusetts newspaper recorded a conversation among those worried about what to eat and desperate to avoid the disease. In an effort to avoid the water, "men and women drink pretty much what they please," while leaving unsold the vegetables radishes, asparagus, "spinage," potatoes, lettuce, and "every green thing." Everyone flocked to eat "lean beef or mutton—broiled or roasted—with boiled rice or stale bread," and boiled milk was recommended for breakfast. In happier times, the newspapers also provided advice on how to enjoy the newest delicacies shipped in from around the world, as in the July 1850 article in a Vermont newspaper, "How to Eat Pineapple."[36]

A remarkable article in *Frank Leslie's Illustrated Newspaper* in 1857 sought to provide an encyclopedic answer to "What Do People Eat?": from British roast beef and French ragouts to Italian "maccaroni," Indian curries, Caribbean yams, and Chinese water-lily soup. "A New York lady's idea of eating may be comprised within one of the little marble tables at Taylor's, loaded with Charlotte Russe [a kind of icebox cake], jellies, tarts, and ices," the article declared, while "a Wall street merchant thinks that he eats when he gulps down a bit of rancid beefsteak, and finishes off with a *pâté-de-foie-gras*." The author also exercised some stereotypes:

> If you go into a log cabin in Virginia or Maryland, you will see Uncle Tom and Chloe enjoying their hoe-cake and fried pork, with a bowl of sour milk to wash it down. If you enter a cottage in a Western prairie, they will cordially invite you to partake of their venison and "corn-fixings!"[37]

The article captured a time when urban Americans were increasingly aware of the differences that remained in what residents of other regions, races, or classes ate. But it also revealed that a New Yorker in 1857 could probably find pasta, venison, fried pork, or a blueberry tart to eat, given the desire and the means to pay for it.

What, then, had this growing abundance of food meant for such northern eaters during the decades leading up to the Civil War? And how are we to know who ate what? We have evidence, such as diaries, stating what someone had for supper on a given day, as well as ephemera such as preserved tavern menus and grocery receipts. But these records are incomplete, so answering these questions requires creative historical thinking. In factories, for example, the girls and young women working in the cotton mills at Lowell, Massachusetts, did not have much influence over the production of their meals, which they took communally.[38] But asking what they— and other men, women, and children—consumed, and how, is a valuable question because food choices provide evidence of how eaters identified themselves, the classes and ethnic groups to which they belonged or aspired, the cash or credit they had available for purchasing foods, their individual talents for producing or procuring dinner, the natural attributes of the region in which they lived as well as its access to larger network of foodstuffs, and of course the seasonal limitations of nineteenth-century food procurement.

Some of the clearest evidence for what and how people ate comes from the advice books directed at white women of means, such as those excerpted in this volume. For these women, urban life meant exclusion from the sphere of business, politics, and economics, and in favor of more complete control over household provisioning, cooking, child care, and education.[39] Middle- and upper-class urban women who, upon marriage, were suddenly saddled with the tasks of running their households and instructing servants were thus increasingly unfamiliar with the art of selecting fresh meat or vegetables, or of tasks such as "trying out" lard.[40] The mistress of the house was often the target audience of moral tracts, etiquette manuals, and—of course—cookbooks, and authors profited from women's uncertainty about how to perform the tasks newly expected of them.

As family incomes rose and class expectations hardened, women of prosperous families reared their daughters to distinguish themselves in arts more esteemed than cookery. Such women increasingly hired female immigrants and women of color as domestic servants. Because so many impoverished Irish women arrived in the United States in the latter 1840s, in particular, the percentages of urban families with hired workers grew at a tremendous clip. In 1845, one in four Boston families had domestic help. This practice spread to other cities and became more common: by 1860, for example, between 85 and 88 percent of professional and managerial households in Milwaukee hired such domestic workers.[41] Immigrants who had so recently escaped famine now confronted foods that they had never before encountered, either at their own meals or in preparing them for employers.

Cookbooks serve as an important lens through which we can see how nineteenth-century Americans negotiated the nation's changing material, economic, and cultural landscapes. As a rule, these documents reveal that meat retained a pride of place in the meals of any who could afford it, whether homegrown beef, pork, or poultry, products of the hunt, or animals—wild or domesticated—bought from the local market. Meat was essential, but the means of its procurement were in flux during the antebellum era and through the Civil War. The cookbooks also show the centrality of grains as used in breads, steamed or boiled puddings, pies made with fruit as well as with meat, cakes, fried foods such as fritters and doughnuts, and an older standby, pickled vegetables.

Most cookbooks published in antebellum America were in English, but the guides by and for immigrants or foreign-language-speaking religious sects afford similar insights into the changing patterns of food procurement and preparation. After examining an 1848 Pennsylvania Dutch cookbook, the historian William Woys Weaver determined that the community preferred to consume locally produced beef rather than send excess cattle to Philadelphia or Baltimore markets. Their turn to beef as a main repast meant that their accompaniments no longer required the sweetness or acidity of fruit to balance pork's flavors, and hence the inclusion of more Anglo-American side dishes that went well with beef.[42]

Such culinary adaptations were a hallmark of many immigrants' food experiences. Although potatoes were the dominant fare in Ireland when the Irish arrived in the United States en masse during the 1840s, they eschewed plain potatoes as a symbol of want and subservience, a reminder of the potato blight and the resulting famine they had left behind. In America, those Irish who could afford to do so returned to the foods they imagined their forebears had eaten before the British dispossessions: cheeses; meats, including goose and ox

HUMAN NATURE.

FEROCIOUS MISTRESS. "Cook, this is the third time you have sent up the joint raw this week, and your Master is much displeased! I must really *entreat* of you in future—to—" (*Awful pause.*)

COOK. "Ah, I see! You've been wexed in the parlor, and so you comes and wents it on me in the kitchen."

In this imagined conversation between a cook and her employer, the cook's pronunciation, which is spelled out for comic effect, would have made it clear to readers at the time that she was a recent immigrant. *Harper's Weekly*, March 18, 1865, 176, Michigan State University Special Collections.

tongue; colcannon (kale or cabbage mixed with potatoes); boxty (a special-event potato dish); stampy (a type of boxty involving cream, sugar, and caraway seeds, and served for Halloween); barm brack (a fruit bread); and variations on oatmeal; and even, for the most well-off, roast beef, mutton browned in butter, mince pies, custards, puddings, celery soups, and apple charlottes.[43]

Cookbooks are also useful historical documents for showing that particular cuisines remained heavily influenced by geography and regional tastes, even as they reflected ethnic heritages, religious values, and socioeconomic realities. In New England, for instance, the Puritans' descendants largely avoided spices and fancy foods, preferring instead meats (baked and boiled), boiled vegetables, and simple pies. Farther south, the Quaker tradition remaining in the Middle Atlantic states encouraged cooks to prepare relatively simple boiled foods. Rural and western farmers, meanwhile, were the most likely to rely on homegrown goods, including corn, greens, and pork, and locally sourced sweeteners such as maple or, during the 1850s, sorghum, a sweet grass.[44]

Scrimping and saving through "economy" is another important trend in antebellum cookbooks aimed at middle-class readers. It is notable that cookbooks and advice manuals published during or just after the era's cyclical economic depressions, such as Lydia Maria Francis Child's *The Frugal Housewife* (1830), stressed economy both in cooking and in housekeeping. To city dwellers, for instance, she advised saving all breadcrumbs and fat scraps for reuse, preserving eggs, obtaining butter from reputable friends in the country when cheapest, and

making bread and cake at home rather than purchasing them from bakers. Likewise, she encouraged readers to consider the age—and therefore the quality and value—of the meats they prepared, and warned that purchased fruit preserves were not for the economically minded. Even so, Child was aware that her readers—women to whom she offered instructions for tending kid gloves, mahogany furniture, and marble fireplaces—*had* access to the cash required to purchase the beef, pork, lamb, chicken, duck, geese, turkey, and pigeon, fish, and veal that would stand at the center of the dishes she recommended.[45] Though she promoted economy, Child's audience at least could dream of a day when such economy would not be necessary.

The idea of economy appears throughout the antebellum cookery and household advice books targeted at the growing middle class, as they offer tips not only for family meals but also for entertaining. Renowned "literary domestics" Sara Josepha Hale and Catharine Beecher, for instance, encouraged readers to "avoid ostentation" when "giving dinners." Not only would lavish entertaining be expensive, Hale cautioned, but also it "will make your guests uncomfortable." Instead, the hostess was to "provide enough, and beware of the common practice of having too much." Beecher, for her part, agreed, and warned American women to avoid the excesses favored by their elite European counterparts.[46] This ideal, however, would be discarded after the Civil War—as menus from the time suggest.

That Hale and Beecher discussed how one should entertain guests, however, and that Child broached matters of kid gloves and marble fireplaces, tells modern readers that their antebellum audiences came from a very select socioeconomic status. The white women to whom they spoke were educated enough to read these texts, and financially comfortable enough to purchase the kitchen tools—including the cookbooks—required to prepare and preserve the foods that their families would enjoy. And in all likelihood, they would have had access to sinks, pumps, servants, and other conveniences of well-to-do households.

But what about the majority of antebellum eaters? We cannot expect to find much evidence for the culinary practices of illiterate members of the working poor or of people of color in the midcentury cookbooks directed at educated white, middle-class American women. How, then, are we to assess what such individuals might have eaten?

Popular images and evidence from literary and material culture afford glimpses of their practices, and no antebellum city provides more evidence than New York. In an 1855 lithograph of New York City's infamous "Five Points" district circa 1827, for instance, every storefront ringing the intersection of Anthony, Cross, and Orange streets is labeled "Grocery." It is an especially revealing historical document because it represents an area of the city that became home to large numbers of African Americans and Irish immigrants and was known for having been a tinderbox of social tensions.

It is entirely possible that owners of these groceries were, in fact, Irish immigrants. Whereas German immigrants had flocked to American farms, the Irish largely avoided returning to the countryside. Instead, they settled in cities, where many became food entrepreneurs: by 1850, Irish families in Boston owned two hundred grocery stores. Irish men and women also became the majority of New York City's fruit and vegetable peddlers, and through 1855, they dominated the city's fish and oyster dealer population. Likewise, nearly one-quarter of all Philadelphia grocers had Irish names in 1857.[47]

German and Irish immigrants introduced new forms of alcohol consumption to the United States, whether through the brewing of light beers, a German specialty, or the mingling of alcohol and religious events, as at an Irish wake.[48] The eating and drinking customs of Germans, Irish, and other immigrant groups tend to appear in the earliest historical records as the butt of jokes and puns: an 1841 newspaper, for example purported to record Caty telling her husband John to "sit down and eat these potatoes, and let your whiskey alone," and she corked the bottle with one hand to emphasize the point; while an 1859 newspaper remarked that "A German at Cincinnati made a bet of fifty dollars that he could drink half a barrel of lager bier in twenty-four hours. Seeing how he was going on, the other party paid him ten dollars to throw up the bet."[49]

While urban Irish bars were frequently dark and patronized only by men, Germans viewed drinking as a social event and preferred well-lit and airy spaces in which whole families, German or not, together ate, drank, and enjoyed music.[50] These shady "beer gardens" were products of the Germans' process for crafting their preferred beverage: because electrical refrigeration did not yet exist, immigrant brewers stored their aging lager (which required long periods of fermentation) in caves or cellars, which they further cooled by planting shade trees, making a perfect space for a beer garden. To help their customers wash the lager down, these brewers often offered free salted pretzels, as well as the infamously fragrant Limburger cheese.[51] In some urban spaces, entrepreneurial brewers catered to Americans' enthusiasm for these venues—and German lager—by creating high-ceilinged indoor beer halls, which they planted with trees and bushes. By so doing, their patrons could enjoy such ambiance year-round.[52]

Some hints of these associations are evident in the New York lithograph, as it depicts some of these grocers as having sold "wiskey," gin, and rum to the motley population carousing in the streets. To the extent that Five Points had a well-deserved reputation for being a raucous part of the city—and that clean water was hard to come by in that vicinity—it is not unlikely that grocers stocked and promoted such spirituous drinks for their clientele.

Other groceries depicted in the image, however, provide important ancillary evidence of what poorer New Yorkers might have eaten: according to the signage on their storefronts, Five Points' grocers plied "Soft Shell Clams" and "Good Fat Hams" and offered oysters, milk, and pickles.[53] Given New York City's proximity to waterways, trade routes, and regional truck farms, Five Points residents could regularly consume such a variety of foods.

The same lithograph sheds light on other dimensions of less-documented antebellum Americans. In particular, it suggests that public spaces brought diverse groups together and encouraged informal food exchanges. For example, in one part of the Five Points vignette, an African American woman hawks her homemade foods on a street corner, perhaps hoping to sell them to the well-dressed white man inspecting her wares. How many foods would they share, and how did those patterns change in this period? Although three decades had passed between the lithograph's publication and the moment it purported to represent, historians have since fleshed out the fact that many New Yorkers bought foodstuffs from street merchants. Between the 1820s and 1840s, African Americans were known to have "danced for eels" at the East River's Catherine Market, while children of French immigrants sold fruit on nearby street corners.[54] On Staten Island, meanwhile, free blacks were permitted to own and work oyster beds, and on the island's sandy southern tip, entrepreneurial freedmen from Virginia and Maryland as well as New York–born African Americans cultivated greens and sweet potatoes in summer gardens for their families. They also grew strawberries and raked oysters, which they sold across the river in Manhattan's Washington Market.[55]

It's difficult to find evidence about what poor Americans ate. The city's sheer population density meant that the poorest people who picked through waste in search of scraps often appeared in and around markets at the same times that well-to-do men (or, later in the century, immigrant servants) tended to the families' marketing needs.[56] In nineteenth-century Baltimore, street scrapers, seamstresses, servants, and dockworkers of every hue and nationality lived hand to mouth. As they were for the rich, bread and meat were their staples, but the working class could afford only a sparse, unpredictable, and nutritionally deficient diet. Stimulants such as coffee, tea, alcohol, and sugar worked to keep these men and women distracted from their hunger.[57] The urban working class had the narrowest menu; rural workers, however poor, frequently had access to farm products, including fruits, vegetables, and dairy, and so ate better. Even those at the almshouse had more options; such eaters, at least, could rely on vegetables every day and meat soup, salt meat, and fish at least once each week.[58]

The problem for hand-to-mouth eaters in Baltimore, New York, and other cities during the antebellum years was that food required ready cash, and even the most spartan diet consumed the bulk of a workingman's income. In fact, wage work was so tenuous during the middle part of the century that the diets of the working class became poor enough to noticeably diminish Americans' average heights.[59] This occurred even as western producers and railroads were bringing an ever-greater bounty into cities during the middle of the century.

This stark contrast of fortunes was evident to the famous British novelist Charles Dickens when he visited the United States in 1842. Dickens recalled having frequented both dance halls and oyster cellars, and he wrote that the cellars "tempt the hungry most at night, for then dull candles glimmering inside, illuminate these dainty words, and make the mouths of idlers water, as they read and linger."[60] George G. Foster, in his exposé of the city's nightlife, noted how near the bars, where men consumed oysters and cheap brandy, were "'private rooms,' where men and women enter promiscuously, eat, drink and make merry."[61]

It is almost certain that the foods brought into cities and prepared on street corners, in almshouses, and in dance halls were far from the minds of authors such as Lydia Marie Child or Catharine Beecher when they were instructing housewives on how they ought to prepare particular recipes before the Civil War. But because neither these foods nor their consumers appear in the more widely available genre of advice manuals, asking what the poor or the marginalized ate, and how, is all the more crucial to understanding how the war would shortly transform their diets, too.

The same can be said for the question of "going west," for emigrating beyond the Mississippi River required creative approaches to the food options. The acquisition of western territory, when combined with the unsettled question of slavery's expansion, precipitated the Civil War. For the up to half a million individuals who crossed to western states and territories between the 1840s and 1850s, the goal was to get between the jumping-off points of Missouri and the rich lands of California and Oregon in a matter of months—and to feed themselves while on the move.[62] To do so, they would need to carry food and supplies or procure them along the way. These movements—whether across the continent by land, or, as more often the case, by sea, either around South America or in two ships and a portage across Central America—led travelers to consume food in new ways and presaged the accomplishments needed to supply troops during the Civil War.

The overlanders who crossed the continent all relied on similar stores of food: bacon, salt pork, beans, flour, cornmeal, sugar, and coffee. Bacon and flour were likely to be purchased, not made, demonstrating the impact of the ongoing revolutions in agricultural production, industrial food processing, and transportation.[63] Some brought cows and were able to enjoy milk and even butter on the trail, while others brought liquor. The majority of their foodstuffs, however, had to be nonperishable and light.

During the California Gold Rush, which began in 1848 and lasted through the middle of the 1850s, the extraordinary surge of prospective miners—largely men—from all over the world created terrific demands and high prices for raw ingredients, preserved foods, and prepared meals in San Francisco and the inland mines. These miners frequently attempted to replicate household units by forming groups of two to ten men. In these groups, they often took weekly turns doing the cooking and laundry. Sometimes, however, they relied on a convalescing group member to do so; at other times, some white men contracted with men of color (whether Native American, Chinese, Mexican, or African American) to do these seemingly unmasculine tasks for them.[64]

The first mineral rushers had no time for agriculture: they would trade gold dust for provisions at the nearest "store," and improvise their meals from what was available. But because provisions were frequently limited to durables that the overlanders carried, gold seekers' foods could be monotonous. When supplies grew scarce, they foraged or hunted—and, in rare cases, planted vegetable gardens, learning that even greater profits could be gleaned from vegetables than from ore.[65] Soon, the world food markets rushed foodstuffs to San Francisco, ready to profit from the high prices. Wheat and flour poured in from Chile and Australia, rice arrived from China, and wine and champagne shipped from France. In fact, so much food arrived during the summer of 1849 that the city's storehouses were overrun and bags of grain were left in the streets.[66] Hungry eaters turned to entrepreneurial restaurants or boardinghouses and sampled French, Mexican, Chilean, or Chinese cuisine.[67]

California soon became a prime market for American canned foods as well. The idea of preserving foods by canning had arisen during the Napoleonic wars, and by the 1820s a nascent canning industry had taken root in Boston and New England. From eastern seaports, canners shipped fruits, berries, mustards, lobsters, and even milk to eaters in far-flung locales.[68] By the 1840s, oyster, lobster, and sardine canning were all flourishing in Baltimore.[69] Although cans would have weighed down overland travelers, ships could carry heavy goods far more easily, and cans provided a food source both for those sailing to California and to feed hungry mouths upon arrival.[70] The canning industry would accelerate again in the years to come, to meet wartime demands.

The Civil War accentuated the ongoing transformations of northern networks of food production and consumption in all of the aspects we have discussed, whether urbanization or immigration, industrialization or food preservation. In fact the triumph of the North has been attributed to its success in "starving the South," and the historian Ted Steinberg has documented how Union soldiers "received more food per person than any other army in the history of warfare."[71] The changes we have outlined had been gradually mounting, but the outbreak of war was an important milestone, as tales of soldiers from the US war with Mexico, twelve years before, make clear. In that conflict, soldiers ate like the others on the overland trails, though with the addition of "hardtack" and some vegetables. However, since the soldiers ate rations shipped from New Orleans and then through central Mexico, they were frequently old, rancid, and inedible when the troops received them. Many men, therefore, supplemented their diets by raiding Mexican villages and farms, or by purchasing food from Mexican vendors.[72]

During the Civil War, however, food producers responded to the surge in demand created by the call-up of Union and Confederate armies in important new ways. Meat and grain production experienced the largest wartime transformations. Over the course of the war, by one account, 1.5 million Union troops consumed more than five hundred million pounds of packed meat.[73] During the 1850s, Chicago developed into a grain-handling and animal-slaughtering juggernaut, and in 1858, packing companies in the city began to harvest winter ice for use in summertime meatpacking, creating new cycles of year-round production.[74] (Ice harvesting was not, however, an entirely novel idea: entrepreneurial Bostonians had done so since the 1810s, using places including Walden Pond to send frozen blocks of Massachusetts water far and wide, including to ports in Cuba, Jamaica, China, and Brazil.)[75] Capturing Great Lakes winter ice for summer use in Chicago eventually proved to be a powerful war measure, enabling greater food production and thereby comprised an important wartime advantage over the Confederacy.

Early in the Civil War, Northern leaders blockaded the Mississippi River in hopes that they could cut the Confederacy off from the world. By doing so, they also prevented northwestern grain and pork from reaching its traditional markets in the South and the Caribbean. Western farmers responded to the blockade by feeding even more of their grain—which they could no longer send south—to growing numbers of hogs, and sending those animals to Chicago for processing. Thus, between the effects of the blockade and the power of a newly harnessed winter, Chicago packers enjoyed rapid growth: between 1859 and 1863, the city's packing capacity increased more than sixfold and surpassed that of the venerable old "porkopolis," Cincinnati.[76] As wartime troop needs for meat, however, combined with the city's newly abundant supply of cattle and hogs, Chicago's businessmen centralized their stockyards.[77] Thus in 1864, nine railroads and the Chicago Pork Packers' Asso-

An advertisement for Heinz Preserved Fruits, circa 1870, The Alan and Shirley Brocker Sliker Culinary Collection, Michigan State University Special Collections.

ciation proposed creating the Union Stock Yards, fueling even greater economies of scale.[78]

Canning also expanded to new foods at the beginning of the war, and the whole pace of production was increased. In 1856, Gail Borden created canned condensed milk, a food that enjoyed terrific popularity during the war, thanks largely to a federal army commissary who discovered that Borden's product withstood the rigors of southern heat without spoiling. By 1863, the company was churning out 17,000 quarts per day, and, by 1864, earning profits.[79] G. C. Van Camp began to can fruits and vegetables in Indianapolis in 1861, while in Boston, William Underwood began to supply canned meat for the army during the Civil War.[80]

Before the war, canneries' rates of production had been limited by the length of time it took to properly heat and preserve each batch of cans—between five to six hours, by one estimate. In Baltimore, wartime innovators turned to calcium chloride to superheat the water in which cans were prepared. This considerably lessened the time required to make each batch, enabling canneries to turn batches out every twenty-five to forty minutes. Thus, by the end of the war, one cannery could produce 20,000 cans per day instead of 2,500.[81] These products, and canning innovations such as the zinc-lidded glass Mason jar, soon enabled Americans to consume perishable foods regardless of season, with greater ease, and—in time—at less cost. It is likely that these factors, born of Civil War needs and soldiers' new preferences for foods preserved in this manner, helped improve the health of Americans for many later generations.[82]

Because of these advances in food production, the Union army could feed its soldiers far more sufficiently than the Confederacy was capable of doing. According to Captain Richard C. Derby, writing in January 1862, Union basic rations were ample: "Every man has each day one and a quarter pounds fresh or salt beef, or three-fourths of a pound of pork; one pound of hard bread like crackers, or twenty-two ounces of baker's bread; beans or rice or hominy; sugar, coffee, or tea; . . . salt, and vinegar, and sometimes molasses and potatoes." With time to cook, the men held a nutritional and at times culinary advantage over their civilian counterparts. One unit, from Bath, New York, hired a local restaurateur and found "such unheard of things in camp life as roast beef, baked ham, fried doughnuts, good, wholesome gingerbread, and the like, made camp life much more agreeable." However, conditions could dictate quick changes. As one surgeon at Chancellorsville reported, under the pressure of incoming shells, "Many of us made a discovery that raw beef, well seasoned, is very grateful to the taste of a hungry man."[83]

Despite advances in food production, the logistics of food delivery to hundreds of thousands of Union soldiers—including those stationed near home, those engaged in battle, those guarding remote but strategic outposts, and those in transit between all those points, perhaps under cover of darkness—remained daunting, and soldiers complained loudly about inedible or inadequate food. Civilian supporters did what they could to help: In August 1861, two steamers filled with new regiments stopped in Ripley, Ohio. Because "the poor fellows has had nothing to eat since the morning before," the newspaper reported, citizens brought out "bread, meat, fruit, and everything that would satisfy hunger" to donate. The officers were especially thankful for the provision of "cool water, of which we stood in great need"—one glimpse into the uncertainties of food facing soldiers long before they reached the battlefield.[84] On the other hand, the *North American and United States Gazette* in Philadelphia found the soldiers' complaints unfounded, citing soldiers' penchant for exaggeration and "the vast amount of unwholesome stuff which the soldiers themselves voluntarily purchase." The "rations, though coarse and hard, are wholesome," the editors argued; not so the "twenty-seven hundred pounds of candy for the regiments at Norfolk" which they saw ordered, paid for, and consumed.[85]

The Civil War influenced the nation's foodways in other, lasting arenas as well. In 1862, the Republican-controlled Congress passed the Homestead Act, which allotted western land to settlers in 160-acre parcels. Because, as the historian Frieda Knobloch has written, "it took 160 acres at least, and often more than that, to support only one family in a society and an agriculture based on the exchange of commodities for cash," this act not only created new farms, which produced more food and in turn lowered prices, but reiterated that western commerce would, in coming decades, be focused on commerce rather than subsistence.[86] That same year, the government reiterated its interest in commercial-oriented agricultural production and in transcontinental trade by funding a transcontinental railroad, which would move people, animals, and commodities east and west; by establishing the Department of Agriculture; and by passing the Morrill Act, which created state-run land-grant colleges in every state, where instructors taught modern methods to American farmers with missionary zeal. During the ensuing decades, these institutions would have tremendous influences on the nature of food production and distribution, and continue to transform Americans' culinary practices and dietary habits—and, many have argued, their passage by a Congress stripped of its Southern members is the most significant legacy of the Civil War after emancipation.[87]

An artist's depiction of General William Tecumseh Sherman's Christmas dinner in Savannah, Georgia, after he had led Union forces in capturing the Southern port in late December 1864. *Harper's Weekly*, January 28, 1865, 53, Michigan State University Special Collections.

What to eat, where to get it, how to cook it, and how to afford it—these were everyday questions and concerns for slaves and free men, native-born Americans and immigrants, urban dwellers and rural homesteaders in the antebellum United States. Food choice and preparation could be so humdrum, or so pressing, as to rarely appear in the historical records. But food was (and is) central to the human experience, and it was essential to the Union victory in the Civil War. In antebellum America and during the Civil War, food was celebrated in literature and arts, debated in political campaigns, and decisive in economic exchanges. Only a fraction of the daily conversations, debates, investments, and gambles around food were documented in the antebellum era's cookbooks—but what a fascinating window into the past they can, nevertheless, provide.

Seeing the Civil War Era through Its Cookbooks

Cookbooks offer a unique and valuable way to examine American life in the era of the Civil War. Their lessons, however, are not always obvious. Direct references to the war were rare in cookbooks, even in those published right in the middle of it. In part, this silence is a reminder that lives went on and that dinner still appeared on most tables most nights, no matter how much the world was changing outside. It's also a reminder, of course, that daily life on the Union home front, especially in the urban North, saw far fewer devastating changes than life in the Confederacy. In addition, writers may have seen cookbooks as an inappropriate space to discuss the repercussions of battles and death tolls. Yet the five cookbooks excerpted in this volume (see the list at the end of this introduction) are all still very much books of their time, and the effects of war and politics on daily life are perceptible in all of them. By reading closely we can glean hints of the turbulence churning outside the kitchen window.

One of the relatively few explicit references to wartime politics that appears in these books was in a recipe called "Tessie's Wheaten Biscuit. (From a Contraband)," which appeared in Mrs. S. G. Knight's 1864 *Tit-Bits; Or, How to Prepare a Nice Dish at a Moderate Expense*. Contrabands were a temporary designation used by Union troops to refer to former slaves who escaped across Union lines but whose legal standing—as free people or as property—remained uncertain. It's not clear whether Knight herself got this recipe directly from an escaped slave named Tessie, whether a friend of hers did, whether she read about the recipe in a newspaper or another source, or—always a possibility—whether she or someone else made it up altogether. In any case, Knight chose to convey the recipe in an imitation of African American speech, which her readers may have seen as humorous or quaint, or as a mark of the recipe's authenticity. For example, according to the recipe, "you beat the dough 'till it begins to go pop, pop, pop,—it'll crack moo' like a whip,—then you know it's done." At a time when photographs of the scarred backs of escaped slaves were appearing in Northern newspapers, readers may have seen this reference to the pop of a whip—a sound they would have assumed ex-slaves knew all too well—as a reference to abolitionist literature. It's also worth noting that even though Knight attributed many of the other recipes in her book to specific women, she never directly quoted anyone else or imitated their speech. And unlike the other women, whom she designated with the respectful titles of Mrs. or Miss, she used only Tessie's first name.

While the Contraband recipe was rare in its direct reference to wartime politics, politics appeared in other forms. Some of Knight's other dishes, like Yankee Pudding and Thanksgiving Pudding, would have struck readers at the time as clear allusions to contemporary events. Thanksgiving only became a national holiday in 1863, the year Knight published her book, after Abraham Lincoln issued a proclamation to that effect because he believed creating a nostalgic American holiday would raise morale.[1] It's also noteworthy that Knight chose to include several southern recipes in her book, such as "Gumbo (a favorite Southern dish)," without further comment on their origins in the self-proclaimed Confederacy. Meanwhile, other recipes with political leanings appeared, too, like Election Cake, a dessert popular since the Revolutionary era, and Railroad Cake, which had become popular during the 1850s as an affordable way for women to celebrate Manifest Destiny at home.[2] Meanwhile, nostalgic recipes like Old Times Johnny Cake and other self-consciously austere dishes harkened back to simpler times.

Many of these cookbooks focused openly on thrift. While economizing was an old theme in American cookery, it would have been especially relevant to families during the Civil War. For instance, the first cookbook ever to focus on leftovers, *What to Do with the Cold Mutton: A Book of Réchauffés, Together with Many Other Approved Receipts for the Kitchen of a Gentleman of Moderate Income*, appeared in the United States in 1865, and its publisher's confidence that leftovers would be a selling point rather than an embarrassment underlines the fact that economizing on food had taken on new urgency in many American families by the end of the war. Hundreds of thousands of Northern families had lost husbands, sons, or fathers, and in many cases that meant they had lost the basis of their economic subsistence. As many Americans knew all too well, turning the scraps left from one dinner into a palatable meal the next day could mean the difference between living within one's budget and sliding into debt.

Besides staying within the changeable family budget, housekeepers would also have been expected to master special cooking repertoires aimed at invalids, and a section on invalid cookery was practically obligatory in cookbooks of the era. The established place of invalid cookery as a specifically female domestic skill gave women significant authority over sickness throughout this era. In fact, the invalid cookery tradition was one reason that women were readily accepted as Civil War nurses at a time when it was generally presumed that women were otherwise too delicate and squeamish to bear the rigors of formal medical training. Food preparation was one of the central tasks of female nurses during the war, and in both the North and the South female nurses established "diet kitchens" connected to military hospitals, based on the widespread cultural assumption that the right kind of nourishing food, delicately prepared by experienced women, would speed soldiers' convalescence.[3]

These cookbooks were also useful because of the widespread migration and immigration occurring throughout this era, and many people eagerly bought cookbooks because they had much to learn and no one to teach them. The American population was a prodigiously mobile one in the early and mid-nineteenth century. Americans were geographically mobile, with some families moving west to claim land on the expanding frontier, sometimes moving from cities to farms, while many other people were moving from farms to cities. At the same time, large numbers of immigrants were entering the United States in the mid-nineteenth century—with particularly large numbers of people coming from Ireland and Germany—and they all would have encountered unfamiliar ingredients, tools, and cooking styles that needed explanation.[4] As people moved, they often moved away from networks of friends and family that women otherwise would have relied upon for domestic knowledge.

At the same time, the mid-nineteenth century was a time of intense class mobility, and that sort of mobility also called for new culinary knowledge and skills. People with newly enlarged incomes who were joining a growing urban middle class would have had access to ingredients they had never used before, as well as more disposable income to spend on food. They would also have faced new social expectations about when, what, and *how* they ate. Even had family members been near enough to give advice, they would not necessarily have possessed the skills or experience considered necessary to new lives and positions.[5] For socially ambitious Americans, cookbooks could be sources of important information about middle-class norms of cooking and dining, which they would not have learned in their childhood homes. But not all class mobility was upward. While some prospered, others struggled, losing fortunes in financial panics, for example, or finding that new forms of industrial production made their artisanal professions obsolete. Several cookbook authors directly addressed the downwardly mobile. Mary Cornelius, in the 1863 edition of *The Young Housekeeper's Friend*, marveled ruefully that "Adversity succeeds prosperity like a sudden inundation. The poor and uneducated are often rapidly elevated to wealthy independence, while the refined and highly educated are compelled to taste the bitterness of poverty." Indeed, it was often a shift in economic fortunes that compelled westward migration in the first place. Thinking about women who were moving west with their families because they could no longer afford to live in the East, Cornelius expressed special sympathy for women who had "passed their youth in affluent ease" but who were now "obliged, by the vicissitudes of life, to spend their time and strength in laborious household occupations." For Americans who were compelled for the first time to provide food for their families on small incomes and to cook without the aid of servants, a good cookbook with clear instructions could be invaluable.

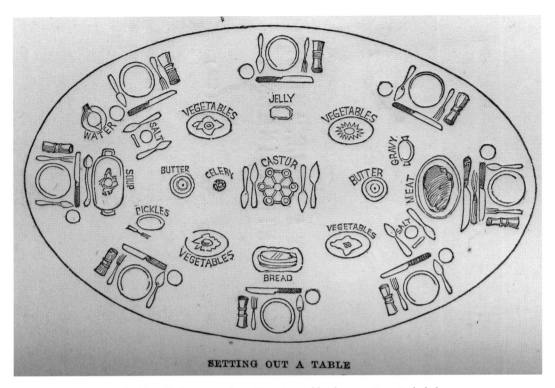

SETTING OUT A TABLE

Besides offering counsel on etiquette, cookbooks sometimes included table-setting diagrams to guide uncertain hosts. *The American Practical Cookery Book* (Philadelphia: John E. Potter & Co., 1859), 214, Michigan State University Special Collections.

Because of both geographic and class mobility, more people than ever in the mid-nineteenth century felt they needed outside guidance when it came to food and cooking. It is little wonder that the cookbook market exploded. In fact, the expanding market for cookbooks was only part of a burgeoning genre of advice literature, as advances in print combined with the growth of cities to create a huge demand for how-to books for a battery of skills including etiquette, dancing, and calculating, as well as cooking.[6]

Reading Cookbooks for History

People accustomed to thinking of cookbooks as a source for recipes, and not much else, can be surprised how much information cookbooks can reveal about the daily lives, social practices, class aspirations, and cultural assumptions of people in the past. While cookbooks offer us a tantalizing glimpse of the past, however, like all historical documents they offer us *only* a glimpse. In fact, cookbooks can be an especially deceptive source, and anyone using them to understand the past has to be on guard. First and foremost, we cannot assume that the recipes or cooking techniques that any single author suggested accurately reflect how Americans in the Civil War era actually cooked and ate. It's important to keep in mind that cookbook authors made decisions about which recipes to include and which to leave out, and they based those decisions in part on guesses about what information would be helpful to readers. The fact that people went to the trouble of recording a recipe at all meant that the writers assumed most people didn't already know it by heart. For instance, Knight wrote that she purposefully omitted most recipes for meat, which she considered "plain cooking," because she supposed readers already knew how to prepare it. This is a good reminder that we can't assume people always, or only, cooked in the way cookbooks describe.

Furthermore, we remain ignorant of the most basic information about the people who read these cookbooks. We don't know who bought them or how they may have modified the recipes—if they tried them at all—once they got them home. We also don't know what they thought of any dishes that resulted. We can infer from the fact that publishing firms accepted the cookbooks in the first place that the editors, at least, believed their recipes would be popular, and we can assume that books that came out in multiple editions were in some demand. But we don't even know with any certainty how many copies 1860s cookbooks sold.

Despite these daunting limitations, however, cookbooks can still tell us all sorts of things. For example, even if cookbook authors sometimes left out dishes they considered too simple or obvious to record formally, recipes with names like Pickle for Daily Use, Common Doughnuts, Every-day Cake, and Good Common Sauce still give valuable clues about what kinds of food people ate regularly. Meanwhile, when authors warned readers against eating certain foods or cooking in certain ways, it's a good clue that they believed many people were already doing so—and should stop. For instance, the author of the 1868 *What Shall We Eat: A Manual for Housekeepers, Comprising a Bill of Fare for Breakfast, Dinner, and Tea, for Every Day in the Year* felt it necessary to caution readers against drinking wine for breakfast. If wine was too strong, the author wrote, "it diminishes business keenness," whereas weak wine "imparts no warmth," an essential quality for breakfast beverages in chilly America. Instead, the author suggested coffee, tea, or hot chocolate for breakfast.

It's also noteworthy that many of the foods that people today consider quintessential American dishes, steeped in age-old tradition, don't appear in these cookbooks or appear only in unfamiliar forms. For example, while there are a few recipes for apple pie, there are many more recipes for blancmange, a popular nineteenth-century custard. While there are occasional recipes for cookies, there are many more recipes for puddings, part of the English culinary tradition that was still thriving in the United States more than eighty years after the Revolution. Likewise, foods that would become mainstays of all-American cooking in the next century, like cheese, ground beef, and chocolate, play very minor roles in these recipes. In contrast, there were whole genres that were popular in the Civil War era that almost totally disappeared from mainstream American cookbooks in the decades that followed. These now defunct genres included *Sweetmeats*, encompassing recipes like Peaches in Brandy, Candied Lemons, and preserved Watermelon Rinds; *Invalid Cookery*, filled with recipes like Wine Whey, Toast Water, and various gruels; and *Common Drinks*, with homemade beverages that were sometimes alcoholic and sometimes not, like Effervescing Drink, Cherry Bounce, and Spring Beer.

Meanwhile, other recipes that seem familiar at first glance turn out to be quite different from what modern readers might assume. In the recipe for Waffles that appears in the 1868 edition of Ann Howe's *American Kitchen Directory and Housewife*, for instance, she sug-gested a salty gravy, rather than a sweet syrup, as an accompaniment. A "pickle" at this time was more likely to refer to a pickled nut or tomato or melon than it was to a pickled cucumber. Macaroni appears regularly in these cookbooks, although rarely with cheese; instead, authors mixed it with fish, served it as a plain side dish, or used it in sweet desserts like Macaroni Pudding. Likewise, Knight's recipe for Coffee Cake was not a cinnamon cake intended to be eaten with a cup of coffee, but instead a cake that actually contained coffee, along with molasses and raisins. At other times the ingredients for dishes were roughly what we might expect, but the methods of cooking—and how people then defined when a food was "done" or not—were wildly different. Note, for instance, that authors routinely instructed readers to boil vegetables for thirty, forty, fifty minutes or more, including tender young vegetables like fresh peas and corn. Cornelius suggested boiling carrots for up to an hour and a half, just as Knight instructed readers to boil rice for a full two hours. By our standards, the mushy pastes that would have resulted would seem disastrously overcooked. But by 1860s standards, of course, these were simply what cooked carrots and boiled rice were.

Readers may also be surprised by different cultural rules about how and when certain foods were eaten. For example, Mary Cornelius outlined strict guidelines concerning which vegetables should properly be served with different styles of meat. According to her, vegetables like carrots, parsnips, greens, and cabbage should only be served with boiled meat, while sweet potatoes, squash, and onions should go with roast meat. Even more striking, as *What Shall We Eat*—the only book here organized around menus—makes clear, breakfasts in this era were filled with items like mutton, pickled pigs' feet, liver, venison, and fish. That might jar modern readers who think of breakfast as a light meal centered around starches, but there was nothing inherently unnatural about it. Indeed, at a time when Americans were much more likely to perform hard physical work all day, large breakfasts centered around meat would have been a valuable source of energy. The different nineteenth-century expectations about food pairings and about what kinds of food were appropriate for which meals call attention to how arbitrary many of our *own* cultural rules about food are.

In their focus on food preservation, the cookbooks also highlight another important aspect of nineteenth-century life. Preserving food and preventing spoilage were urgent tasks in an era before electric refrigeration because food that wasn't consumed in a timely manner, especially in summertime, could quickly spoil. Americans were more accustomed to eating questionable or moldy food at this time, and Civil War soldiers on both sides routinely ate moldy hard tack or rancid meat.[7] In her section on preserves and jellies, Cornelius noted that "a thick, leather-looking mould" on top of a preserve was good because it would effectively seal out air, but she cautioned readers that if the preserves were merely speckled with mold they should taste them to determine how much could be salvaged. Food spoilage could be dangerous as well as wasteful, and people who ate food that had gone bad could get seriously ill or even die. Nineteenth-century Americans had good reason to fear food spoilage, and housekeepers mastered a diverse range of skills to keep it at bay. To preserve meat, they might dry it, salt it, smoke it, pickle it, can it, pot it, pack it in snow, or make sausages. Cookbooks were also filled with recipes for preserved vegetables, fruits, eggs, and nuts. Cheese was a good way to preserve milk, just as beers, ciders, and other alcohols were good ways to preserve grains and fruits. In addition, cookbooks almost always included whole sections on pickles, jams, syrups, and relishes.

In fact, these homemade condiments were more than a good way to keep foods from spoiling. The cookbooks' heavy reliance on boiling and baking may make their vegetable and meat recipes seem straightforward by today's standards, and modern readers might casually assume that eaters then subsisted on hearty but plain meat-and-potatoes fare. These stereotypes are right, in part. Ann Howe, for instance, warned cooks "not to have the natural flavor of the food disguised by the seasoning," and she cautioned against using excessive spices. Yet what comes through most clearly in the cookbooks is not the blandness of 1860s meals, but rather how diverse and flavorful they must have been, especially when supplemented with condiments like tomato figs, burned butter sauce, East India Pickle, pepper vinegar, and pickled nasturtium buds. In fact, highly seasoned condiments including ketchups, chou chous, pickles, curries, sauces, sweetmeats, and slaws were more prevalent in mainstream cookbooks, and perhaps more

Advertisement for Ceresota flour. The Queen of Hearts Ceresota flour advertisement, Northwestern Consolidated Milling Co. (Minneapolis, Minn.: Northwestern Consolidated Milling Co., ca. 1870), The Alan and Shirley Brocker Sliker Culinary Collection, Michigan State University Special Collections.

unabashedly appreciated, than they would be again in this country for more than a century. The arsenal of recipes for ketchups alone—including recipes not just for tomato ketchup but also for walnut ketchup, oyster ketchup, and mushroom ketchup—shows that some aspects of twenty-first-century cooking might seem straightforward and bland by 1860s standards, and not the other way around.

Besides an array of homemade condiments, Americans during the Civil War era also produced many items at home that people today think of as things you get from grocery stores and *only* from grocery stores. Foods regularly made at home in the 1860s included not just bread and butter, but also gelatin, carbonated drinks, vinegar, yeast, cheese, shortening, and bouillon cubes, also called portable soup. Yet Americans in the 1860s— especially the middle-class northeastern Americans targeted by these cookbooks—were hardly off the industrial food grid. For instance, recipes sometimes called for boxed gelatin or for Maizena, a commercial brand of cornstarch. In her section on bread, Mary Cornelius gave instructions for people who grew their own wheat as well as for those who bought theirs at the store. For this second group, she stressed the importance of buying flour under trusted brand names, an acknowledgment of the rapidly changing geography of American wheat production, which meant in practice that consumers often had little idea about where their wheat came from. Recipes at this time also called for processed items that would likely have come from stores, like cream of tartar, saleratus (or baking soda), or isinglass, a collagen made from fish bladders that served roughly the same role as gelatin.

Another development that might surprise modern readers is that Americans in the 1860s responded with growing interest to recipes whose titles loudly declared them to be foreign. These cookbooks are filled with recipes like Chicken Pillau, Calcutta Curry, Vermicelli Soup, Charlotte Russe, Mullagatawnee Soup, and Sauce Piquant, and authors also casually used generic national titles for recipes like French Rolls, German Cake, Spanish Soup, and Irish Stew. Most notably, as French cooking was increasingly exalted as the highest and most artful cuisine in the world, authors touted cooking styles that wore their French influence on their sleeves, like fricassees, soufflés, sautés, and ragouts.

Moreover, all these cookbooks, even the humblest, demanded ingredients that would have been transported across the country and the globe. Among others foods grown far from the northern United States—and often outside America—cookbooks called for chocolate, tea, coffee, sugar, vanilla, cinnamon, mace, nutmeg, cloves, cayenne, curry, pepper, olive oil, almonds, figs, citrus fruits, coconut, bananas, pineapples, gum arabic, and starches from tropical plants like sago, arrowroot, and tapioca. The fact that these cookbook authors didn't hesitate to call for imported ingredients, even in the midst of the Civil War, is one more reminder that these were Northern cookbooks, since virtually none of these far-flung ingredients would have been readily available in the South by the middle of the war because of the blockade.

The man depicted in this engraving had to carry a fifty-pound sack of flour down the street after losing a bet. It is noteworthy that the flour was produced under a brand name, which was increasingly common by the 1860s. *Harper's Weekly,* January 21, 1865, 45, Michigan State University Special Collections.

Cranberries, which Americans in the mid-nineteenth century celebrated as a uniquely American ingredient. *American Practical Cookery Book*, 139.

In general, though, what's remarkable isn't that Americans in the 1860s thought of themselves as cosmopolitan eaters, but the fact that they *didn't*. Although authors sometimes acknowledged the distant provenance of their ingredients, usually they did not, even as they were increasingly interested in foreign cuisines.[8] American food systems had been global long before the Revolution, and by the mid-nineteenth century their international reach was thoroughly normalized. It seems likely that readers of these cookbooks rarely thought of imported ingredients like cinnamon or olive oil as particularly exotic at all. The regular use of imported ingredients also highlights how contemporary nostalgia

about "returning" to local, regional eating is based on a simplistic understanding of the past.

Yet while many of the spices and flavorings used by northern Americans were imported long distances, most of their core foods were domestically produced throughout this era, and many in fact were actually native to the Americas. All of the American cookbook authors here gave recipes for strikingly American dishes like succotash, Indian Fritters, and Corn Dodgers, and they all regularly called for native American ingredients like cranberry, pumpkin, sweet potato, squash, corn, and turkey. It's noteworthy, in contrast, that virtually none of those American ingredients appeared in the one book originally published in England, *What to Do with the Cold Mutton*.

If food in the Civil War era was not strictly local, it was more seasonal than it is today. Seasonal availability of ingredients was a serious constraint, an issue present in all the cookbooks but clearest in the monthly menus of *What Shall We Eat*, in which fresh produce abounds only in the summer months, meats like lamb are only suggested in spring, and shellfish appears only in the winter. Of course, those food preservation techniques discussed above would have expanded cooks' options, but cookbook writers—and presumably ordinary eaters, too—were sensitive to the differences between fresh and preserved foods. Another issue nineteenth-century cooks grappled with, and one that modern readers are less likely to consider when thinking about seasonal foods, is that cooking techniques also had to be adjusted depending on whether the weather was hot or cold.

Cookbook writers at the time routinely referred to this daily reality. Ann Howe, for example, wrote that venison tasted better when it had been stored for about ten days before cooking it, but she knew that this was only possible in cold weather. Similarly, in a recipe for Rennet Pudding, Knight instructed readers that in cold weather they should warm the milk "enough to remove the chill," though she noted it would already be warm enough in summer. The phrase "room temperature," a commonplace cookery term by the mid-twentieth century, virtually never appeared in the mid-nineteenth century, a time when room temperatures would have varied enormously during the year.

The variability of household temperatures was only one of the challenges 1860s cooks faced as they ran their kitchens, the most thoroughly demanding job in any home. Among many other tasks, housekeepers or their servants had to pump and haul water, tend kitchen gardens, and care for animals like chickens, pigs, and cows. They carried coal and sometimes chopped wood, and they had to start and supervise the fire, the most complicated and dangerous job of all. Getting the cook stove to a desired temperature and keeping it there was an art form. Heated by coal or by wood, ovens were notoriously hard to control, and cooks would not have had thermometers to help them gauge the temperature. As a result, cookbook authors did not specify precise temperatures but instead used broad terms to describe levels of heat, like "a slow oven," "a moderate oven," "a quick, but not furiously-hot oven," or simply "bake until you think it is done." In other words, they relied heavily on their readers' experience to know how hot to get the oven and how long to leave the food inside. Of course, for people with little cooking experience to draw upon, cookbooks could offer frustratingly meager help on this point.

Like instructions about oven temperatures and baking times, cookbook authors described food quantities with what can seem like jarring imprecision. At least a generation before the use of measuring cups and spoons was standardized in the United States, measurements tended to be relative and impressionistic.[9] Authors described quantities of food in terms like "the size of a hen's egg" or "about the size of a Spanish silver dollar." Although the use of cups, rather than scales, would become one of the leading distinctions between American and British cookery by the early twentieth century, authors in the 1860s still varied, sometimes from page to page, over whether quantities appeared in terms of cups, like a "wineglass" or a "coffee cup," or in terms of weight, as in the popular phrase "the weight of six eggs in sugar."

In the 1860s, Americans who could afford to do so generally ate large quantities of animal products, building their meals on milk, butter, cream, eggs, lard, and, especially, meat. Indeed, middle-class cooking centered around meat, incorporating it into virtually every meal and making use of a diversity of animal species and cuts that would dizzy a contemporary eater accustomed to the paucity of modern supermarkets. Desserts routinely called for meat products, too. Beyond gelatin or mincemeat, nineteenth-century desserts regularly contained suet, lard, and salt pork—and sometimes pounds of them.

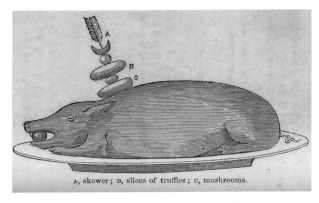

A, skewer; B, slices of truffles; c, mushrooms.

A roasted suckling pig. Pierre Blot, *Hand-Book of Practical Cookery for Ladies and Professional Cooks* (New York: D. Appleton, 1868), 236, Michigan State University Special Collections.

Americans in this era were also generally comfortable eating—and thinking about—a much greater variety of animal body parts than Americans today. For instance, in Cornelius's recipe for Souse—which meant meat that had been boiled and then soused, or soaked, in vinegar and spices—she instructed readers to remove "the horny parts of the feet and toes of a pig, and clean the feet, ears, and tail very thoroughly." In another recipe, she instructed the reader to cut off the feet of a freshly slaughtered piglet, to stuff the body cavity and skewer it on a spit, and then to make a gravy with the feet, liver, and brains while the piglet turned before the fire. And how would the reader know when the piglet was done? That was easy: when the eyes fell out. Ann Howe thought it a nice touch to serve the calf's feet on a platter right alongside the calf's head. Recipes routinely instructed readers to work with appendages and organs, to remove eyes or brains or to saw bones.

Together, excerpts from five cookbooks from the Civil War era present a compelling portrait of cooking and eating in the urban North of the 1860s United States. Many different kinds of people used cookbooks in the 1860s, and the intended audiences of these books were diverse. Mary Hooker Cornelius's *Young Housekeeper's Friend* and Ann Howe's *The American Kitchen Directory and Housewife* are both classic examples of domestic encyclopedias. Detailed works aimed at inexperienced housekeepers, both offered relatively explicit instructions that would have been useful to young women keeping house for the first time as well as to anyone hoping to learn about the cooking styles of the urban middle class. That would have included the many families living in cities for the first time and families with newly enlarged incomes, among other groups. The fact that both books went through multiple editions—*The Young Housekeeper's Friend* was first published in 1845 and then many times thereafter, including in 1863, while *The American Kitchen Directory and Housewife* was published first in 1863 and then again in 1868—shows that a real demand existed for their variety of detailed domestic advice.

Yet the cookbook genre itself was changing in the 1860s, and the Civil War accelerated those changes. Demand was steadily rising for a range of specialized cookbooks that focused exclusively on food, rather than for thick reference works in which cooking featured as one among a host of domestic topics. Knight concentrated on the cost of food, tailoring her concise recipes for women who could regularly afford meat and desserts but who still needed to prepare such dishes in a relatively economical way. The 1865 *What to Do with the Cold Mutton: A Book of Réchauffés, Together with Many Other Approved Receipts for the Kitchen of a Gentleman of Moderate Income*, first published the year before in London by an author identified only as P. K. S., demonstrates the strong continuing influence of British cookery in American kitchens well into the mid-nineteenth century. The author aimed the book at women who were forced to prioritize economy when they planned their meals. The book focuses on the humble categories of leftovers, which the author called *réchaufés*, presumably because he or she thought the French term sounded more elegant. Finally, with notably less concern for economy than the other cookbooks, the author of the 1868 *What Shall We Eat? A Manual for Housekeepers, Comprising a Bill of Fare for Breakfast, Dinner, and Tea, for Every Day in the Year* aimed squarely at ladies in charge of overseeing prosperous households. Anticipating the heavy multicourse dinners that would become chic in the Gilded Age, the author organized the book around menus, offering valuable hints about how Americans may have organized their meals, although the elaborate spreads suggested on a daily basis here would have been prohibitively expensive for the great majority of Americans.

Grammar, spelling, and capitalization were all somewhat idiosyncratic in the mid-nineteenth century. In a few cases, I made minor changes in the capitalization of the recipe titles in order to make the style consistent across the cookbooks. Otherwise, I have kept the authors' original text except in cases where there was clearly a typographical error.

The Cookbooks

Mary Hooker Cornelius. *The Young Housekeeper's Friend*. Boston: Taggard & Thompson, 1863.

Mrs. S. G. Knight. *Tit-Bits; Or, How to Prepare a Nice Dish at a Moderate Expense*. Boston: Crosby and Nichols, 1864.

P. K. S. *What to Do with the Cold Mutton: A Book of Réchauffés, Together with Many Other Approved Receipts for the Kitchen of a Gentleman of Moderate Income*. New York: Bunce and Huntington, Publishers, 1865.

Ann Howe. *The American Kitchen Directory and Housewife*. Cincinnati: Howe's Subscription Book Concern, 1868.

What Shall We Eat? A Manual for Housekeepers, Comprising a Bill of Fare for Breakfast, Dinner, and Tea, for Every Day in the Year. New York: G.P. Putnam & Son, 1868.

Mary Hooker Cornelius,
The Young Housekeeper's Friend

Throughout the first half of the nineteenth century, a time when professionally printed cookbooks were first becoming widely available in the United States, they served mainly as encyclopedic domestic references. Recipes were a crucial part of these books, but they were usually only a part, along with sections on laundry, housecleaning, etiquette, childrearing, treating the sick, and making household supplies, among other subjects. Throughout the first half of the nineteenth century, when even financially comfortable families might have only one domestic book in their homes, authors felt it incumbent on themselves to provide comprehensive guidance. By the Civil War era, however, as books became more widely available and more broadly affordable, cookbook authors started to focus more exclusively on food and cooking. Mary Cornelius's *The Young Housekeeper's Friend*, first published in 1845 and then again several times thereafter, including in 1863, clearly shows the transition occurring within the genre. She devoted the great majority of her book to food and even specifically noted that she was *not* including instructions

for general care of the household. Yet she did in fact write at length about managing servants, Christian piety, and the importance of creating schedules for all domestic tasks, as well as concluding the book with a thirty-page section that touched on everything from killing insects to washing clothes to caring for houseplants and making cologne.

Writers providing domestic information often personified their books as friendly teachers, and many actually called them a "friend" or "companion" or "guide," just as Cornelius called her book *The Young Housekeeper's Friend*. Cornelius claimed that she was motivated to help other women because she had "seen many a young lady, just entered upon the duties of married life, perplexed and prematurely care-worn, for want of experience, or a little good instruction, in regard to the simplest domestic processes." The idea that cookbooks were helpers and friends was an old one in American cookery. In Amelia Simmons's 1796 *American Cookery*, the book widely recognized as the first American cookbook, Simmons advertised the fact that she herself was an "American

Orphan" precisely because she wanted her book to help other women who had no mother nearby to guide them in the kitchen.[1]

While domestic references like Cornelius's would have appealed to a range of people who wanted to learn more about cooking, she aimed her book specifically at newly married middle-class women with limited budgets. She intended her instructions "to be so minute, and of so practical a character, that the observance of them shall prevent very many of the perplexities which most young people suffer during their first years of married life." Although her brief and sometimes vague instructions might frustrate modern readers, they were actually quite explicit relative to the cursory style of most cookbooks in the first half of the century, where recipes were often little more than an imprecise list of ingredients. It's also noteworthy that what might frustrate a modern reader as a cook can be revealing to a modern reader as a historian; all recipes, old and modern, detailed and curt, are limited by the assumptions they make about a reader's prior knowledge, and those recipes that provide the least information give a sense of the skills even a relatively inexperienced cook may have been presumed to have possessed in the mid-nineteenth century.

Foreshadowing the claims of the home economics movement in the decades that followed, Cornelius argued that diet had a profound effect on both the body and the mind, and she elevated cooking as an intellectual achievement and as an occupation worthy of educated women. Cornelius opened her book by calling

for women to have more "symmetrical" educations, by which she meant that they should be educated not only in classical subjects but also in the domestic arts. It had become common, she lamented, to find highly educated young women who were profoundly ignorant about basic household tasks. As a result, their management of food was often "little else than a series of experiments; often unsuccessful, resulting in mortification and discomfort in the parlor, and waste and ill temper in the kitchen." Vigorously fighting the idea that domestic work was fit only for mindless drudges, she argued that, on the contrary, the "most elevated minds fulfil best the every-day duties of life."

Cornelius's readers would have needed to know how to plan menus and grocery budgets, to understand how food was prepared, and to oversee the kitchen work, but they very possibly did not do the bulk of the cooking themselves. Although Cornelius said she was writing for women who had "neither poverty nor riches," it's important to note that she still assumed her middle-class readers would have at least one or two servants helping them in the kitchen, and she wrote at length about the treatment of servants. By the mid-nineteenth century, it had become fashionable for elite Americans to express humane and even parent-like concern for the welfare of servants and slaves, at least rhetorically if not in practice. Cornelius went out of her way to counsel her readers on the art of enlightened management of servants, and she specifically recommended that mistresses teach any illiterate servants to read, advice that readers at the time would have readily contrasted with the slave codes in southern states that made it illegal to teach slaves to read. Cornelius also cautioned northern readers against thinking too well of their own treatment of domestic help simply because they hired servants, rather than owning slaves: "The situation of a waiting-maid is, in some families, one of hard bondage. It seems as if her employers had forgotten that she is made of flesh and blood, and is therefore capable of having an aching head and weary limbs." But Cornelius also warned readers against coddling servants. For example, she wrote that they should not indulge the cook by giving her the leftovers.

Americans in the 1860s relied heavily on preserved foods, yet when they ate fresh food, it was often exceedingly fresh. For example, Cornelius told her readers to buy fish only if it had been caught a few hours before, and she gave detailed instructions about how they could distinguish a truly fresh fish: "Of this you can judge by their being hard under the pressure of the finger. Fish lose their best flavor soon, and a few hours make a wide difference in the taste of some sorts." In another recipe for roasted pig she stated that the piglet should be no more than a month old and that "it should be killed on the morning of the day it is to be cooked." Her recipes also highlight the degree to which the availability of many ingredients was strictly seasonal. In her recipe for pickled butternuts, for instance, she instructed readers to gather the nuts "between the twenty-fifth and thirtieth of June." Meanwhile, she imagined her recipe for Old Potatoes would be most useful in the spring, when potatoes harvested the previous summer were driest and least appealing.

Preface, 1845

In preparing this little volume, my aim has been to furnish to young housekeepers the best aid that a book can give in the departments of which it treats. No printed guide can perfectly supply the place of that experience which is gained by early and habitual attention to domestic concerns. But the directions here given are designed to be so minute, and of so practical a character, that the observance of them shall prevent very many of the perplexities which most young people suffer during their first years of married life.

The receipts, with the exception of about twenty which are copied from books, are furnished from my own experience, or that of my immediate friends. An ample variety is given for furnishing the table of any American family; but especial reference has been had to those who have neither poverty nor riches; and such directions have been given as will enable a housekeeper to provide a good and healthful table, or, if desired, a handsome one, at a moderate expense.

To save repetition, very minute directions are given at the head of every chapter, by attending to which, the least experienced cook will learn how to proceed in making each article for which a receipt is given.

I do not attempt to give directions in regard to the best methods of taking care of all sorts of furniture, and performing all the various kinds of household labor, because there are works already published which furnish copious and judicious instructions on these subjects.

It may be asked, "Why then publish a book of counsels and receipts, for there surely are many receipt-books?" This is true; but while some of them are not ample guides on the subjects which they treat, others are based upon a plan both expensive and unhealthy, and all of them that I have seen, leave an inexperienced housekeeper at a loss in regard to many of the things most necessary to economy and comfort.

I have seen many a young lady, just entered upon the duties of married life, perplexed and prematurely care-worn, for want of experience, or a little good instruction, in regard to the simplest domestic processes; and often have felt, with the sincerest sympathy, an earnest wish to render her some effectual aid. If I succeed in affording it through this little book, I shall esteem myself happy; and I have only to ask, in conclusion, that my numerous young friends, and all the youthful housekeepers into whose hands it may fall, will receive it as a token of my friendly interest and best wishes.

M. H. C.

Andover, 1845

Preface to the Revised Edition, 1859

My aim in the revision of this little book has been to make the arrangement of the receipts and of the index more convenient, the directions more simple and clear, and the entire collection more select and reliable. In place of some of the old receipts many choice new ones are substituted, which, so far as I know, have not been in print before. All of them have been attested by experience, either my own, or of friends in whose judgment in such matters I have entire confidence. The last chapter, written long since in compliance with frequent requests from young friends, is appended in the hope that it will increase the usefulness of the book to those for whose benefit it was originally designed.

I trust it is not improper for me to add, that among the motives which have led to the present revision, is the favor with which many ladies have regarded this book in its original form, notwithstanding its confessed imperfections. It has been my earnest wish for years to make it more worthy of such estimation; and hoping that it will prove a better Friend to Young Housekeepers than it has hitherto been, I ask for the continued patronage of those who have so long and so kindly overlooked its faults.

M. H. C.

March, 1859

Counsels and Suggestions

A symmetrical education is extremely rare in this country. Nothing is more common than to see young ladies, whose intellectual attainments are of a high order, profoundly ignorant of the duties which all acknowledge to belong peculiarly to women. Consequently many have to learn, after marriage, how to take care of a family; and thus their housekeeping is, frequently, little else than a series of experiments; often unsuccessful, resulting in mortification and discomfort in the parlor, and waste and ill temper in the kitchen.

So numerous are these instances, that excellence in housekeeping has come to be considered as incompatible with superior intellectual culture. But it is not so. The most elevated minds fulfil best the every-day duties of life. If young women would resolve, let the effort cost what it will, to perfect themselves in their appropriate duties, a defective domestic education would soon be remedied. Observation and persevering attention would give the requisite knowledge, and their efforts would bring a speedy and ample reward . . .

How often do we see the happiness of a husband abridged by the absence of skill, neatness, and economy in a wife! Perhaps he is not able to fix upon the cause, for he does not understand minutely enough the processes upon which domestic order depends, to analyze the difficulty; but he is conscious of discomfort. However improbable it may seem, the health of many a professional man is undermined, and his usefulness curtailed, if not sacrificed, because he habitually eats *bad bread*.

How frequently, in case of students in the various professions, is the brightest promise of future attainment and honor overshadowed by a total loss of health; and the young scholar, in whom the choicest hopes were garnered up, is compelled to relinquish his studies, and turn his unwilling thoughts to other pursuits; or, worse than this, he becomes a helpless invalid for life. Yet even this is an enviable lot, compared with his, whose noble intellectual powers have become like the broken chords of an instrument that shall never again utter its melody. But are such evils as these to be traced to the use of unwholesome food? Every intelligent physician, every superintendent of our insane hospitals, testifies that in very many instances, this is the prominent cause . . .

In concluding these suggestions, the writer cannot refrain from adding a few words of sympathy and encouragement for those who, having passed their youth in affluent ease, or in the delights of study, are obliged, by the vicissitudes of life, to spend their time and strength in laborious household occupations. There are many such instances in this country, particularly in the great Western Valley. Adversity succeeds prosperity like a sudden inundation, and sweeps away the possessions and the hopes of multitudes. The poor and uneducated are often rapidly elevated to wealthy independence, while the refined and highly educated are compelled to taste the bitterness of poverty; and minds capable of any attainment, and that would grace any station, are doomed to expend their energies in devising methods for the hands to earn a scanty livelihood.

Let not such persons feel themselves degraded by the performance of the humblest domestic labor . . . However lowly the common duties of life may be, a faithful and cheerful discharge of them is always honorable, and God smiles on those who patiently fulfil them.

Ovens, Bread, &c.

Directions Respecting Bread

There is no one thing upon which health and comfort in a family so much depend as *bread*. With good bread the coarsest fare is tolerable; without it, the most luxurious table is not comfortable.

It is best economy to purchase *the best* flour, even at an extra cost. Good flour adheres slightly to the hand, and if pressed in it, shows the impress of the lines of the skin. Dough made of it is a *yellowish white*, and does not stick to the hands after sufficient kneading. There is much bad flour in market, which can in no way be made into nutritious food.

When you find good flour, notice *the brand* and afterwards purchase the same kind. The writer knows a family that for eleven years purchased flour in this way, without once having a poor barrel; then the mills passed to another owner, and though the brand was the same, the flour was good no more.

If you raise wheat, or buy it in the grain, always wash it before sending it to the mill. Take two or three bushels at a time, pour in water and stir it, and then pour off the water. Repeat this till the water is clear. Do not let the grain stand in the water, as it will swell and be injured; spread it on a large cloth in the sun, or where it will have warmth and fresh air, and stir it often, and in a day or two it will be dry. The flour is much improved by this process.

Newly ground flour which has never been packed, is very superior to barrel flour, so that the people in Western New York, that land of finest wheat, say that New England people do not know what good flour is.

Indian meal, also, is much the best when freshly ground. The meal made of Southern corn is often injured by salt water, or *dampness* acquired in the hold of a ship.

Rye flour is very apt to be *musty* or *grown*. There is no way to detect this but by trial. It is well to engage a farmer to supply you with the same he provides for his own family.

Good Family Bread

For five common-sized loaves, make a pint and a half of thin water gruel. Use half a teacupful of fine Indian meal. Salt it a little more than if it were to be eaten as gruel, and boil ten or fifteen minutes. This is of importance, as, if the meal is only scalded the bread will be coarse. Add enough milk to make two quarts of the whole. If the milk is new, the gruel may be poured into it in the pan; if not, it should be scalded in the kettle with the gruel. This is particularly important in the summer, as at that season milk which is but a few hours old, and is sweet when put into the bread, will sour in the dough in a short time. When the mixture is cool, so that you are *sure* it will not scald, add a teacupful of yeast, and then stir in sifted flour enough to make a thick batter. This is called a sponge. This being done in the evening, let it stand, if in summer, in a cool place, if in winter, in a moderately warm place, till morning. Then add flour enough to make it easy to mould, and knead it very thoroughly.

This process of kneading is very important in making bread, and there are but few domestics whom it is not necessary to instruct how to do it. They generally work over the dough without expending any strength upon it. The hands should be closely shut, and the fists pressed hard and quickly upon the dough, dipping them into flour whenever the dough sticks to them. A half an hour is the least time to be given to kneading a baking of bread, unless you prefer, after having done this till it ceases to stick to your hands, to chop it with a chopping-knife four or five hundred strokes. An hour's kneading is not too much.

All this looks on paper like a long and troublesome process; but I venture to say that no lady, after having learned the benefit of it, will be willing to diminish any portion of the labor and attention necessary to secure such bread as these directions, observed, will make. Practice will make it easy, and no woman of sense will hesitate in choosing between sour, tough, ill-baked bread, with heaps of wasted pieces, a dyspeptic husband, and sickly children on the one hand, and comfort, economy, and health on the other.

But to return to the bread. After it is thoroughly kneaded, divide it into four or five equal pieces, and mould according to the form of the pans in which you bake it. These being greased with clean drippings, put in the dough and set it in the sun or near the fire (according to the season) to rise. Loaves of this size will bake in an hour; if the oven be rather hot, in a few minutes short of an hour. Practice and good judgment must direct these things. If the bread rises rather slowly, take a dish of warm water and wet the top with your hand.

When the loaves are baked, do not lay them flat upon the table; good housewives think it makes them heavy. Set them on the side, one against another, and put a coarse cloth closely over them; this makes the crust tender by keeping in the steam. If bread is baked too hard, wring a towel in cold water, and wrap around it while it is yet hot. Care is necessary that bread does not rise too much, and thus become sour, especially in warm weather; and it becomes dry sooner by long rising. No exact rule can be given; experience and observation must teach. When dough becomes so light as to run over after being moulded and put into pans, it is best to mould it again, kneading it hard two or three minutes, but using as little flour as possible; then lay it back into the pans, and put it immediately into the oven; this prevents its being tasteless and dry; it will be perfectly light, but of a different sort, and much preferred by some persons.

Some people invariably use saleratus in bread, and there are tables where the effluvia of this article, and the deep yellow color of the bread, offend the senses before it is tasted. If all the materials used are good, and the dough has not been permitted to sour, white bread except that which is made with water, is far better without saleratus. If dough has become sour, a teaspoonful of saleratus for every quart of the milk or water that was used for wetting the bread, will be sufficient to correct it. The tray or pan in which the bread is made, should be scalded after being washed, every time it is used, except in cold weather. It is not good economy to buy skimmed milk, as some persons do, for making bread. It renders it tough and indigestible, if used in the ordinary way. In case it is used for this purpose, it should be boiled, and thickened with a little Indian meal in the same way, and the same proportions as directed for making gruel, in the receipt for Good Family Bread. Use no water with it.

To Make Stale Bread, or Cake, Fresh

Plunge the loaf one instant in cold water, and lay it upon a tin in the stove ten or fifteen minutes. It will be like new bread without its deleterious qualities. Stale cake is thus made nice as new cake. But bread or cake heated over thus, should be used immediately.

Biscuits, Tea Cakes, Griddle Cakes, &c.

Butter-milk Biscuit

Take a half pint of butter-milk, or sour milk, and a pint of flour. Rub into the flour a piece of butter half the size of an egg. Add a little salt and stir the milk into the flour. Dissolve a teaspoonful of saleratus in a very little hot water, and stir into it.

Add flour enough barely to mould it smooth; roll it out upon the board, and cut out and bake exactly like the tea biscuit. The advantage of putting in the saleratus after the dough is partly mixed, is, that the foaming process occasioned by combining the sour milk and alkali, raises the whole mass; whereas if it stirred first into the milk, much of the effervescence is lost, before it is added to the flour.

Whigs

Half a pound of butter, the same of sugar, six eggs, two pounds of flour, a pint of milk, a gill of yeast, and a little salt. Melt the butter in the milk, and pour into the flour; beat the sugar and eggs together and stir in. Add the yeast last, and be careful to mix the whole very thoroughly. Bake in tin hearts and rounds, in the stove, or baker.

Waffles

To a quart of milk, put six eggs, a quarter of a pound of butter, a large gill of yeast, a little salt, and flour enough to make a batter the thickness of griddle cakes. The iron must be heated on hot coals, and then buttered or greased with lard, and one side filled with batter, then be shut and laid on the fire. After a few minutes turn it upon the other side. It takes about twice the time that it would to bake them on a griddle, and they are really no better, but look more inviting.

Fritters or Pan-Cakes

Make a batter of a pint of milk, three eggs, salt, and flour to make a rather thick batter. Beat it well, then drop it with a spoon into hot fat, and fry like doughnuts. These, and the snow fritters are usually eaten with sugar and cider, or lemon juice.

Snow Fritters

Stir together milk, flour, and a little salt, to make rather a thick batter. Add new-fallen snow in the proportion of a teacupful to a pint of milk. Have the fat ready hot, at the time you stir in the snow, and drop the batter into it with a spoon. These pancakes are even preferred by some, to those made with eggs.

Washington [Cake]

To one pound of flour, put one pound of sugar, three quarters of a pound of butter, eight eggs, two nutmegs, one pound of raisins, and one of currants.

Composition [Cake]

A coffee cup of butter (small measure), two of sugar, three of flour, one and a half of good ground rice, one of sour milk, half a nutmeg, a little essence of lemon, a large teaspoonful of saleratus, and three eggs. If you have sour cream, instead of the milk, use a half a cup of butter.

Measure [Cake]

Twelve fresh eggs, three cups of flour, three of sugar, a little salt, and spice or lemon as you prefer. Break the eggs together, and put them without beating into the sugar, then beat steadily with a smart stroke half an hour, then stir in the flour, and bake in rather thick loaves three quarters of an hour.

No one but a person having a very strong arm can make this kind of sponge cake well. It is elegant when well made.

Federal [Cake]

A pound each of butter and sugar, a pound and two ounces of flour, a pound of raisins, five eggs, a cup of sour cream (or, if milk is used instead of cream, add a quarter of a pound more of butter), half a nutmeg, a wineglass of brandy, and a teaspoonful of saleratus. Stir the butter, sugar, and nutmeg to a cream, then add the eggs, then the cream and saleratus mixed, next the flour (a little at a time), except a handful in which to mix the raisins, and last, the brandy and fruit.

Very delicious for persons who like rich cake.

Gold [Cake]

A pound each of flour and sugar, three quarters of a pound of butter, the yolks of fourteen eggs, and the juice and grated rind of two lemons. Stir the sugar and butter to a cream, and add the yolks well beaten, and strained. Then put in the lemon peel, and the flour (dried), and a teaspoonful of saleratus dissolved in a spoonful of hot water. Beat it fifteen minutes, and just before it goes into the oven, stir in the lemon juice very thoroughly. Bake it in a square, flat pan, ice it thickly, and cut it into square pieces.

Silver [Cake]

One pound of sugar, three quarters of a pound of dried flour, six ounces of butter, the whites of fourteen eggs. Add mace and citron. Beat the sugar and butter to a cream, and add the whites, cut to a stiff froth, next the flour, and then the mace and citron. Bake in a pan of the same size as for the golden cake. They are not difficult to make, and are very beautiful together.

Cream Cakes, Cookies, Wafers, Kisses, Jumbles, Gingerbread, Etc.

Cookies

To one teacup of butter, three of sugar, half a cup of milk or cream, three eggs, one small teaspoonful of saleratus, and flour to make it rather stiff. Flavor with nutmeg and cinnamon.

Kisses

Beat the whites of nine fresh eggs to a stiff froth, then mix with it fifteen spoonfuls of finest white sugar, and five or so drops of essence of lemon. Drop them on paper with a teaspoon, sift sugar over them, and bake them in a slow oven.

Hard Sugar Gingerbread

Two cups of butter, four of sugar, two eggs, a cup and a half of milk, two teaspoonfuls of ginger, and one of saleratus. Flour to make rather a stiff dough.

Ginger Crackers

A pint of molasses, two cups of butter, one and a half of sugar, one teaspoonful of saleratus, and two of ginger; add flour enough to make it easy to roll out. Stir the butter and sugar together, boil the molasses and pour it into the pan, and stir steadily until the butter and sugar are melted, then put in a few handfuls of flour, and add the saleratus. Stir it a few minutes, and then work in all the flour. To be rolled very thin, and baked but a few minutes.

New York Ginger Snaps

Half a pound each of butter and sugar, two and a half pounds of flour, a pint of molasses, a teaspoonful of saleratus, caraway seeds, or ginger. Mix it just like the ginger crackers, and bake them thin.

[Pie] of Stewed Apple

Stew the apple with water enough to prevent its burning; sweeten and flavor it to your taste, and, while it is hot, add butter in the proportion of a dessert spoonful to a quart of apple. The spices most appropriate are nutmeg and lemon, cinnamon and orange. Two kinds are enough; one does very well. When you have laid the under crust in the plate, roll out the upper one, so that it may be laid on the moment the apple is put in, as the under crust will be clammy if the pie is not put immediately into the oven.

Whortleberry [Pie]

Fill the dish not quite even full, and to each pie of the size of a large soup plate, add four large spoonfuls of sugar (for blackberries and blueberries, five). Dredge a very little flour over the fruit before you lay on the upper crust. Close the edge with special care.

Cranberry [Tarts]

Take the sauce as prepared to eat with meat; grate a little nutmeg over it, put three or four thin shavings of butter on it, and then lay on the upper crust. If not sweet enough, add more sugar. Make it without an upper crust, if you prefer, and lay very narrow strips across diagonally.

[Pie of] Green Currants and Gooseberries

These require a great deal of sugar, at least two thirds as much in measure as of fruit. Currant pies should be made in a deep plate or a pudding dish, and with an upper crust.

Gooseberries should be stewed like cranberries, sweetened to suit the taste, and laid upon the under crust, with strips placed diagonally across the top, as directed for the cranberry tarts. Currants that are almost ripe make a nice pie, and require the same measure of sugar as blackberries.

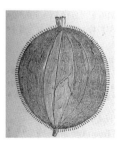

A gooseberry.
American Practical Cookery Book, 137.

Rich Mince [Pie]

To one beef's tongue, allow a pound of suet, a pound of currants, another of raisins, a pound and a quarter of sugar, half a pound of citron, eight large apples, a quart of wine or boiled cider, salt, a nutmeg, cinnamon, cloves, the juice and pulp of a lemon, and the rind chopped fine. Let the meat be chopped very fine, then add the apples and chop them fine also. Put the sugar into the cider or wine, and just boil it up so as to skim off the top; let it stand a few minutes, and then pour it off into a pan containing all the other ingredients. Be careful, in pouring it, not to disturb any sediment there may be from the sugar. Use loaf sugar if you choose.

Temperance [Pie]

Boil five pounds of meat in water enough to have one quart when it is done; chop the meat very fine when it is cold, and add a quarter of a pound of suet, or salt pork, three pounds and a half of sugar, three of chopped apple, two and a half of box raisins and one of Sultana raisins, one of citron, and a pint of syrup of preserved peach, quince, or both; or any other syrup you may have; add salt, nutmeg, and powdered clove. To mix the ingredients, remove the fat from the juice of the meat and put it into a kettle with the apple, sugar, raisins, and citron, and let them boil a few minutes; if froth rises, take it off; have the meat ready in a pan mixed with the spices, pour the mixture boiling hot upon it, and stir it together; add, if you choose, the juice and pulp of three lemons. This process cooks the ingredients so thoroughly that, if you prefer, you can bake the paste first and then fill the dishes; and if you choose to reserve part of it, it will keep in a cool place several weeks.

Puddings

Directions about Puddings

The eggs for all sorts of puddings in which they are used, should be well beaten, and then strained. If hot milk is used, the eggs should be added after all the other ingredients. Milk for pumpkin, squash, coconut, tapioca, ground rice, sago, arrowroot, and sweet potato puddings, should be boiled; for bread and plum puddings also, unless the bread is soaked in milk over night. When suet is used in puddings, it should be chopped fine as possible.

In making batter puddings, but a small portion of the milk should be put to the flour at first, as it will be difficult to stir out the little lumps, if the whole quantity is mixed together at once. After the flour is stirred smooth, in a part of the milk, add the eggs not beaten, and beat the mixture well; then add the remainder of the milk, and stir all together till equally mixed. A flour pudding is much lighter, when the materials are all beaten together, than if the eggs are done separately. When berries or cherries are to be used, put them in last. A batter pudding, with berries, requires at least a third more flour than one without. For cherry pudding but a small addition of flour is needed.

A buttered earthen bowl, with a cloth tied up close over it, is a very good thing in which to boil a pudding or dumpling; but some persons think they are lighter boiled in a cloth. A large square of thick tow or hemp cloth does very well; but if a bag is preferred, it should

A typical pudding, steamed or baked in a mould. Most nineteenth-century puddings were not creamy dairy desserts, but rather heavier dishes made from a batter of flour and eggs. Blot, *Hand-Book of Practical Cookery*, 444.

be so cut that the bottom will be several inches narrower than the top, and the corners rounded. The seam should be stitched close with a coarse thread on one side, and then turned and stitched again on the other, in order to secure the pudding from the water. When used, let the seam be outside. A strong twine, a yard long, should be sewed at the middle to the seam, about three inches from the top of the bag. When the bag is to be used, wring it in cold water, and sprinkle the inside thick with flour, and lay it in a dish; pour in the batter and tie up the bag quickly, drawing the string as tight as possible. Allow a little room for the pudding to swell. (An Indian pudding made with cold milk, swells more than any other.) Lay it immediately into the boiling pot, and after ten minutes, turn it over to prevent the flour from settling on one side. If there is fruit in the pudding, it should be turned three or four times during the first half hour. Keep it covered by adding water from the tea-kettle if necessary, and be careful that it boils steadily. If it does not, the pudding will be watery. When you take it up, plunge it for a moment in a pan of cold water; then pour off the water, untie the twine, and gently lay back the top of the bag. Have a dish ready, and turn the pudding out upon it. A batter pudding without berries cooks very nicely in a tin pudding pan, set upright in a kettle of boiling water.

To cut a boiled pudding without making it heavy, lay the knife, first one side and then the other, upon it, long enough to warm the blade.

If these directions seem needlessly minute, it should be remembered that those things which seem perfectly obvious to the experienced, are often very perplexing to the uninitiated.

Apple Pudding

To a quart of stewed sour apple, put while it is hot, a piece of butter the size of an egg, and sugar enough to make it quite sweet. Beat it several minutes in order to mix it thoroughly. Beat four eggs and stir into it, add lemon or any essence you choose. Butter a cold dish thick, with cold butter, and strew the bottom and sides with cracker crumbs, or very fine bread crumbs; then pour in the mixture, sift plenty of the cracker crumbs on the top, grate a little nutmeg upon it, and sprinkle it with sifted sugar. Bake forty or fifty minutes in one dish, or half an hour in two. It is as good cold, the second day, as when first baked. It is an improvement to eat it with cream.

Bird's Nest [Pudding]

For a pint of cold milk allow three eggs, five spoonfuls of flour, six medium sized, fair apples, and a small teaspoonful of salt.

Pare the apples, and take out the cores; arrange them in a buttered dish that will just receive them (one in the centre and five around it). Wet the flour smooth in part of the milk, then add the eggs and beat all together a few minutes; then put in the salt, and the rest of the milk. Stir it well and pour it into the dish of apples. Bake it an hour, and make a melted sauce. For a large family make double measure, but bake it in two dishes, as the centre apples of a large dish will not cook as quickly, as those around the edge.

Cracker [Pudding]

To a pint of boiled milk, put four crackers, pounded and sifted, three eggs, and a small teaspoonful of salt. Add whortleberries if convenient, and in that case, half of another cracker. Make a sweet sauce. Bake half an hour, or forty minutes. The same mixture made with cold milk is a nice pudding boiled an hour and a half.

Plum [Pudding]

A pound of bread or six pounded crackers, one quart of milk, six eggs, a large spoonful of flour, a teacup of sugar, one nutmeg, a teaspoonful of cinnamon, half a one of powdered clove, a piece of butter the size of an egg, the same quantity of chopped suet, and a pound of raisins. Boil the milk. It is very well to soak the bread in the milk over night; then the entire crust becomes soft, and mixes well with the other ingredients.

These puddings are served with a rich sauce, if eaten warm, but are excellent cold, cut up like cake. People that are subject to a great deal of uninvited company, find it convenient in cold weather to bake half a dozen at once. They will keep several weeks, and when one is to be used, it may be loosened from the dish by a knife passed around it, and a little hot water be poured in round the edge. It should then be covered close, and set for half an hour into the stove or oven.

Sago [Pudding]

A pint of milk, a table-spoonful and a half of pearl sago, two eggs, two large spoonfuls of sugar, and half a tea-spoon of salt. Wash the sago in warm, but not hot water, twice; then put it with the milk into a pail and set it into a kettle of hot water. Stir it very often, as it swells fast, and will else lie in a compact mass at the bottom. When it has boiled two or three minutes, take the pail from the kettle, add the salt, and the eggs beaten with the sugar. Flavor it with vanilla or a few drops of essence of lemon, put it into a dish, and grate nutmeg over it. Set it immediately into the oven, and bake it about three quarters of an hour. If you make a quart of milk, three eggs answer very well. It should then bake an hour. With this number of eggs, the sago settles a little. To have it equally diffused take five eggs.

Baked Indian [Pudding]

Boil a pint of milk, and set it off from the fire. Then stir in a large teacup of Indian meal, a cup of finely chopped suet, half a cup of white flour, the same of molasses, and a teaspoonful each of salt, ginger, and cinnamon. Grease thick by a deep fire-proof patty pan, or a brown earthen one with a small top, such as are made for baking beans, and pour in the mixture; then stir in half a pint of cold milk. Bake it in a moderate heat two hours. If you object to using suet, substitute two eggs well beaten. An excellent sauce for this, and all kinds of Indian pudding, is made by mixing sour cream and sugar, seasoned with nutmeg.

The modern ovens do not bake this kind of pudding as well as a brick oven.

Suet [Pudding]

A pint of suet chopped very fine, a pint of chopped apples, two gills of milk, a gill of molasses, a large teaspoonful of salt, and flour enough to make it rather stiff. Boil it four hours. This, and the last before it, should be boiled in a close tin pail or pudding pan, in a kettle of water.

Such a pudding as this is too hearty to be eaten after meat, and is substantial enough to constitute a dinner.

Dumplings, Flummeries, and Other Inexpensive Articles for Dessert

Baked [Apples]

Pare large, fair apples, and take out the cores, lay each one into a piece of plain pie crust, just large enough to cover it. Fill the centre of the apple with brown sugar, and add a little cinnamon, or small strips of fresh orange peel. Close the crust over the apple, and lay them, with the smooth side up, into a deep, buttered dish, in which they can be set on the table. Bake them in a stove an hour and a half. If, after an hour, you find that the syrup begins to harden in the bottom of the dish, put in half a gill of hot water. Make a cold, or melted sauce as you choose.

Roley Poley

Make a potato crust, or a paste of light bread, with butter rolled in, or one of cream tartar biscuit, as you prefer; roll it narrow and long, about a third of an inch thick; spread it with raspberry jam or apple sauce; take care that this does not come too near the edge of the crust; roll it up and close the ends and side as tight as possible, to keep the sauce from coming out and the water from soaking it. Sew it up in a cloth, and boil it an hour and a half or two hours, according to its size. Make a sauce.

[The quart measure used in the following articles, and throughout this book, is the beer quart, except where a small quart is specified.[2] In cooking such dishes as those which immediately follow, the milk should always, as in making custards, be boiled in a pail set into a kettle of hot water. They are much more delicate than when it is boiled in a saucepan; and then there is no danger of its being burned.]

Potato Starch Flummery

To one quart of boiled milk, put four beaten eggs and four spoonfuls of potato starch, wet in a little milk. Add the starch and a little salt first; then the eggs, and boil the whole a minute more. Take it up in a mould and eat it with sauce. Boil a few peach leaves in the milk if you like the flavor.

Sweet Dishes

In making blanc-mange, custards, ice-creams, &c., do not boil the milk in a saucepan, but set it, in a tin pail, into a kettle of boiling water. The milk does not rise, when boiled thus, as it does in a sauce-pan, but when the top is covered with foam, it boils enough.

In making ice cream, it is an improvement to churn the cream until it becomes frothy, before adding the other ingredients.

Arrow-Root Blanc-Mange

To three large spoonfuls of pure Jamaica arrowroot, a quart of milk, a large spoonful of fine sugar, a spoonful of rose-water, and a little salt. Reserve a gill of milk to wet the arrow-root, and boil the rest. When it boils up, stir in the arrow-root, and boil it up again a minute or two; add the sugar, salt, and rose-water, and put it into the mould.

Isinglass Blanc-Mange

Wash an ounce and a half of calf's-foot isinglass, and put it into a quart of milk over night. In the morning add three peach leaves, and boil it, slowly, twenty minutes or half an hour. Strain it into a dish upon a small teacupful of fine sugar. If it is to be served soon, add two or three beaten eggs while it is hot. Put it into the mould and set in a cool place. In hot weather this should be made over night, if wanted at dinner the next day, as it hardens slowly.

Calf's Foot Blanc-Mange

Put four calf's feet into four quarts of water; boil it away to one quart, strain it, and set it aside. When cool, remove all the fat, and in cutting the jelly out of the pan, take care to avoid the sediment. Put to it a quart of new milk, and sweeten it with fine sugar. If you season it with cinnamon or lemon peel, put it in before boiling; if with rose or peach-water, afterwards; or, if you choose, boil peach leaves in it. Boil it ten minutes, strain it through a fine sieve into a pitcher, and stir it till nearly cold. Then put it into moulds.

Charlotte Russe

Make a boiled custard of a pint of milk and four eggs; season it with vanilla, or any essence you prefer; make it very sweet, and set it away to cool. Put a half an ounce of isinglass or English gelatine into a gill of milk where it will become warm. When the gelatine is dissolved, pour it into a pint of rich cream, and whip it to complete froth. When the custard is cold, stir it gently into the whip. Line a mould that holds a quart with thin slices of sponge cake, or with sponge fingers, pour the mixture into it, and set it in a cold place.

Directions for Making Ices

Mix equal quantities of coarse salt and ice chopped small; set the freezer containing the cream into a firkin, and put in the ice and salt; let it come up well around the freezer. Turn and shake the freezer steadily at first, and nearly all the time until the cream is entirely frozen. Scrape the cream down often from the sides with a knife. When the ice and salt melt, do not pour off any of it, unless there is danger of its getting into the freezer; it takes half an hour to freeze a quart of cream; and sometimes longer. A tin pail which will hold twice the measure of the cream, answers a good purpose, if you do not own a freezer. In winter, use snow instead of ice.

Several nice receipts for ice-creams will be given under this head, but a common custard, made of rich milk, two or three eggs, and a little arrow-root, and seasoned with lemon or vanilla, makes an excellent ice-cream.

A Rich Ice-Cream

Squeeze a dozen lemons, and strain the juice upon as much fine sugar as it will absorb; pour three quarts of cream into it very slowly, stirring very fast all the time.

Apricot [Ice]

Pare, stone, and scald twelve ripe apricots; then bruise them in a marble mortar. Then stir half a pound of fine sugar into a pint of cream; add the apricots and strain through a hair sieve. Freeze and put it into moulds.

Peaches would be a good substitute for the apricots, using, if they are large, nine, instead of twelve.

Currant [Ice]

Take a gill of fresh currant juice, make it very sweet, and stir in half a pint of cream and freeze it. In the winter, or when fresh currants are not to be had, beat a teaspoonful and a half of currant jelly with the juice of one lemon, sweetened, and put to it half a pint of cream.

Wine Custard

Beat the yolks of three eggs with two spoonfuls of crushed sugar, and cut the whites to a stiff froth; put them into the dish which is to go to the table, and add a quart of milk, and a few drops of peach or rose-water, and when these are well mixed, stir in a spoonful and a half of rennet wine. In a cold weather, the milk should be warmed a little; in warm weather it is not necessary. It should be immediately set where it will not be disturbed. It will harden soon, perhaps in five minutes. This depends somewhat on the strength of the rennet, and the measure of wine necessary to harden a quart of milk will depend on this. Sometimes a spoonful will prove enough. There is no way to judge but by trying, as in using rennet for making cheese. The strength of this article varies exceedingly.

To Preserve Fruit and Make Jellies

A kettle should be kept on purpose. Brass, if very bright, will do. If acid fruit is preserved in a brass kettle which is not bright, it becomes poisonous. Bell-metal is better than brass, and the iron ware lined with porcelain, best of all.

The chief art in making nice preserves, and such as will keep, consists in the proper preparation of the syrup, and in boiling them *just long enough*. English housekeepers think it necessary to do them very slowly, and they boil their sweetmeats almost all day, in a jar set into a kettle of water. Brown sugar should be clarified. The crushed and granulated sugars are usually so pure as not to require being clarified. Loaf sugar is the best of any. Clean brown sugar makes very good sweetmeats for family use; but the best of sugar is, for most fruits, necessary, to make such as will be elegant, and keep long.

Sweetmeats should be boiled very gently lest the syrup should burn, and also that the fruit may become thoroughly penetrated with the sugar. Furious boiling breaks small and tender fruits. Too long boiling makes sweetmeats dark, and some kinds are rendered hard and tough.

Preserves keep best in glass jars, which have also this advantage, that you can see whether or not fermentation has commenced, without opening them. If stone jars are used, those with narrow mouths are best, as the air is most easily excluded with them; and small sized

Depictions of an apple, both whole and halved, and a cherry. *American Practical Cookery Book*, 127.

ones, containing only enough for once or twice, are best, as the frequent opening of a large jar, injures its entire contents, by the repeated admission of the air. When sweetmeats are cold, cover them close, and if not to be used soon, paste a paper over the top, and with a feather, brush over the paper with white of egg. When you have occasion to open them, if a thick, leather-looking mould covers them, they are in a good state, as nothing so effectually shuts out the air; but if they are specked here and there with mould, taste them, and if they are injured, it should be carefully removed, and the jar set into a kettle of water (not hot at first, lest it should crack) and boiled. If the taste shows them to be uninjured, this mould may be the beginning of a leather-mould; therefore wait a few days, and look at them again, and scald them if necessary. A very good way of scalding them, and perhaps the easiest, is to put the jar (if it is of stone ware) into a brick oven as soon as the bread is drawn, and let it stand three or four hours. If the oven is quite warm a shorter time will do. This, or setting the jar into a kettle of water, as mentioned above, is much better than to scald them in the ordinary way, as they are exposed to the air when poured into the preserving kettle, and also when returned to the jar.

In making jellies, the sugar should be heated and should not be added, until the fruit-juice boils; and for this reason,—that the process is completed in much less time than if they are put together cold. Thus the diminution of the quantity, which long boiling occasions, is avoided, and the color of the jelly is much finer. Sometimes ladies complain that, for some inexplicable reason, they cannot make their currant jelly harden. The true reason was doubtless this,—that while making it, it was suffered to stop boiling for a few minutes. Let it boil gently but steadily, until by taking a little of it into a cold silver spoon, you perceive that it quickly hardens around the edges. A practised eye will readily judge by the movement of the liquid as it boils. Put jelly in little jars, cups, or tumblers; when it is cold, paste paper over the top and brush it over with white of egg. When *this* is used, the old method of putting brandy papers upon jelly is unnecessary. *Particular attention is requested to these suggestions in regard to making jellies.*

Crab Apples [Preserves]

Weigh them, and put them into water enough to almost, but not quite, cover them. Take them out when they have boiled three or four minutes, and put into the water as many pounds of sugar as you have fruit, and boil it till clear, then set it aside till it is cold; skim it, and return the fruit to the kettle, and put it again on the fire. The moment it actually boils take it off; lay the fruit into the jar with care, so as not to break it.

Pine-Apples [Preserves]

Take equal quantities of pine-apple and the best of loaf sugar. Slice the pine-apple, put nearly or all the sugar over it. Put it in a deep pan, and let it stand all night. In the morning take the apple out and boil the syrup. When it begins to simmer, put the apple in and boil fifteen or twenty minutes. Tie a piece of white ginger in a bit of muslin, and boil it in the syrup before adding the apple. After boiling the whole ten or fifteen minutes, take out the apple and boil the syrup ten minutes longer; then pour it over the pine-apple. The apples should be ripe, and yet perfectly sound. If the syrup does not taste enough of ginger, boil it with the ginger till it suits the taste.

Cranberries [Preserves]

Pour scalding water upon them, as this will make it much more easy to separate the defective ones from the good, than if they are washed in cold water. Measure the fruit, and allow two quarts of sugar for five of fruit. Boil the cranberries till they are soft in half as much water as fruit. Stir them very often. When they are soft add the sugar, and boil gently as possible half an hour more. They are very liable to burn, and therefore should be carefully attended to. If you like cranberry sauce very sweet, allow a pound of sugar for a pound of fruit.

Cranberries keep very well in a firkin of water in the cellar, and if so kept, can be stewed fresh at any time during the winter.

Strawberries [Preserves]

Take large strawberries not extremely ripe; weigh equal quantities of fruit and best sugar; lay the fruit in a dish, and sprinkle half the sugar over it; shake the dish a little, that the sugar may touch all the fruit. Next day make a syrup of the remainder of the sugar and the juice which you can pour off from the fruit in the pan, and as it boils lay in the strawberries, and boil them gently twenty minutes or half an hour.

Apple Jam (which will keep for years)

Weigh equal quantities of brown sugar and good sour apples. Pare and core them, and chop them fine. Make a syrup of the sugar, and clarify it very thoroughly; then add the apples, the grated peel of two or three lemons, and a few pieces of white ginger. Boil it till the apple looks clear and yellow. This resembles foreign sweetmeats. The ginger is essential to its peculiar excellence.

Currant Jelly

Pick over the fruit, but leave it on the stems. Put it into the preserving kettle, and break it with a ladle or spoon, and when it is hot, squeeze it in a coarse linen bag until you can press out no more juice. Then weigh a pound of sugar to a pint of juice. Sift the sugar, and heat it as hot as possible without dissolving or burning; boil the juice five minutes very fast, and while boiling add the hot sugar, stir it well, and when it has boiled again five minutes, set it off. The time must be strictly observed. Jelly to eat with meat does very well made with brown sugar, but must boil longer.

Vegetables and Sauces Appropriate for Different Meats

Potatoes are good with all meats. With fowls they are nicest mashed. Sweet potatoes are most appropriate with roast meat, as also are onions, winter squash, cucumbers, and asparagus.

Carrots, parsnips, turnips, greens, and cabbage are eaten with boiled meat; and corn, beets, peas, and beans are appropriate to either boiled or roasted meat. Mashed turnip is good with roasted pork, and with boiled meats.

Tomatoes are good with every kind of meat but specially so with roasts. Apple-sauce with roast pork; cranberry-sauce with beef, fowls, veal, and ham. Currant jelly is most appropriate with roast mutton. Pickles are good with all roast meats, and capers or nasturtiums with boiled lamb or mutton. Horseradish and lemons are excellent with veal.

Directions for Cooking Meats

Alamode Beef (in a plain way)

Take a thick piece of flank, or, if most convenient, the thickest part of the round, weighing six or eight pounds, for a small family of four or five persons. Cut off the strips of coarse fat upon the edge, make incisions in all parts, and fill them with a stuffing made of bread, salt pork chopped, pepper, and sweet marjoram. Push whole cloves here and there into the meat; roll it up, fasten it with skewers, and wind a strong twine or tape about it. Have ready a pot in which you have fried to a crisp three or four slices of salt pork; take out the pork, lay in the beef, and brown every side. When well browned, add hardly water enough to cover it, chop a large onion fine, add eighteen or twenty cloves, and boil it gently, but steadily, three or four hours, according to size. The water should boil away so as to make a rich gravy, but be careful it does not burn. When you take up the beef, add browned flour to the gravy, if it needs to be thickened.

Stewed Brisket of Beef

Put three or four pounds of brisket into a kettle, and cover it with water. Take off the scum as it rises. Let it boil steadily two hours. Then take it from the pot and brown it with butter in a spider. When it is browned on every side, return it to the kettle, and stew it gently five hours more. Add more water if it boils away. Put in a carrot and a turnip or two, cut small, an onion also; a few cloves, and salt and pepper as you think necessary. Half an hour before dinner add tomato or mushroom catsup. To serve it, lay the beef upon a dish, and strew capers over it. The water in which it was stewed is a nice soup.

Stewed Tongue

Boil a fresh tongue three hours, and if the skin does not easily come off, boil it longer. Remove the skin; strain the water in which it was boiled. Wash the pot, and return the tongue to it, with enough of the strained liquor to cover it. Put in it a carrot, a turnip, and an onion, cut fine, and a table-spoonful of powdered clove and also of ground pepper, tied up in muslin bags. Boil the tongue gently two hours and a half. About fifteen minutes before it is taken up, toast two slices of bread without the crust, cut it up in small bits, and put it into the pot. When you dish it up, put about a pint of the liquor and vegetables round the tongue in a fricassee dish.

Veal Pot Pie

Take the neck, the shank, and almost any pieces you have. Boil them long enough to skim off all the froth. Make a paste and roll it about half an inch thick. Butter the pot and lay in the crust, cutting out a piece on each side of the circle in such a way as to prevent its having thick folds. Put in a layer of meat, then flour, salt and pepper it, and add a little butter or a slice or two of salt pork, as you choose. Do this until you have laid in all your meat; pour in enough of the water in which the veal was boiled to half fill the kettle, then lay on the top crust and make an incision in it to allow the escape of the steam. Watch that it does not burn, and pour in more of the water through the hole in the crust if necessary. Boil an hour and a half. The objection to this dish is, that boiled crust is apt to be heavy, and therefore unhealthy; but if it is made after the receipt for cream tartar biscuit, or of potato crust, it will be light.

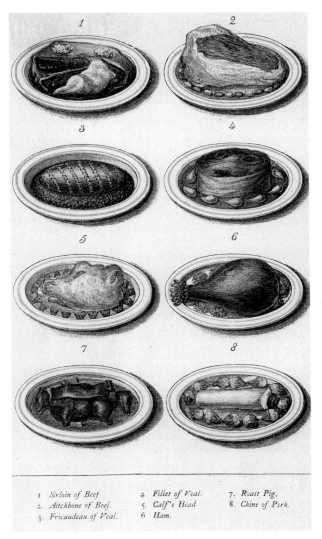

1. Sirloin of Beef.   4. Fillet of Veal.   7. Roast Pig.
2. Aitchbone of Beef.   5. Calf's Head.   8. Chine of Pork.
3. Fricaudeau of Veal.   6. Ham.

This colored plate showcased a variety of prepared meat dishes. Mrs. N. K. M. Lee, *The Cook's Own Book: An American Family Cook Book* (New York: James Miller, 1864), front matter, Michigan State University Special Collections.

Calf's Head

Let the head, feet, liver and lights, soak some hours in a plenty of cold water.[3] Take out the brains. Boil the head, &c., till very tender, which will require from two hours to two and a half. Throw some salt into the water, and skim it thoroughly. Boil the brains ten or fifteen minutes, tied up in a piece of muslin; chop them, and put them with melted butter, and parsley cut fine. If you choose, boil an egg hard, cut it up and add it. Cold calf's head is good. It is also good hashed.

To Roast a Pig

It should not be more than a month old. It is better a little less, and it should be killed on the morning of the day it is to be cooked. Sprinkle fine salt over it an hour before it is put to the fire. Cut off the feet at the first joint. Make stuffing enough to fill it very full, of bread crumbs moistened with a little milk, a small piece of butter, sweet marjoram, sage, pepper, and salt. When placed on the spit, confine the legs in such a manner as to give it a good shape. Rub it all over with butter or sweet oil, to keep it from blistering. Flour it at first a little. As soon as it begins to brown, dredge on a very thick covering of flour. Turn the spit every three or four minutes. If the flour falls off, instantly renew it. When it has all become of a dark brown color, scrape it off into a plate and set it aside. Put a piece of butter into the gravy in the roaster, and baste the pig very often, till it is done, which it is when the eyes fall out. The feet and liver should be boiled an hour or two, and the gravy from the roaster be poured into the water in which they were boiled. The liver should be cut or mashed fine, and the feet cut open and returned to the sauce-pan, the brains taken out and added, and the gravy thickened with the browned flour reserved in the plate. A pig of a month old will roast in two hours and a half.

Frizzled Smoked Beef

Shave thin slices, and put them in a teacupful of milk into a small kettle or sauce-pan; boil it a few minutes, and then add a small bit of butter and an egg beaten with a teaspoonful of flour, and stir well. Put a little more milk to it if needed.

[Smoked beef is good in poached eggs, but in that case the beef should be boiled a few minutes in the milk before the eggs are added. The last remnants of a ham may be scraped from the bone, and put into poached eggs, but will not need the boiling which is necessary in the case of the smoked beef.]

To Select Poultry and Prepare It for Being Cooked

To Boil a Turkey

Stuff a young turkey, weighing six or seven pounds, with bread, butter, salt, pepper, and minced parsley; skewer up the legs and wings as if to roast; flour a cloth and pin around it. Boil it forty minutes, then set off the kettle and let it stand, close covered, half an hour more. The steam will cook it sufficiently. To be eaten with drawn butter and stewed oysters.

Chicken Salad

Boil or roast a nice fowl. When cold, cut off all the meat, and chop it a little, but not very small; cut up a large bunch of celery and mix with the chicken. Boil four eggs hard, mash, and mix them with sweet oil, pepper, salt, mustard, and a gill of vinegar. Beat this mixture very thoroughly together, and just before dinner pour it over the chicken.

To Roast Pigeons

Pick out the pin feathers, or if there are a great many, pull off the skin. Examine the inside very carefully. Soak them half an hour in a good deal of water, to take out the blood. Then boil them with a little salt in the water, half an hour, and take off the scum as fast as it rises. Take them out, flour them well, and lay them into a dripping-pan; strain the water in which they were boiled, and put a part of it into the pan; stir in it a little piece of butter, and baste the pigeons often. Add pepper and sweet marjoram if you prefer. Roast them nearly two hours. Pigeons need to be cooked a long time.

Pigeons in Disguise

Prepare them just as directed in the receipt above, and boil them long enough to remove all the blood, then pepper and salt them, make a good paste, roll each pigeon close in a piece of it; tie them separately in a cloth, taking care not to break the paste. Boil them gently an hour and a half, in a good deal of water. Lay them in a hot dish, and pour a gravy over them made of cream, parsley, and a little butter.

Calcutta Curry

Boil and joint two chickens. Fry three or four slices of salt pork, and when they are nearly brown add a large spoonful of butter. Cut three or four onions fine, and fry them a light brown; then remove them, and the pork, and fry the chickens gently in the fat; strew over the meat while it is frying a spoonful and a half of good curry powder, and dredge in flour. Then add hot water to make sufficient gravy; if the gravy is not thick enough, mix a little flour smooth in cold water, and stir in. Add salt to suit your taste. This dish is best when stewed slowly. Garnish with slices of lemon.

Partridges, pigeons, rabbits, sweet-breads, breasts of mutton, lamb, and veal, are all used for curries.

There is a difference in the quality of curry powder. The above measure, is for the strongest kind, and is enough for a quart of gravy. The East Indians never use flour in thickening the gravy, but depend on curry powder.

To prepare rice for Calcutta curry, wash a pint in several waters, and put it into a kettle, containing a gallon of warm water, with salt in it. Cook it ten minutes from the time it begins to boil; then pour it into a sieve, and when the water is entirely drained out, shake the sieve, and the particles of rice will separate, and it is ready to serve.

Soups

Roast Beef Bone Soup

Boil the bones at least three hours, or until every particle of meat is loose; then take them out and scrape off the meat and set aside the water; the next day take from it all the fat, cut up an onion, two or three potatoes and a turnip, and put into it. Add, half an hour before dinner, powdered sweet marjoram, catsup, and some salt. Boil it an hour.

Ox-tail Soup

Take two tails, divide them at the joints, soak them in warm water. Put them into cold water in a gallon pot or stew-pan. Skim off the froth carefully. When the meat is boiled to shreds, take out the bones, and add a chopped onion and carrot. Use spices and sweet herbs or not, as you prefer. Boil it three or four hours.

White Soup

Boil a knuckle of veal to shreds, add a quarter of a pound of vermicelli, half a pint of cream, and lemon peel and mace.

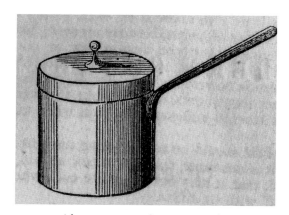

A large copper pot for soup or stock.
Acton, *Modern Cookery*, 38.

Vegetable Soup

Take two turnips, two carrots, four potatoes, one large onion, one parsnip, and a few stalks of celery or some parsley. Cut them all fine, or chop them in a tray; put them, with a spoonful of rice, into three quarts of water, and boil the whole three hours. Then strain the soup through a colander or coarse sieve, return it to the kettle, and put it over the fire. Add a piece of butter of the size of a nut, stir the soup till the butter is melted, dredge in a little flour, let it boil up and then serve it.

Mutton or Lamb Broth

Take the water in which a leg of mutton or lamb was boiled on the previous day, take off the fat and boil it two hours with a turnip, an onion, and a carrot, cut small. Add some minced parsley and a spoonful of rice. All these, except the parsley, should be put in while the water is cold. Any little pieces of the neck, ribs, or shank will make excellent broth.

Directions Respecting Fish

Purchase those which have just been caught. Of this you can judge by their being hard under the pressure of the finger. Fish lose their best flavor soon, and a few hours make a wide difference in the taste of some sorts.

Cod are best in cold weather. Mackerel are best in August, September, and October. Halibut, in May and June. Oysters are good from September to April; but are not very good or healthy from the first of May to the last of August. Lobsters are best at the season when oysters are not good.

Minced Salt Fish

Pick out all bones and bits of skin the day that the fish is boiled, as it is most easily done while it is warm. Next day chop it fine, and also all the potatoes left of the previous dinner; they are better for this purpose than those that are just boiled. Lay three or four slices of salt pork into a spider, and fry till they are crisped; take them out, and put the chopped fish and potato into the middle, and press it out equally, so that the fat will be at the sides. Cover it close; after about five minutes put into the centre a gill of milk, and cover it again. In a few minutes more stir it, but so carefully as not to disturb the sides and bottom, else a brown crust will not form. Add more milk if it is too dry. When thoroughly heated through, stir in a small piece of butter, loosen the crust from the sides with a knife, and turn it out upon a hot dish. If it is done right, it will come out whole, and nicely browned.

Fish-Balls

Chop and mix fish and potatoes in the same manner as directed in the other receipt [Minced Salt Fish]; melt a small piece of butter in a little milk, and when you have stirred it into the fish, make it up into little flat cakes, roll them in a plate of flour, and fry in hot lard, droppings, or the fat of fried pork.

To Boil Salmon

Clean a salmon in salt and water. Allow twenty minutes for boiling every pound. Wrap it in floured cloth, and lay it in the kettle while the water is cold. Make the water very salt. Skim it well; in this respect it requires more care than any other fish. Serve it with drawn butter and parsley.

If salmon is not thoroughly cooked it is unhealthy. When a piece of boiled fresh fish of any kind is left of dinner, it is a very good way to lay it in a deep dish, and pour over it a little vinegar, with catsup, and add pepper or any other spice which is preferred.

Pickled Oysters

Boil the liquor of an hundred oysters and pour it over them. When they have stood a few minutes, take them out and boil the liquor again, with a gill of vinegar, a few whole black peppers, and two or three blades of mace. When this is cold, pour it over the oysters, and cover them closely. This is a very good way to keep them.

Baked Bass

Make a stuffing of pounded cracker or crumbs of bread, an egg, pepper, clove, salt, and butter. Fill it very full, and when sewed up, grate over it a small nutmeg, and sprinkle it with pounded cracker. Then pour on the white of an egg, and melted butter. Bake it an hour in the same dish in which it is to be served.

Directions for Salting Meat, Fish, &c.

To some young housekeepers, the salting of meat, and taking care of it, and of smoked meat, are perplexing. Perhaps the following directions may assist them. The best pieces to corn are the end of the rump, the thin end of the sirloin, and the edge-bone. If you like it with alternate streaks of fat and lean, the pieces at the ends of the ribs, called by butchers the rattle-ran, are very good. The edge-bone affords the most lean meat.

The best piece of pork to corn is the shoulder. It is a good way to divide it, if large, and stuff half of it with sage and bread crumbs, and roast it; and corn the other half.

In winter, hang fresh killed meat up two or three days before putting it into brine, as it will thus become more tender. Make a brine of four quarts of water, three pints of salt, half a table-spoonful of saltpetre, and a pint of molasses, or a pound of coarse brown sugar. Mix it thoroughly without boiling it. In this lay the meat, and see that it is entirely covered. It is well to look at it after a day or two, and if necessary, turn it the other side up. It will be good in a few days, but it is better to let it lie three or four weeks before boiling it. The same brine will do for many successive pieces in winter. But for a family that like salt meat, it is the best way to make a double measure, and put into it at once as much meat as it will cover. It should be kept in a firkin or tub, with a close cover.

After a considerable quantity of meat has thus been cured, scald and skim the brine, add a little more molasses, salt, and saltpetre, and let it become cold before meat is put into it.

A brine like this, only a little more rich with molasses, is very good for salting tongues, and pieces that are to be smoked. But they should lie in it four or five weeks. Meat should never be salted for smoking, later than February or the middle of March.

In warm weather, it will not do to use the same brine more than once, as the blood from the meat will become tainted. Therefore a less expensive mixture, that may be thrown away after being used once, is better. Two quarts of salt to four of water, is a good rule for brine in hot weather.

In the summer, the strong membrane that covers the rib bones, must be cut open with a sharp knife before the meat is put into brine; for, as the salt will not penetrate this membrane, the bones will else become tainted, and the meat soon be spoiled. Meat, at this season, should be cooked within three or four days after being put into brine.

To Salt Pork

Allow a bushel of salt for a barrel of pork, or a peck for fifty weight. The salt called coarse-fine, is commonly used by butchers; but the best way in a private family, where no more than twenty-five or fifty weight is put down for the year's use, is to use fine salt. Put water enough to cover it. Examine it in a few days, and if the salt is all dissolved, add more. The only sure way of keeping pork sweet, is to have the brine so strong that some of the salt remains undissolved. A board, with a stone upon it, should always be kept on the top of pork, as it will soon become rusty if the edges lie above the surface of the brine.

It is not fit for use, until it has been in brine six weeks.

To Cure Hams

[This receipt is furnished by a person whose hams are celebrated in the eastern part of Massachusetts, for their superior quality.]

For curing fifty weight, allow three quarts of coarse salt, half a pound of saltpetre, and two quarts of good molasses. Add soft water enough just to cover the hams. Common sized hams should be kept in this pickle five weeks; larger ones six. They should all be taken out once a week, and those which were on the top laid in first, and the lower ones last. They should be smoked from two to three weeks with walnut wood or with sawdust and corn-cobs, mixed. Meat smoked with cobs is very delicate.

Pieces of beef for smoking, may be laid in this pickle, after the hams are sent to the smoke house; but more salt should be added.

The Knickerbocker Pickle

To three gallons of soft water, put four pounds and a half of salt, coarse and fine, mixed; a pound and a half of brown sugar, an ounce and a half of saltpetre, half an ounce of saleratus, and two quarts of good molasses.

Boil the mixture, skim it well, and when cold pour it over the hams or beef. Beef laid down in this pickle, does not become hard, and is very fine, when boiled gently and long.

Some persons consider this the best of all methods for curing beef and hams.

To Make Sausages

A common fault is, that the meat is not chopped enough. It should be chopped very fine, and this is most easily done if it is a little frozen. When ready for the seasoning, put in just cold water enough to enable you to mix the ingredients equally; but be careful not to use more than is necessary for this purpose.

The following excellent rule for seasoning sausages is furnished by the same person whose receipt for curing hams I have been allowed to copy.

To twelve pounds and a half of meat put a gill of fine salt, large gill of powdered sage, and half a gill of ground pepper. Let the measures be exact.

Some persons find it most convenient to keep sausage meal in a cloth. It is done by making a long bag of strong cotton cloth, of such a size that, when filled, it will be as large round as a common half pint mug. It should be crowded full, and each end tied up. If you have not a sausage-filler, it can be filled with the hand. Sew up only a quarter of a yard, then fill it tight, so far; then sew another quarter, and fill it, and so far until you reach the end. When the meat is to be used, open one end, rip up the seam a little way, and cut off slices rather more than an inch thick, and fry them. It may be kept good from December to March, in a cold dry place. Dip the bag in strong salt and water, and dry it, before filling it.

To Try Lard

The fat should not be suffered to stand long without being new, because, even in cold weather, some parts of it may then become musty, and nothing can then restore its sweetness.[4] Remove all the lean bits, as they will adhere to the kettle, and cause the fat to burn. Cut it into pieces a little more than an inch square, and take care to have them nearly of a size. Put a little water into the kettle, and keep a steady, good fire, without much blaze, and stir the fat often. Attention to the kettle and the fire will be necessary, through the process. It will require three hours to do it. When the fat no longer bubbles, but is still, it is done enough. It is best to squeeze it through a tow cloth bag, made by folding half a square in such a way that the corner will form the end, and it should be rounded off a little at the bottom, and the seam made exactly as directed for a pudding-bag. Two pieces of wood fastened together, somewhat like a lemon-squeezer, will facilitate the process of straining it. Strain all that flows off without much pressure into one jar, and that which is extracted last, into another. There is no advantage in putting salt into lard. It does not mingle with it, as appears by its being always found at the bottom of the kettle, un-dissolved. Stone jars are best for keeping lard, but potter's ware does very well. It should stand in a cold place, and in warm weather, a fireplace with a close board, in a cool room, is a very good place to keep it.

Scraps are a favorite dish with many persons. Put salt, pepper, and pulverized sage to them, while they are still warm, break them small, and stir them well so that the seasoning may be equally distributed.

Tomatoes

Pickle (an excellent condiment)

Put eight pounds of skinned tomatoes, and four of brown sugar, into a preserving kettle. Stir often and see they do not burn. Boil them to the consistency of molasses, then add a quart of sharp cider-vinegar, a teaspoonful of mace, another of cinnamon, and half a teaspoonful of clove, and boil five minutes longer.

Catsup

Slice the tomatoes and sprinkle them with salt. If you intend to let them stand until you have gathered several parcels, put in plenty of salt. After you have gathered all you intend to use, boil them gently an hour, strain them through a coarse sieve; slice two good-sized onions very thin for every gallon; add half a spoonful of ginger, two spoonfuls of powdered clove, two of allspice, and a teaspoonful of black pepper. Boil it twenty minutes after the spices are added. Keep it in a covered jar.

This kind of catsup is specially designed to be used in soup, and stewed meats.

Another Catsup (retaining the color and flavor of the fruit)

Skin and slice the tomatoes, and boil them an hour and a half. Then put to one gallon not strained, a quarter of an ounce of mace, the same of nutmegs and cloves, one handful of horseradish, two pods of red pepper, or a large teaspoonful of cayenne, and salt as you like it. Boil it away to three quarts, and then add a pint of wine and half a pint of vinegar. Bottle it, and leave the bottles open two or three days; then cork it tight. Make this catsup once, and you will wish to make it every year.

On Cooking Vegetables

Potato Balls

Mash boiled potatoes fine, stir into them the yolk of an egg, and make them into balls; then dip them into a beaten egg, roll them in cracker crumbs, and brown them in a quick oven; or, fry them in a small quantity of nice drippings, and in that case flatten them so that they can be easily turned, and browned on both sides.

Old Potatoes

When potatoes are poor, as they often are in the spring, pare, soak, and boil them as directed in the first receipt, then take two together in a coarse cloth, squeeze and wring them. You can, with care, turn them into the dish in shape; but if not, it is no matter. The broken pieces will still be far better than before, for they will be dry and mealy. Keep a cloth for the purpose.

A "vegetable spoon" was used to carve hard vegetables into balls. Blot, *Hand-Book of Practical Cookery*, 41.

String Beans

Beans should never be used in this way after the pod has become old enough to have a string, or tough fiber upon it. Cut off each end, and cut them up small. Boil them in as little water as will keep them from burning. Just before you take them up, add salt and butter, and dredge in a little flour. They should have only as much liquor in them as you wish to take up in the dish, else the sweetness is wasted. String beans and peas are good boiled together.

Peas

If peas are round and fresh (and none others are good), they will boil in half an hour or thirty-five minutes. They should be put into cold water, without salt. The same quantity should be used as for string beans, and for the same reason. When they are tender, add salt and butter. It is an improvement to boil a single small slice of pork in them. It need not be laid into the dish, and the same will do for another boiling.

Asparagus

Wash it, trim off the white ends, and tie it up in bunches with a twine of a strip of old cotton. Throw them into boiling water with salt in it. Boil twenty-five minutes or half an hour. Have ready two or three slices of toasted bread, dip them in the water and lay them in the dish.

Spread them with butter and lay the bunches of asparagus upon the toast. Cut the strings with a scissors and draw them out without breaking the stalks; lay thin shavings of butter over the asparagus, and send it to the table.

Salad

Gather lettuce and pepper-grass early, before the dew has evaporated; pick them over, and lay them in cold water. If the weather is very warm, change the water before dinnertime, and add ice. Just before it is served, cut it small, and prepare the dressing in the following manner. Boil three eggs twelve minutes, and throw them into cold water; remove the shell, and take out the yolks; mash them fine in a spoonful of water and two of oil; add salt, powdered sugar, made mustard and vinegar; pour the mixture over the salad, cut the whites of the eggs in rings and garnish the top.

Macaroni

Procure that macaroni which looks white and clean. When it is to be used, examine it carefully, as there are sometimes little insects inside. Wash it, and put it in a stew-pan in cold water enough almost to cover it. Add a little salt. Let it boil slowly half an hour; then add a gill of milk and a small piece of butter, and boil it a quarter of an hour more. Then put it into the dish in which it is to go to the table, grate old cheese over it, and heat a shovel red-hot and hold over the top to brown it. It may be browned in a stove, but if the dish would be injured by it, the better way is to use the shovel.

Carrots

These are not considered by most people very good; but they are so in broth and soup. To eat with meat they should be boiled three quarters of an hour, if fresh from the garden; in the winter, an hour and a half. They make very good pies after the fashion of pumpkin of squash; but they must be boiled very tender, and in a good deal of water, else a strong taste will pervade the pies.

Onions

Boil them twenty minutes, and pour off the water entirely; then put in equal parts of hot water and milk, or skimmed milk alone, and boil them twenty minutes more. When they are done through, take them up with a skimmer, let them drain a little, and lay them into the dish. Put on butter, pepper, and salt.

Spinage

Put it into a net, or a bag of coarse muslin, kept for the purpose, and boil it in plenty of water with salt in it, ten or twelve minutes. All kinds of greens should be boiled in plenty of water, else they will be bitter.

One method of serving spinage[5] is, to press it between two plates, then put it into a saucepan with a small bit of butter, salt, and a little cream, and boil it up. Another is to drain it thoroughly, lay it in the dish, put upon the top hard boiled eggs, sliced, and pour melted butter over it.

Succotash

Cut off the corn from the cobs, and, an hour and a half before dinner, put the cobs, with a few shelled beans, into cold water to boil. After one hour take out the cobs, put in the corn and boil it half an hour. There should be no more water than will be necessary to make the succotash of the right thickness; as having too much occasions a loss of the richness imparted by the cobs. When you take it up, add a small piece of butter. This is much better than to boil the corn on the cob and then cut it off.

It is a very good way, when a family is tired of fresh meat in hot weather, to boil a piece of pork in another pot until the grossest fat has boiled out, and then put it with the succotash for the remainder of the time. It gives a very good flavor to the corn, and makes an excellent dinner.

Pickling

Pickles

Pickles[6] should never be kept in potter's ware, as arsenic and other poisonous substances are used in the glazing; and this is sometimes decomposed by vinegar. Whole families have been poisoned in this way; and where fatal effects do not follow, a deleterious influence may be operating upon the health, from this cause, when it is not suspected. Pickles should be made with cider vinegar.

Mangoes

Select small musk-melons (the common kind is much better for this purpose than cantelopes);[7] cut an oval piece out of one side.[8] You must have a sharp knife, and be careful to make a smooth incision. Take out the seeds with a teaspoon. Fill the melons with a stuffing made of cloves, mustard-seed, peppercorns, scrapings of horseradish, and chopped onion if you like it. Sew on the piece with a needle and coarse thread, or bind a strip of old cotton around each one and sew it. Lay them in a jar, and pour boiling vinegar on them with a little salt in it. Do it two or three times, then lay them in fresh vinegar and cover them close.

Peaches

Select peaches that are ripe, yet not quite soft enough to eat; push a clove into each one at the end opposite the stem. Put two pounds of brown sugar to a gallon of vinegar, and boil it up; skim off the top, boil it up once more, and pour it, hot, upon the peaches. Cover them close.

It may be necessary to scald the vinegar again in a week or two; after that, they will keep any length of time. They retain much of the flavor of a fresh peach.

Nasturtiums

Gather the seeds while green, let them lie a few days, then throw them into vinegar. They need no spice except a little salt, being themselves sufficiently spicy. Boil the vinegar and pour on them. They are considered by many persons better than capers, and are much like them. They should be kept six months, covered close, before they are used.

Eggs

Boil them twelve minutes, and throw them immediately into cold water, which will cause the shell to come off easily. Boil some red beets till very soft, peel and mash them fine, and put them into cold vinegar enough to cover the eggs; add salt, pepper, cloves, and nutmeg. Put the eggs into a jar and pour the mixture over them.

Butternuts

Gather them between the twenty-fifth and thirtieth of June. Make a brine of boiled salt and water, strong enough to bear up an egg after it is cold. Skim it while it boils. Pour it on the nuts, and let them lie in it twelve days. Then drain them; lay them in a jar, and pour over them the best of cider vinegar, boiled with pepper-corns, cloves, allspice, mustard, ginger, mace, and horseradish. This should be cooled before it is poured on. Cover close, and keep them a year before using them. Walnuts are done in the same way. The vinegar becomes an excellent catsup, by many persons preferred to any other.

Convenient Common Dishes, and Ways of Using Remnants

Souse

Take off the horny parts of the feet and toes of a pig, and clean the feet, ears, and tail very thoroughly; then boil them till the large bones slip out easily. Pack the meat into a stone jar, with pepper, salt, and allspice sprinkled between each layer. Mix some good cider vinegar with the liquor in which it was boiled, in the proportion of one third vinegar to two thirds liquor, and fill up the jar.

Foods and Drinks for the Sick, and for Infants

Beef Tea

Cut a piece of lean, juicy beef into pieces an inch square, put them into a wide-mouthed bottle and cork it tight. Set the bottle into a kettle of cold water and boil it an hour and a half. This mode of making beef tea concentrates the nourishment more than any other.

Calf's Foot Broth

Boil two feet in three quarts of water, until it is wasted to three pints. Strain it, and set it aside in a cool place. When cold, take off the fat. Heat a little at a time as it is wanted, and add salt, nutmeg, and, if approved, a spoonful of good wine.

Wine Whey

To a pint of milk put two glasses of wine; mix it, and let it stand twelve minutes, then strain it through a muslin bag or a very fine sieve. Sweeten it with loaf sugar.

If it is necessary to have the whey weaker, put a little hot water to the milk.

Barley Water

Boil an ounce of pearl barley a few minutes to cleanse it, pour off the water, and put a quart of cold water and a little salt to it. Simmer it an hour.

Milk Porridge

Put to half a pint of boiling water, two teaspoonfuls of flour wet smooth in cold water, and add salt. Then put in half a pint of milk, stir it well, and let it boil up again. Vary the proportions of milk and water as the case requires. Made wholly with milk it is a very hearty dish.

Oatmeal Gruel

Put two large spoonfuls of oatmeal, wet in cold water, into three pints of boiling water; boil it gently half an hour, skim it, add a little salt, sugar, and nutmeg. If raisins are also used, a large teacupful stoned, will be enough. But gruel with raisins should be boiled longer than without.

A Nutritious Jelly

Take of rice, sago, pearl barley, and hartshorn shavings, each an ounce; add three pints of water, simmer it till reduced to one, and then strain it.[9] When cold, it will be a jelly, to be given dissolved in broth, milk, or wine, as directed by the physician.

Crust Coffee

Take a large crust of bread; brown is to be preferred, but Graham bread will answer. Dry it in the toaster, and at last almost burn both sides; lay it in a saucepan and pour boiling water on it; boil it up a minute or two, and then strain off the coffee; return it to the saucepan with a little milk, or cream, and boil it up again. It should be made strong enough to look like real coffee, of which it is a very good imitation when well made.

Miscellaneous Receipts and Directions

Currant Shrub

Boil currant juice five minutes with loaf or crushed sugar—a pound of sugar to a pint of juice. Stir it constantly while cooling, and when cold, bottle it. A spoonful or two in a tumbler of water affords a refreshing beverage.

English Ginger Beer

Pour four quarts of boiling water, upon an ounce and a half of ginger, an ounce of cream of tartar, a pound of clean brown sugar, and two fresh lemons, sliced thin. It should be wrought twenty-four hours, with two gills of good yeast, and then bottled. It improves by keeping several weeks, unless the weather is hot, and it is an excellent beverage. If made with loaf instead of brown sugar, the appearance and flavor are still finer.

Maple Beer

To four gallons of boiling water, add one quart of maple syrup and a small table-spoonful of essence of spruce. When it is about milk warm, add a pint of yeast; and when fermented, bottle it. In three days it is fit for use.

Rennet Wine

Wash a third, or a half of a salted rennet; wipe it dry and put it into a bottle of wine. The wine will be fit to use for custard the next day. To keep the remainder of the rennet till more is needed, put it into a strong brine and cover it close.

Cologne Water

To one gallon of alcohol, put twelve drachms each, of oil of lavender, oil of bergamot, and essence of lemon; four drachms of oil of rosemary, and twelve drops of oil of cinnamon.

Tooth Powder

Two ounces of Peruvian bark, two of myrrh, one of chalk, one of Armenian bole, and one of orris root.

To Kill Cockroaches and Beetles

Strew the roots of black hellebore, at night, in the places infested by these vermin, and they will be found in the morning dead, or dying. Black hellebore grows in marshy grounds, and may be had at the herb shops.

To Take Out Iron Mould

Dissolve a teaspoonful of salts of tin in two table-spoonfuls of water. Dip the iron-mould into the solution, and let it remain five minutes. Then dip it into a mixture of equal parts of muriatic acid and water. Dip the mould spots alternately into these mixtures, or make the first one stronger with the salts of tin, and apply it with a soft rag on the end of a stick. Last of all, rinse the articles very thoroughly in cold water.

A simpler method of removing iron-mould succeeds well, provided it is recent, and not very dark. Tie up a teaspoonful of cream of tartar in the moulded place, and put it into cold water without soap, and boil it half an hour.

Mrs. S. G. Knight, *Tit-Bits; Or, How to Prepare a Nice Dish at a Moderate Expense*

Modesty was the rule in introductions to nineteenth-century literature, whether the author was presenting a novel, a book of poems, or an instruction manual. And the introductions to cookbooks were often excessively humble. After all, cookbooks written by female authors served as surrogates for women entering the public sphere, and their introductions were meant to showcase their authors' caution and modesty in doing so.

Mrs. Knight's introduction to *Tit-Bits; Or, How to Prepare a Nice Dish at Moderate Expense*, is a prime example of authorial modesty, and in it she practically apologized for bothering the world with yet another book about cooking. Knight stressed that she did not intend for her book to replace "any of the valuable 'Cook Books' already in the market," but rather to serve as "an accompaniment to them." Furthermore, she declined to take full credit for the book, calling herself a mere "compiler" rather than an author, and stating forthrightly that most of the book's recipes came from friends. Indeed, she underlined the fact that she was only producing a

book in the first place because her friend encouraged her to do so. Her friend, not her ego, urged her to publish, in other words. Even the name Knight chose for her book, *Tit-Bits*, reflected this general humility: a "tit-bit," or a "tidbit," meant a small and unassuming morsel.

Make no mistake, however. While Knight's tone was humble, she made savvy use of the introduction to sell her book. In fact, by writing that her friends contributed recipes and encouraged her to publish a cookbook she not only demonstrated her modesty but also the fact that other people already judged her recipes to be valuable. Value, indeed, was a central theme, and Knight praised her recipes as exceptionally affordable. Even while claiming that she did not intend her book to replace cookbooks that already existed, she noted, "The universal cry among the less wealthy classes is, 'We can do nothing with Cook Books, the receipts are so *extravagant!*'" By contrast, she assured readers that her recipes "combin[e] economy with excellence" because they came from people "who love a nice dish, and have found a way to prepare it, without spending all their substance in riotous living." Far from costing money, she implicitly promised that her book would save people money in the long run. For Americans in precarious financial circumstances, as many families were throughout the mid-nineteenth century, such attention to economy would have been an invaluable consideration.

Knight was not exaggerating when she said that many of her recipes came from others. She often gave credit to other women in her recipe titles, such as Mrs. Faben's Economy Cakes, Mrs. Parsons' Rusk, or Miss Pindar's Dyspepsia Bread, the last of which was meant to ease digestion. Recipes with her own name on them, like Mrs. Knight's Currant Shrub, were presumably ones she developed or heavily modified herself. In her recipe titles, Knight also sometimes included editorial comments like "Poverty Rice Pudding (very nice)," "Plum Cake (good)," or "Berwick Pie (delicious)." As a result, the book sometimes has the casual feel of a community cookbook, already marked up in the margins. Besides using her recipe titles to give credit to her friends, Knight also used the titles to point to her recipes' regional provenance, and they frequently mention Massachusetts cities and towns like Lowell, Salem, Marblehead, Brookline, and Boston, among many others.

Knight's cooking instructions were less explicit than those in the previous book in this volume, and she generally seems to have assumed that she was providing additional ideas for people who already knew how to cook. The recipe format she chose reflected this assump-

A plum. *American Practical Cookery Book*, 167.

tion. Unlike modern cookbooks, which have clear lists of ingredients followed by step-by-step instructions, Knight wrote her recipes in prose, often providing frustratingly vague information about quantities, temperatures, and timing. Sometimes she included no real cooking instructions whatsoever, such as her recipe for Common Doughnuts, which simply listed ingredients: "Two cups of sugar, one and a half of milk, two eggs, one nutmeg, two tea spoonfuls of cream of tartar, one of soda." In contrast, Knight occasionally provided explicit details about recipes modern readers might think of as ordinary, like rice. Her meticulous instructions for Boiled Rice, for example, revealed her assumption that her average northern reader would *not* know how to cook it.

Knight's desserts may surprise contemporary readers, especially sweet dishes like Potato Pudding, Squash Cake, and Macaroni Pudding that used ingredients subsequent generations would designate as inappropriate for desserts. Knight also combined categories of sweet and savory in ways that would come to seem strange in later decades. Her dessert recipes not only routinely called for animal fats like lard and suet, but they also sometimes called for hefty quantities of meat itself. Her recipe for "Pork Cake," for example, called for half a pound of finely chopped salt pork, which would have imparted a strong, salty taste to the cake. And her Mince Pie recipe called for a full two pounds of chopped beef as well as half a pound of suet.

In everyday cookbooks, recipes for the sick were usually relatively simple, including gruels, porridges, teas, and broths designed not to tax the feeble digestive tracts of the ill. Sometimes invalid recipes were simply intended to be especially appealing to people who were uninterested in food. Knight said that invalids would "relish" Toast Water, a dish made of stale bread that had been toasted, cut up, and soaked in boiling water, then mixed with fresh nutmeg and white wine. Invalid cookery in the 1860s made regular use of alcohol, which was thought to have medicinal and warming qualities. At the same time, such recipes may also simply have served as a socially acceptable way for people—and perhaps women in particular—to drink alcohol in the midst of an increasingly powerful temperance, or anti-alcohol, movement. Hop Tea, for instance, which Knight praised as "a quieting drink, most excellent for nervous headache," combined hops, hot water, sugar, and gin. More than anything else, it was really a mild cocktail.

Introduction

In presenting this book to the public the compiler wishes it to be understood that it is not designed to supersede any of the valuable "Cook Books" already in the market, but as an accompaniment to them; being intended to fill a place which is not yet filled.

The universal cry among the less wealthy classes is, "We can do nothing with Cook Books, the receipts are so *extravagant*!"

For the last twenty years the writer has been collecting receipts for her own private use.

Many of these were so valuable, combining economy with excellence, she was constantly giving them to her friends. One lady remarked that one single receipt given her was worth five dollars to her.

A year or two since a friend suggested that these receipts should be given to the public, and that as many new ones as possible should be gleaned from private sources and added to those already in possession.

A large majority of cake receipts are for common use, and made by *cup* measure, to avoid the trouble of weighing.

A small space is given to meats, it being deemed unnecessary to fill the book with receipts for plain cooking, which it is to be supposed all housekeepers are familiar with, and thereby make it a more costly one. Two of the receipts are from the Washington family in Virginia; a number from the private manuscript of a deceased relative, collected with great care; but the large majority are from the stray leaves of friends, who love a nice dish, and have found a way to prepare it, without spending all their substance in riotous living.

Meats

TO SELECT BEEF

Nice beef may be known by its color; the fat will be of oily smoothness, and incline to white, rather than yellow, while the lean will be of an open grain, bright red. Yellow fat is a sure sign of an inferior quality.

Spiced Beef

Cover a round of beef, weighing about sixteen pounds, with a pound of salt, and turn it every day for a week.

At the end of that time, wash it in cold water, rub it well with two ounces of black pepper and quarter of an ounce of mace.

Fry three or four onions sliced, add a few cloves, then put in the meat, cover it with water, and bake in a stone-covered stewing pan for five hours.

To be eaten cold, for breakfast or supper.

Beef Heart

Wash it carefully, and stuff it nicely; roast or bake it, and serve with the gravy, which should be thickened with some of the stuffing. It is very nice hashed, with a little port wine added.

Alamode Beef

Make a stuffing of rich herbs, spice, suet, and stuff the beef with it; one and a half bottles of port or claret wine, according to the size of the beef, and five quarts of water. Do not let it boil, but simmer until it is done.

Corned Beef

The brisket is the best. A piece of eight pounds will require four hours slow boiling. Put it into cold water, and take off the scum as it rises; the slower it boils the better. The liquor which the beef is boiled in is very nice for gravies and soups, and should be saved for that purpose.

Beef Stew

Take a pound and a half of nice beef, and cut it into small pieces.

Place in the bottom of your saucepan a layer of sliced potatoes, a few slices of onion, a pinch of pepper, one of salt; then a layer of meat, another layer of potatoes, onions, salt, and pepper, with a layer of meat, and continue in this way till you have disposed of all of your meat; let the top layer be of potatoes, onions, and seasoning. Cover all with water, and let it stew for an hour and a half.

Beef Tongue

If it is corned, it should be soaked for twenty-four hours before boiling.

It will require from three to four hours, according to size. The skin should always be removed as soon as it is taken from the pot. An economical method is to lay the tongue, as soon as the skin is removed, in a jar, coiled up, with the tip outside the root, and a weight upon it. When it is cold, loosen the sides, with a knife, and turn it out. The slices being cut horizontally all round, the fat and lean will go together.

Savory Beef

Take a shin of beef from the hind quarter, saw it into four pieces, put it in a pot, and boil it until the meat and gristle drop from the bones; chop the meat very fine, put it in a dish, and season it with a little salt, pepper, clove, and sage, to your taste; pour in the liquor, in which the meat was boiled, and place it away to harden.

Cut in slices and eaten cold.

In fresh pork the flesh is firm, smooth, a clear color, and the fat set. Dairy fed pork bears the palm over all others. In young pork, the lean, when pinched, will break.

Excellent bacon may be known by the lean being tender and of a bright color, the fat firm and white, yet bearing a pale rose tinge, the rind thin, and the lean tender to the touch. Rusty bacon has yellow streaks in it. The test of a sweet ham is to pass a sharp knife to the bone, and when drawn out smell it; if the knife is daubed greasy, and the scent disagreeable, it is bad.

Corned Pork

It should be soaked a few hours before boiling, then well washed and scraped, and put into a fresh water.[1] It must not be boiled fast, but put into cold water, and gradually warmed through; skim frequently while boiling.

A leg or shoulder, weighing seven or eight pounds, should boil slowly for four hours. When taken up it must be skinned carefully, though some prefer the skin remaining on, as it loses much of the juice by skinning. It is very nice cold.

To Fricassee Pork

Cut a small sparerib or chine of pork into pieces, cover with water and stew until tender; remove the meat, and flavor the gravy with salt, pepper, and thicken with a little flour. Serve in a deep dish, in the gravy, and garnish the dish with rice.

Raised Pie.

A large meat pie like this was "raised" in a decorative lard crust, in contrast to common potpies that were cooked in vessels. The author stressed that cooks should not aim for flaky pastry because the crust had to be strong to hold up its savory contents. A tough crust need not be eaten, she assured readers, and could simply serve as an attractive vehicle for gravy and vegetables mixed with beef, mutton, poultry, or game. Acton, *Modern Cookery*, 257.

Pork Pie

Prepare your pork as above [To Fricassee Pork], or take any nice bits of cold roast pork. Line a deep dish with paste, fill in with the meat, pour the gravy over it, and cover all with the paste; make a small hole in the middle of the paste, and bake until nicely browned.

Pig's Feet

Boil four pig's feet until the bones drop out. Draw out the long bones and place them in a dish to cool.[2] Split each foot, take the liquor in which it is boiled, add the juice of a lemon and some salt, and turn over the feet. They may be dipped in batter, and fried in salt pork.

Pig's Head

Have the head nicely cleaned, and boil it till very tender. Chop it very fine, and season with salt, pepper, sage, and a little clove, while hot. Put in a deep dish, and cover with a plate that is smaller than the dish, that it may rest on the meat. Place on the plate a very heavy weight, and let it stand for twenty-four hours. This makes the famous "Pig's Head Cheese."

TO SELECT VEAL

When the kidney is well surrounded by fat, you may be sure the meat is of good quality. Always choose that which is whitest and fattest.

If the vein in the shoulder, which is very perceptible, is a bright red or blue, it is a sure sign that the meat is fresh.

Knuckle of Veal Stewed

Break the bone in two or three places, put to it five pints of water, some sweet herbs, whole black peppers, a little salt and mace.

When the meat is done, take it out with the herbs and spices, and thicken the liquor with a little flour, and boil it up well; then put back the meat, add two glasses of Madeira wine, and the juice of a lemon. Let it come to a boil, but be careful that it does not burn. It is much more apt to after the flour is added.

Veal Sweetbread

Take two or three fresh sweetbreads, parboil them for a few minutes, then take them from the hot water, and put them into cold. Take some bread crumbs, and add the yolks of two eggs, well beaten, to the crumbs.

When the sweetbreads are perfectly cold, place them on a skewer, and roll them in the prepared crumbs, lay them in a stew-pan with a small bit of butter and a little veal gravy, and cook them a nice brown.

Take the gravy in which they are cooked, add the juice of a lemon, a little salt and pepper; toast some slices of bread, dip them into the gravy, and lay the sweetbreads on.

Calf's Head

Let the butcher split the head in halves. Take out the eyes and the snout bone; then lay it in cold water, to soak two hours before boiling; take out the brains, and wash them well in several waters, then lay them in cold water. Put the head together, and lay it in a good sized pot, cover it with cold water, and throw in a table spoonful of salt. Let it boil slowly for two hours and a half, or three hours, according to size.

When it has boiled a little more than an hour, take some of the liquor, about a quart, and put into a stew-pan for the gravy; add to this liquor some salt, pepper, a little parsley chopped fine, a table spoonful of lemon pickle, and put over the fire to boil.

Beat up an egg lightly, with two table spoonfuls of flour, then remove carefully the skin from the brains, and beat them up with the egg and flour. When well beaten, thicken the gravy with it, and stew about ten minutes.

MUTTON AND LAMB

The best Mutton is of a fine grain, the fat firm and white.

Lamb should be eaten very fresh. In the fore quarter, the vein in the neck being any other color than blue, betrays it to be stale.

Mutton Kidneys

Take half a dozen fine mutton kidneys, clear them of fat and skin, and cut them into thin slices, powder them immediately with sweet herbs in fine powder, a little cayenne and salt.

Put into a stew-pan two ounces of clarified butter or fresh lard; put in the slices of kidney, and fry them nicely; dredge a little flour over them, and moisten with lemon juice, and in five minutes they will be done; lay them on a hot dish, around which are slices of fried bread.

Pour into the gravy two glasses of white wine, give it a boil, pour over the kidneys, and serve hot.

Leg of Lamb

Boil it in water to cover it; when half done add two cups of milk to the water, with a large spoonful of salt. It should be served with spinach and caper sauce. It will cook in an hour and a quarter, or half, according to size.

Fish, Fowl, Soups, Eggs, Etc.

Alamode Pigeons

Wash them very clean; make a stuffing of bits of salt pork, pounded biscuit, thyme, or summer savory, a little salt, and one or two eggs. Stuff the breasts sufficiently to make them look plump, lay them in a stew-pan or pot, cover them with water, add a little thyme, and half a pint of red wine.

If young, two and a half hours moderate stewing is sufficient; if old, three or four hours. Add more seasoning before you take them off, if required.

Oyster Sauce for Turkeys, &c.

Strain fifty oysters, put the juice into a sauce-pan, add one pint of new milk, let it simmer, and skim off any froth which may rise; then rub a large spoonful of flour and two of butter together; stir this into the liquor; add a little salt and pepper. Let it simmer five minutes, but do not add your oysters till just as they are to be sent to the table, as if they are too much cooked they are hard.

Anchovy Sauce

Boil a pound of beef in water enough to cover it, with a slice of toasted bread. When boiled, remove it from the water, and add four or five anchovies, and a glass of claret wine, with a little clove; boil up, and strain into your tureen boiling hot.

Forcemeat Balls

Take one pound of tender lean beef, and half a pound of nice beef suet, chopped very finely, the crumbs of a stale loaf of bread, soaked in cold water for a few moments, and squeezed very dry, the grated rind and juice of a lemon, half a tea spoonful of ginger, the same of salt and summer savory, with a little cayenne. Mix well together, and add the yolks of three eggs, well beaten. Divide in halves; put one half in a stew-pan, with a wine glass of ketchup; stew half an hour. The other half make into balls, the size of a walnut, and fry brown. Place round the dish in which the stew is served.

Fish Chowder

Take a fresh haddock, of three or four pounds, clean it well, and cut in pieces of three inches square. Place in the bottom of your dinner-pot five or six slices of salt pork, fry brown, then add three onions sliced thin, and fry those brown. Remove the kettle from the fire, and place on the onions and pork a layer of fish; sprinkle over a little pepper and salt, then a layer of pared and sliced potatoes, a layer of fish and potatoes, till the fish is used up. Cover with water, and let it boil for half an hour. Pound six biscuits or crackers fine as meal, and pour into the pot; and, lastly, add a quart or pint of milk; let it scald well, and serve.

Stewed Trout

Clean and wash the fish with care, and wipe it perfectly dry; put into a stew-pan two table spoonfuls of butter, dredge in as it melts a little flour, grate half a nutmeg, a few blades of mace, a little cayenne, and a tea spoonful of salt; mix it all together, then lay in the fish, let it brown slightly; pour over some veal gravy, a lemon thinly sliced, stew very slowly for forty minutes, take out the fish, and add two glasses of wine to the gravy. Lay the fish on a hot dish, and pour over it some of the gravy. Serve the rest in a sauce tureen.

Gumbo (a favorite Southern dish)

Cut up a pair of good sized chickens, as for a fricassee, flour them well, and put into a pan with a good sized piece of butter, and fry a nice brown, then lay them in a soup pot, pour on three quarts of hot water, and let them simmer slowly for two hours. Braid a little flour and butter together for a thickening, and stir in a little pepper and salt. Strain a quart or three pints of oysters, and add the juice to the soup. Next add four or five slices of cold boiled ham, and let all boil slowly together for ten minutes. Just before you take up the soup, stir in two large spoonfuls of finely powdered sassafras leaves, and let it simmer five minutes, then add your oysters. If you have no ham, it is very nice without it. Serve in a deep dish, and garnish the dish with rice.

Chicken Soup

Boil a pair of chickens with great care, skimming constantly, and keeping them covered with water. When tender, take out the chicken and remove every bone from the meat; put a large lump of butter into a frying-pan, and dredge the chicken meat well with flour, lay in the hot pan; fry a nice brown, and keep it hot and dry. Take a pint of the chicken water, and stir in two large spoonfuls of curry powder, two of butter, and one of flour, one tea spoonful of salt and a little cayenne; stir until smooth, then mix it with the broth in the pot; when well mixed, simmer five minutes, then add the browned chicken. Serve with rice.

Pickles, Ketchup, &c.

Sweet Tomato Pickles

Eight pounds peeled tomatoes, four of powdered sugar, cinnamon, cloves, and allspice, each one ounce. Boil one hour, and then add a quart of boiling vinegar.

Pickled Cucumbers (very nice)

To a gallon of water add a quart of salt, put in the cucumbers, and let them stay over night. In the morning wash them out of the brine, and put them carefully into a stone jar. Boil a gallon of vinegar, put in, while cold, a quarter of a pound of cloves and a table spoonful of alum; when it boils hard, skim it well and turn over the cucumbers. In a week they will be fit for use.

Chou Chou

A peck of tomatoes, two quarts of green peppers, half a peck of onions, two cabbages cut as for slaw, and two quarts of mustard seed. Have a large firkin, put in a layer of sliced tomatoes, then one of onions, next one of peppers, lastly cabbage; sprinkle over some of the mustard seed, repeat the layers again, and so on till you have used up the above quantity. Boil a gallon of vinegar, with a bit of alum, two ounces of cloves and two of allspice tied in a little bag, and boiled with the vinegar; skim it well and turn into the firkin. Let it stand twenty-four hours, then pour the whole into a large kettle, and let it boil five minutes; turn into the firkin, and stand away for future use.

Tomato Chowder

Slice a peck of green tomatoes, six green peppers, and four onions; strew a tea cup of salt over them. In the morning turn off the water, and put them in a kettle with vinegar enough to cover them, a tea cup of sugar, one of grated horseradish, a table spoonful of cloves, allspice, and cinnamon, each. Boil until soft.

Pickled Cabbage

Cut a cabbage in about eight pieces; soak it in cold water two or three hours; strain it thoroughly from the water, put it into the jar, sprinkling a little salt on each layer, add a few cloves, a little allspice and pepper, and a few slices of onions. Pour boiling vinegar sufficient to cover it. After standing twenty-four hours scald the vinegar again. In two or three days it is fit for use.

Oyster Ketchup (Philadelphia)

Take a gallon of fresh oysters, drain off the liquor, and pound or mash them well with a pestle. To a quart of the oysters add a quart of wine, one half ounce of mace, one of ground allspice, quarter of a pound of salt, simmer all together for ten or fifteen minutes, then strain through a sieve, and when cold bottle and seal.

Picollilly

Of cut cucumbers, beans, and cabbage, each four quarts, of cut peppers and onions two quarts each, celery and nasturtions four quarts each.[3] Pour on boiling vinegar, flavored strongly with mustard, mustard seed, and ground cloves.

Pickle for Daily Use

A gallon of vinegar, three quarters pound of salt, quarter pound of ginger, an ounce of mace, quarter ounce of cayenne pepper, and an ounce of mustard seed, simmered in vinegar, and when cold put in a jar. You may throw in fruits and vegetables when you choose.

Pickled Oysters

Take two quarts of oysters, put them in a sauce-pan, and if they are fresh, salt them; let them simmer on the fire, but not boil; take out the oysters, and add to the liquor in the sauce-pan a pint of vinegar, a small handful of whole cloves, quarter of an ounce of mace, and two dozen peppercorns. Let it come to a boil, and when the oysters are cold in the jar pour the liquor on them.

Pickled Peppers

Do not pick them till just as they begin to turn red; then soak them for ten or twelve days in strong salt and water; take them from the brine and soak them in clear water for a day. Wipe them dry, and put them away in cold vinegar; or if you wish them milder, remove the seeds and scald the vinegar, not boil.

Cold Slaw

A white, hard head of cabbage, cut in halves and laid in cold water, then shave it very fine.[4] Boil from a half to a pint of vinegar, stir into it the well-beaten yolk of an egg, and then turn over the cabbage, but not till a short time before using.

Tomato Ketchup

One peck of tomatoes, one great spoonful of cloves, allspice, cinnamon, and nutmeg each, half a large spoonful of black pepper, half a tea spoonful of cayenne, and a pint and a half of vinegar. Stew the tomatoes and strain them, and then add the spice and vinegar. This will make three bottles.

Pickled Peaches

Boil together one gallon good vinegar and four pounds of brown sugar for a few moments, and skim it well. Take ripe clingstone peaches, remove the down with a flannel cloth, and stick a few cloves in each. Put them in a glass or earthen vessel, and pour the liquor upon them boiling hot. Cover them, and let them stand in a cool place a week or ten days; then pour off the liquor, and boil as before; after which, return it boiling to the peaches, cover carefully and place away for future use.

Tomatoes Fried (very nice)

Do not pare them, but cut in slices, as an apple; dip in cracker, pounded and sifted, and fry in a little good butter.

Bread, Biscuits, Fritters, Corn Cakes, &c.

Soda Biscuits

Into a quart of flour, rub one table spoonful of lard and one of butter, with two tea spoons of cream of tartar. Dissolve a tea spoon of soda, and one and a half of salt in half pint of water, and if this will not wet the flour sufficiently add a little more cold water; roll it out, handling as little as possible, and cut with a tin into rounds. Bake in a quick oven,—quarter of an hour should bake them. Everything depends on a quick oven. Many use milk instead of water, but if made and baked properly water is nice enough to render them fit for any epicure.

Sour Milk Biscuits

To be made as the above, with the exception that sour milk is used in the place of cream of tartar, and the soda is dissolved in the milk.[5] Tea spoon of soda to a pint of sour milk.

Mrs. Reed's Brown Bread

Two cups of Indian meal even full, three cups of flour or Graham meal heaped, a pint and a half of sour milk, a cup of molasses, tea spoon and a half of soda, one of salt, steamed four hours. Brown lightly in the oven afterwards.

Mrs. Faben's Economy Cakes

Rusked bread, or that which is old and sour, can be made into very nice fritters. The bread should be cut in small pieces, and soaked in cold water till very soft. Drain off the water and mash the bread fine.

To three pints of bread thus prepared, add two eggs, four table spoonfuls of flour, a little salt, one tea spoon of soda in a cup of milk, which must be stirred into the bread, and a little more milk added, until thin enough to fry.

Potato Rolls

Boil four good sized potatoes, with their skins on; squeeze them in a towel, to make them dry and mealy, then remove the skin, and mash them perfectly smooth, with a spoonful of butter and a little salt; add the yolks of three eggs, well beaten, and stir into the potatoes, then add one pint and a half of milk, and a large spoonful of yeast; beat in flour enough to make a stiff dough; set it to rise, and when risen make it into cakes the size of an egg; let them rise again, and bake a light brown.

Slapjacks

One pint of milk, three eggs, tea spoon of soda, tea spoon of salt, flour enough to make a thin batter. Butter your griddle, and fry them the size of a plate; when one is done turn it on the dish, sprinkle on a little white sugar, and continue in this way till they are all fried. Always fry them with butter. Some people grate over a little nutmeg with the sugar on each one. The charm is to eat them while hot.

Johnny Cake

One quart of buttermilk or sour milk, one quart Indian meal, one quart of flour, one cup of molasses, tea spoon of soda (two scant tea spoons if the milk is sour), tea spoon of salt.

Aunt Chloe's Biscuits

One pint of rich milk, one tea spoon of soda dissolved in it, tea spoon of salt, two table spoonfuls of molasses, two eggs, Indian meal to make a batter to fry.

Malden Indian Cake

One cup of molasses, one cup of sour milk, tea spoon of soda dissolved in the milk, three cups of meal, three cups of flour, tea spoon of salt. To be baked.

Old Times Johnny Cake (very nice)

A quart of Indian meal, tea spoon of salt, scalded well with boiling water. Baked about half an inch thick. When done split through the middle, cut in pieces for table, and dip in melted butter.

Mrs. Courtney's Waffles

A pint bowl of cold boiled rice, thin it with cold milk, beaten well, one egg, a small piece of butter, and flour to make a batter stiff enough to bake.

Use pork to grease your waffle iron, not butter.

Hoe Cake

One pint of Indian meal, tea cup of flour, two table spoonfuls of molasses, a quart of cold milk, tea spoon saleratus, tea spoon salt.

Bake with a good fire, half an hour.

Brand-name baking soda, like the Arm & Hammer baking soda advertised here, was increasingly replacing generic saleratus and other leavening agents in American pantries. Advertisement for Church and Co.'s Arm & Hammer baking soda, Church and Dwight Co., New York, N.Y., ca. 1870, The Alan and Shirley Brocker Sliker Culinary Collection, Michigan State University Special Collections.

Miss Pindar's Dyspepsia Bread

One pint bowl of Graham flour, dissolve one half tea spoonful of soda in two thirds of a cup of homemade yeast, and add to the mixture one tea cup of molasses; pour in sufficient warm water to make it somewhat thinner than flour bread.

Mrs. Parsons' Rusk

One pound of flour, small piece of butter big as an egg, one egg, quarter pound white sugar, gill of milk, two great spoonfuls of yeast.

Miss Clarke's Graham Bread

One quart of water, one cup of molasses, one cup of yeast, mix in Graham flour to make a thin dough, stand over night to rise, stir in the morning, put in pans, let it rise in the pan and bake.

Indian Fritters

Scald one quart of corn meal with milk (half milk and half water will answer), stir in half pint of flour, half pint of yeast, and a little salt; let it rise, and fry on griddle.

Milk Bread

One pint of boiling water, one pint of new milk, one tea spoon soda, the same of salt, flour enough to form a batter; let it rise, and add sufficient flour to form a dough, and bake immediately.

Puddings

If you intend to boil a pudding, always have the water boiling before you put in the pudding.

Many people use a pudding cloth, kept expressly for the purpose, made of the thickest twilled cotton, and always, before using it, wash it out in clean water, and flour it well, before pouring in the pudding, allowing room for the pudding to swell according to the size designed.

I much prefer the *tin* pudding boiler, which is hollowed in the centre, that the pudding may be thoroughly cooked. This should be well buttered before the pudding is turned in, which will prevent it from adhering to the boiler. The cover should be tied on, and a thick cloth tied tightly over the cover.

All puddings in which berries are used require more flour than those without; and it must be remembered fruit should always be added the last thing. In *baking* puddings, always be sure and butter the dish well before the pudding is turned in.

Yankee Pudding

One quart of milk boiled, one pint Indian meal, two cups of molasses, a dozen sweet apples cut in small pieces, and bake it with a steady fire three hours.

Green Corn Pudding

Three cups of grated sweet green corn, two quarts of milk, eight eggs, half a cup of melted butter, one nutmeg, tea spoon of salt.

Bake it one hour, and eat with nice sauce.

Potato Pudding

Boil six or seven good sized potatoes, and when thoroughly done, peel and mash with milk to a thin batter; add half a pound of white sugar, four eggs, the grated peel and half the juice of a lemon. Bake three quarters of an hour.

Cranberry Pudding

One pint of milk, three eggs, and flour enough to make a thick batter, then add one pint of cranberries, and boil two hours. It must be eaten with nice sauce.

Boiled Cracker Pudding

Split four soft crackers, pour a pint of boiling milk over them, and add immediately a cup of suet well chopped; when cool, add five eggs well beaten, a little mace, and as many raisins as you like. Boil three hours, and eat with sauce.

Poverty Pudding

Soak your bread in milk the night before using; when ready, butter your pudding dish, and place in a layer of the bread. Have a dozen apples pared and sliced, and place a layer of apples on the bread, another layer of bread, then of apples, and so on, till your dish is filled; let the last layer be bread, and bake it an hour. To be eaten with sauce.

Baked Bread Pudding

Soak all your nice bits of bread the evening previous; in the morning add half a cup of butter and four eggs. Raisins if you like.

Bake an hour and a half, and eat with sauce.

Lemon Pudding

Peel of three lemons grated, and juice of two, one pound of sifted white sugar, half a pound of melted butter, a pint of cream or milk, eight eggs, a gill of rose water, and bake until you think it is done.

Squash Pudding

Boil half a squash, good size, and sift through a sieve, add to it two table spoonfuls of butter, a cup and a half of white sugar, six eggs, a quart of milk, three table spoonfuls of rose water, one biscuit, pounded very fine. Cover the bottom of your pudding dish with a nice paste, fill with the squash, and bake till done.

Mrs. Appleton's Pudding

Half a baker's white loaf, nine eggs, half a pound of suet chopped fine, half a pint of rose water, glass of wine. Sugar and spice to your taste. Raisins chopped as you please. Baked.

Mrs. Hopper's Bird's Nest Pudding

Pare and core as many apples as will stand in a dish, and fill the holes with sugar.

Make a custard of a quart of milk, eight eggs, and quarter of a pound of sugar. Pour it over the apples, grate a nutmeg over the top, and bake one hour.

Poverty Rice Pudding (very nice)

Boil a large cup of rice in three cups of water and a little salt; when cooked add one cup of molasses, table spoonful of cinnamon, three pounded soft crackers, and a pint of milk. Put in two table spoonfuls of butter while the rice is hot. To be baked until browned.

Macaroni Pudding

Break one pint of macaroni into short pieces and boil till soft; when cool, add four eggs, half pound of sugar, half cup of butter, nutmeg, and pint and a half of milk. Bake till nice brown.

State Ship Pudding (very nice)

Three cups of flour, one of molasses, one of water, one of suet chopped fine, one of raisins also chopped, tea spoonful of allspice, half a tea spoon of soda dissolved in the molasses. To be boiled three hours and a half, and eaten with butter or sauce. The same pudding is very nice taking four instead of three cups of flour, and using apples instead of raisins.

Thanksgiving Pudding

Pound twenty crackers fine, add five cups of milk, and let it swell. Beat well fourteen eggs, a pint bowl of sugar, tea cup of molasses, two small nutmegs, two tea spoonfuls of ground clove, three of ground cinnamon, two of salt, and half a tea spoonful of soda, and add to the cracker lastly a pint bowl heaped of raisins, and citron if you like. This quantity will make two puddings.

Carrot Pudding

Boil six large carrots, strain them through a sieve, and add half a pound of melted butter, half a pint of cream, eight eggs, cinnamon, rose water, wine and sugar to your taste; allow one hour to bake it.

To be baked in a dish lined with paste.

Maizena Pudding

Four table spoonfuls of maizena, stirred into two eggs, and milk enough to make it smooth.[6] Set a quart of milk to boil, and just before it boils stir in the above, constantly stirring the same way till it thickens; remove from the fire, and flavor. To be cold, and eaten with milk or cream, and sugar. It is very nice to omit the eggs, and take six table spoonfuls of maizena to a quart of milk (stirring the same way), and eaten warm with wine sauce.

Apple Pancakes

Add to one quart of flour milk enough to make a stiff batter, one large spoonful of good yeast, and set to rise.[7] When risen, add the grated rind of two lemons and two well beaten eggs to the batter. Pare and slice your apples one inch thick, dip into the batter, and drop into boiling lard.

Brown on both sides, sift sugar over, and send to table.

Pastry

COMMON PASTE

Rub half a pound of butter and one spoonful of lard into a quart of flour, add a little salt, and cold water enough to make a dough; flour your moulding board and roll out the dough. Be sure and not mould it, but handle as little as possible.

Mince Pie

Two pounds of beef, boiled and chopped; half a pound of suet, chopped fine; six large apples, pared and chopped; two pounds of currants, half pint of wine, glass of rose water, sugar and spice to your taste.

Cream Pies

Put on pint of milk to boil. Break two eggs into a bowl, and add a cup of white sugar, half a cup of flour, and after beating well, stir into the milk just as it commences to boil; keep on stirring one way till it thickens; take it off, and flavor with vanilla, or any other flavor you may prefer.

Previous to making the cream, make the paste for three pies, roll out and cover your plates, then roll out and cover a second time, and bake. When baked, and while warm, separate the edges gently with a knife, and lift the upper from the lower paste; fill in the cream, and put on the upper paste.

Apple Pie (very nice)

Stew a dozen good-sized greenings; when done, add a table spoonful of butter, a cup of white sugar (more if you like them sweet), half a glass of rose water, and a grated nutmeg. Make and bake your paste as for cream pie, and fill with apple instead of cream.

Pan Pie

Take a deep earthen pudding pot, fill it with slices of apple, then pour on as much molasses as the apple requires to sweeten it; sprinkle over a little cinnamon, put over a paste, with a small slit in the middle, and place in the oven. After the first paste is baked it may be taken off, and another put on in its place. This should be taken off, and the apple remain long enough to be a deep red. When cooked enough, take from the oven, and immediately break the paste in small pieces, and stir into the sauce while hot. To be eaten cold. It is a favorite dish with many people, and very nice.

Squash Pie

Boil a squash that weighs about six pounds, sift it through a sieve, add two quarts of milk, four eggs, well beaten, with three soft crackers, pounded as fine as meal. If the squash is watery, add another egg or a cracker as you prefer. Flavor with ginger or nutmeg, and sweeten to taste. A table spoonful of butter, while the squash is hot, is a great improvement. Bake in pie plates lined with paste. It may be baked deeper in a pudding dish, and is very much liked as a pudding by most people.

Pumpkin Pie

One quart of pumpkin to one quart milk, two cups sugar, two table spoonfuls of rose water, one of ginger, if you like, and four eggs. Baked in deep plates lined with paste. One or two eggs less may be used by substituting two or three table spoonfuls of maizena, or a soft cracker finely powdered.

Berwick Pie (delicious)

Make a rich paste, line a deep dish and bake it. Pare and core as many apples as will fill the dish (one layer), put them into a stewpan with four table spoonfuls of white sugar, a wine glass of sweet wine, and a little thin lemon peel or rose water as you please. Cover the stew-pan and let them stew until tender, then let them cool. Make a rich, boiled custard; when quite cold put the apples into the dish in which is the paste, and pour over the custard.

Baltimore Pie

Roll out some rich puff paste, not quite an inch thick; cut into any shape you please, making each piece of the same shape, but smaller than the preceding one, till the last is about the size of a cent. Between each piece spread some rich preserve or jam; turn up the edges of the paste, and brush the sides and top with the beaten yolk of an egg. Lay the pyramid on a tin sheet, and bake light brown. Serve hot.

Peach Pie

Fill a pudding dish with pared peaches (stones left in), sprinkle over as much sugar as the peaches require, a very little water, and cover with puff paste.

Cake

DIRECTIONS FOR MAKING CAKE

The flour used for making cake should always be dried and sifted; always break the eggs separately in a cup. It is a good plan to lay the eggs, to be used, for a few hours in very cold water before breaking; they whip better for being cold.

When soda is used, always dissolve it before adding it to the general mixture.

In winter, soften but do not melt the butter in the milk used.

Never add the fruit to cake until it is ready for baking.

In baking cake which requires long baking, take white paper and lay on the sides, bottom, and top; it is easily removed when the cake is done.

To ascertain when a loaf of cake is done, take a fine knitting-needle and insert in the thickest part of the loaf; if it does not stick to the needle, the baking is finished.

In whipping the whites of eggs, always use a shallow dish, and whip them in a cool place.

Never stop after you commence until they are light, and whip them until you can turn the dish over without their slipping.

It is better to beat the yolks and whites of eggs separately, except in cake that contains yeast or soda.

The ingredients of the cake should be well beaten together before the flour is mixed in, for it does not benefit the cake by beating after all the flour is added.

I find by experience that the granulated sugar is purer, sweeter, and better in every respect for cakes and all pastries than brown sugar.

The butter and sugar should always be worked to a cream, and the other ingredients added afterwards, the flour always the last.

The cake should be turned from the tins as soon as it comes from the oven. It requires a much hotter oven for cake with soda in it, than for that which is raised with yeast.

Cup Cake

Five cups of flour, three of sugar, one and a half of butter, six eggs, one cup of milk, with a scant tea spoon of soda, one grated nutmeg, and three quarters of a pound of currants. It is very nice without the currants.

French Sponge Cake

The yolks of eighteen eggs, well beaten for two hours, two pounds of sugar, one pound of flour, and beat well together; the whites of eighteen eggs, whipped to a froth, and put into the cake the last thing before putting it into the oven.

Plum Cake (good)

Five cups of flour, two of sugar, one of molasses, one of butter, half cup of lard, tea spoon of salt, tea spoon of soda dissolved in a cup of sour milk, two tea spoons of ground clove, two of allspice, one of mace, one pound chopped raisins, two ounces of citron sliced thin.

Pork Cake.

Half pound of salt pork chopped fine, two cups of molasses, half pound raisins chopped well, two eggs, two tea spoons each of clove, allspice, and mace, half a table spoonful of saleratus or soda, and flour enough to make a stiff batter. Bake in a moderate oven.

Nothing Cake

One egg, a piece of butter the size of an egg, one cup of sugar, one cup of milk, one pint of flour, two tea spoonfuls of cream of tartar, one of soda. Divide the milk, and dissolve the cream of tartar in one, and the soda in the other, and pour one into the other to effervesce, then add to the other ingredients.

Poverty Cake

One cup of sugar, one egg, butter as large as an egg, three cups of flour, one tea spoon of soda, two tea spoons cream tartar, one cup milk, one nutmeg.

Mrs. Page's Gold Cake

Yolks of one dozen eggs, five cups of flour, three of white sugar, one of butter, one and a half of cream or sour milk. If the milk is sour, one tea spoon of soda dissolved in it; if cream, half a tea spoon of soda.

Wafers

One pound of flour, three quarters of a pound of granulated sugar, half pound of butter, five eggs, and a gill of rose water.

Every-day Cake

One cup molasses, one cup of sugar, one cup of butter, two eggs, two thirds of a cup of milk, with one tea spoon of soda dissolved in it. Two tea spoons of cream tartar, and flour enough to make it as other loaf cake, one tea spoon of salt, one of clove, one of cinnamon, one nutmeg.

Cookies

Six cups of flour, two of sugar, one of butter, one of milk, tea spoon of soda, flavored with cinnamon or nutmeg, as you like.

Mrs. Briggs' Election Cake

Lay a sponge over night with milk, next morning add to the sponge a pint of flour, one coffee cup of sugar, one of butter, one nutmeg, tea spoon of soda, and fruit if you choose.

Jenny Lind Cake

Four cups of flour, two of sugar, one of butter, one of milk, five eggs, one tea spoon cream tartar, half tea spoon of soda. Flavored with rose or lemon.

Railroad Cake

One cup sugar, one table spoon of butter beaten to a cream, three eggs beaten to a froth, one cup flour, three table spoonfuls sweet milk, one tea spoon cream tartar, half tea spoon soda, half tea spoon salt.

Squash Cake

One cup of squash, after it is sifted, three of flour, one of milk, and if the squash is very dry a little more, two table spoonfuls of sugar, one of butter, one egg, two tea spoons yeast powder.

Boston Soft Gingerbread (nice)

Nine eggs, a pound and a half of sugar, three quarters of a pound of butter, a scant pound of flour, and ginger to your taste.

Caraway seeds are a great improvement.

Mrs. Lincoln's Doughnuts

Two cups of sugar, two eggs, cup and a half of milk, half a tea spoon cream of tartar, half tea spoon of soda, butter size of an egg, flour to roll out thin.

Lemon Sponge Cake

Take ten eggs, separate them, a pound of granulated sugar, half pound of flour, the grated peel of two lemons, and the juice of one; beat the yolks with the sugar, and the whites alone; then add them, and sift in the flour by degrees; beat well, and bake with a quick heat.

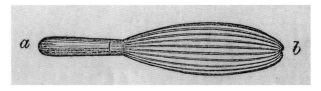

The author suggested that if readers didn't already possess a good eggbeater, they could take this engraving to a tinsmith so that he could make them one using the image as a model. Blot, *Hand-Book of Practical Cookery*, 24.

Common Doughnuts

Two cups of sugar, one and a half of milk, two eggs, one nutmeg, two tea spoonfuls of cream of tartar, one of soda.

Mrs. Emerson's Sponge Cake

The weight of six eggs in sugar, the weight of four in flour, and a few drops of essence of lemon. Beat the eggs and sugar together for half an hour, stir in the flour, and bake twenty minutes.

Mrs. Burrage's Coffee Cake

Five cups of flour, one cup of made coffee, one cup sugar, half cup molasses, one cup of butter, tea spoon soda, two tea spoonfuls of cinnamon, one of clove, raisins or currants.

Common Plum Cake

Three cups of flour, one of sugar, one of sour cream,—if you have not cream, half of butter, and half of milk,—two eggs, tea spoon of soda, cup of raisins, little spice.

Preserves, Jellies, Blanc-Mange, &c.

Mrs. Curtis' Velvet Cream

Half an ounce of isinglass dissolved in one and a half cups of white wine; then add the juice and grated peel of a lemon, three quarters of a pound of loaf sugar; simmer all together until mixed well; strain and add one and a half pints of rich cream, and stir until cool; pour it into moulds, and let it stand till stiff enough to turn out.

Currant Jelly

Three pounds of juice of red currants, one pound of juice of white currants, boil quickly for fifteen minutes; then take from the fire and stir in two pounds of granulated sugar, stirring till dissolved; place again on the fire, and boil hard for eight minutes.

After it is put in the glasses, set it for two or three days in a hot sun.

Mrs. Hooper's Whip Syllabubs

One quart of rich cream, the juice of three lemons, three quarters of a pound of sugar, and wine to your taste; whip all well together, put the froth in your glasses as fast as it rises.

Preserved Quinces

A pound of sugar to each pound of quince (after paring, coring, and quartering); take half of the sugar and make a thin syrup; stewing a few of the quinces at a time till all are finished, make a rich syrup of the remaining sugar and pour over them.

Blanc-Mange

Three pints of cream boiled well and flavored and sweetened to taste, one and a quarter ounce of gelatine, or half an ounce of isinglass dissolved in warm water enough to cover it; when dissolved cover with cream and boil up once or twice till rather thick, then pour it on the seasoned cream; stir it well and put it in the moulds.

Apple Jam

Core and pare a good quantity of apples, chop them well, allow equal quantity of weight, apples and sugar, make a syrup of your sugar by adding a little water, boiling and skimming well, then throw in some grated lemon peel, a little white ginger with the apples, boil until the fruit looks clear.

Preserved Pine Apple

A pound of sugar to a pound of pine apple; put the slices in water, and boil a quarter of an hour; then remove them, and add the sugar to the water; put in the apple, and boil fifteen minutes. Boil the syrup till thick.

Grapes. *American Practical Cookery Book*, 178.

Grape Jam

Boil the grapes in a little water long enough to make them tender, then add a pound of sugar to a pound of grapes, and boil half an hour.

Preserved Tomatoes

A pound of sugar to a pound of tomatoes. Take six pounds of each, the peel and juice of four lemons, and quarter of a pound of ginger tied up in a bag; put on the side of the range, and boil slowly for three hours.

Preserved Pears

Select sound, medium-size pears; pare, halve, and core them; lay them in a sauce-pan for preserving; cover them with cold water, with quarter of a pound of ginger tied in a muslin bag and put into the water; let them simmer slowly till soft, then drain them on a sieve, weigh them, and allow sugar equal in weight.

Pare thinly the rind of three fresh lemons, and put with the juice into the syrup; when it boils lay in the pears, and let them cook slowly for twenty minutes; then lay the pears on a dish, and return the syrup to the fire, and let the watery particles evaporate; when the pears are cold put them in your jar, and pour on the syrup when quite cold. Cork tightly.

Moss Blanc-Mange

Take an ounce of moss, wash thoroughly, and put into two quarts of new milk; let it simmer slowly till it thickens;[8] strain through a sieve, flavor, and put it into moulds.

Snow

Pour on to half a box of gelatine a pint and a half of boiling water, let it thicken; beat together the whites of two eggs, one cup of sugar, and juice of two lemons, stir into the gelatine and put into your mould to cool.

Sauces

TO CLARIFY SUGAR

To two pounds of granulated sugar put a pint of water, and dissolve it. When dissolved place to boil, and before hot stir in well the whites of two eggs; watch it carefully, skimming well. When clear cool and bottle it. This will keep a long time if kept in a cool place.

Beacon Street Sauce

Two cups of white granulated sugar, one even cup of butter worked back to a cream, add a glass of wine, and a little rose or nutmeg as you like. Stir a scant half tea spoon of soda into a cup of sour milk, and when it effervesces add it, and stir all well together; then add four table spoonfuls of boiling water without stirring at all, and put into the sauce tureen, disturbing it as little as possible.

Good Common Sauce

Half a pint bowl of brown sugar, two table spoonfuls of butter, a glass of rose water whipped to a cream. Then dredge in about a table spoonful of flour, and add half a pint of boiling water, stirring well for two or three minutes.

Egg Sauce

Take quarter of a pound of butter and braid it well into three even spoonfuls of flour; then turn on a scant pint of boiling water, chop well three boiled eggs, and stir into the butter as it goes to the table.

Caper Sauce

Is to be made as egg sauce, and two table spoonfuls of capers stirred in instead of eggs.

Oyster Sauce

Put on a pint of water to boil; when it boils stir in a quarter of a pound of butter, and three table spoonfuls of flour (even full), let it boil once, and add a pint of solid oysters.

Mint Sauce

Strip off the tender leaves of the mint, and chop them fine; powder it well with sugar, and cover with vinegar half an hour before serving.

Cranberry Sauce

A quart of cranberries, a large pint of sugar, and half a pint of water. Boil slowly, and beat the cranberries to a jelly. When thoroughly bruised put in your moulds.

Haverhill Cranberry Sauce

One quart of cranberries, pint and a half of white sugar, half pint of water.

Boston Cranberry Sauce

One pint cranberries, three quarters pint of sugar, simmer slowly, and be sure not to burn.

Superior Sauce

Turn a pint of boiling cream on to the well-beaten yolks of six eggs; add four table spoonfuls of white sugar, and three of butter, which have been previously worked to a cream; put all on the fire, and stir it till it begins to thicken, then add a glass of sherry.

Apple Sauce

Pare, core, and cut up a quart of apples, add half a cup of water, boil them till tender, then add sugar and nutmeg to taste.

Salem Apple Sauce

Prepare the apple sauce as above, and when done, stir in a lump of butter, and flavor with rose water.

Quince Sauce

Cut, pare, and core a quart of quinces, cover in water and boil till perfectly tender, then add three quarters of a pound of sugar, and continue boiling for ten or fifteen minutes, that the sugar may penetrate the quince.

Beverly Sauce

Two cups of sugar, and three quarters of butter worked back to a cream; add a little flour, stir it into two gills of boiling water, put over the fire, and let it boil two minutes; take off, and add immediately two glasses of wine.

Lemon Sauce

Put two cups of milk on to boil; when it boils, stir in two tea spoonfuls of flour, two cups of sugar, and the beaten yolks of three eggs; take from the fire, and add the juice and grated rind of the lemon.

Cream Sauce

Beat the yolks of three eggs, three table spoonfuls of white sugar, and vanilla flavor. Turn on it a pint of boiling milk, and stir it well.

Wine Sauce

One pint bowl of white sugar, not quite a quarter of a pound of butter, one glass of wine, one grated nutmeg, and a table spoonful of warm water; beat together steadily for half an hour.

Set a sauce-pan on the fire, with about a gill of water in it; when it boils, put in the sugar, &c., but do not stir it nor let it boil, but simmer gently till all is dissolved; pour into the tureen, and do not cover till cold.

Good Common Sauce

To eight table spoonfuls of sugar add four of butter, and stir it together until white; then put into a sauce-pan, with a cup of hot water; set on the fire, and stir till it boils; then add a spoonful or two of wine, or, if you please, flavor with lemon and rose water.

Miscellaneous

Mulled Wine

Put a little cinnamon or allspice to half a pint of hot water, and steep it; add three eggs, well-beaten, with sugar, heat to a boil a pint of wine; then put in the spice and eggs while boiling, and stir for three minutes.

Boiled Rice (very nice)

Wash a cup of rice, and add four cups of water, and a tea spoon of salt; let it simmer on the back of the range for two hours, and do not stir it.

Jellied Rice

To three pints of milk put a tea cup of rice, and a little salt; cover it close, and let it simmer about three hours; beat it well, and put it into moulds, and eat as blanc-mange.

Cracker Toast

Separate a dozen hard crackers, lay them in a dish, and pour water over them; put on a little salt, and when soft put in two or three nice bits of butter and a little milk; put in the oven till heated through.

Mush, or Hasty Pudding

Set on a quart of water to boil; in the mean time stir half a pint of sifted Indian meal into water enough to make it smooth, with two tea spoonfuls of salt. When the water boils, stir in one spoonful and let it boil, then another and let it boil, and so on till you have thickening in; then add enough sifted raw meal gradually, stirring all the time till thick enough, and it is done. This is a very nice receipt.

Fried Mush

Made as above [Hasty Pudding], the day before it is wanted, and cut in slices, and fried with fat enough to prevent it from sticking to the griddle.

Oatmeal Gruel

Put on a cup of raisins in a quart of water, to boil; boil them hard for half an hour. Take two table spoonfuls of oatmeal, and make smooth with cold water; a little salt; when the raisins are boiled enough, stir in the thickening; let it boil up and skim it well, then add a bit of butter, a little white sugar, and grate a little nutmeg on the top when it is served.

Toast Water

Two slices of stale bread, toasted brown, cut in pieces, and a pint of boiling water poured over. Invalids relish it with a glass of white wine added, and a little nutmeg grated over.

Fresh Egg for an Invalid

Break an egg into a tumbler, add two tea spoonfuls of white sugar, and whip briskly; then add a glass of wine, and fill up the tumbler with milk.

Hop Tea

Take a large spoonful of hops, and simmer in a pint of water; when strong enough of hops, strain off and add white sugar and a table spoonful of gin. It is a quieting drink, most excellent for nervous headache.

Egg Nogg

The yolks of six eggs, with four table spoonfuls of sugar, a little nutmeg, a glass of wine, and two glasses of brandy; then add, when well mixed, a quart of milk. It is refreshing in summer to add ice, pounded very small.

Excellent Yeast

Two table spoonfuls of hops to a quart of water; let them steep well; make a thickening of six potatoes mashed fine, and three table spoonfuls of flour worked into the potatoes; strain the hop water upon it, stir it well, and when cool enough add yeast to work it. Bottle, and keep in a cool place.

Cherry Rum

A peck of black wild cherries, soaked in cold water for twenty four hours. Put them in a demijohn, add two pounds brown sugar, two quarts blackberries, and a gallon of best New England rum.[9] The older it is the better, if kept well corked; it is excellent for summer complaints.[10]

Ginger Beer

Two ounces of ginger to a pint of molasses, add a gallon of warm water, stir it well, and add half a pint of lively yeast.

Mrs. Knight's Currant Shrub

To a quart of juice add a scant pint of water, and a pound and a half of crushed sugar; boil well; add a little brandy, a gill to a bottle of the shrub, and cork, after standing for ten or twelve days.

Wine Whey

Boil a quart of milk, add to it half a pint of wine, put on the fire till it boils again, then set aside till the curd settles, pour off the whey, and sweeten to taste. It is said good country cider is nice as the wine.

Succotash

Cut off corn from the cobs, and put the cobs in just water enough to cover them, and boil one hour; then remove the cobs, and put in the corn and a quart of Lima beans, and boil thirty minutes. When boiled, add some cream or milk, salt, and butter.

Tripe

Must be washed in warm water, and cut into squares of three inches; take one egg, three table spoonfuls of flour, a little salt, and make a very thick batter by adding milk. Fry out some slices of pork, dip the tripe into the batter, and fry a light brown.

Aunt Emily's Cake

Four cups of flour, two of sugar, one cup of butter, one of milk, three eggs, whites beaten separately, fruit if you like, flavor as you please.

A raspberry. *American Practical Cookery Book*, 166.

Raspberry Wine

Bruise the raspberries with the back of a spoon; strain them through a flannel bag; one pound of loaf sugar to one quart of juice; stir well and cover closely, letting it stand for three days, stirring well each day. Pour off the clear juice, and add one quart of juice to two quarts of sherry wine; bottle it and use in two weeks. Brandy instead of wine, it will be Raspberry Brandy.

Tessie's Wheaten Biscuit (from a contraband)

Make a quart of flour short with butter and lard; wet with cold water, and made pretty stiff; put on a wooden block or board, beat out thin, sprinkle with flour; then fold up and repeat the beating (with a mallet or pestle), "till it begins to go pop, pop, pop,—it'll crack moo' like a whip,—then you know it's done." Cut into thin biscuits and bake.

P. K. S., *What to Do with the Cold Mutton: A Book of Réchauffés, Together with Many Other Approved Receipts for the Kitchen of a Gentleman of Moderate Income*

What to Do with the Cold Mutton promised to provide appealing methods of using up food left over from one meal to another. Although the author attempted to elevate the subject with the French word *réchauffés*, or reheated dishes, what that meant was leftovers, a humble category of cooking that had rarely if ever been placed center stage before. Although originally published in England in 1864, the book's specificity was perfectly in line with a publishing trend going on in the United States, too, as cookbooks continued to evolve away from big compendiums of domestic information toward smaller volumes with specialized themes. The title of the book also anticipated twentieth-century publishing trends in its humor, its promise to solve an annoying daily problem, and its frank emphasis on economy.

While the subtitle states that the recipes were intended for "the Kitchen of a Gentleman of Moderate Income," this did not mean that the food was meant only for bachelors or widowers. Rather, the author was casually referring to economic reality: in England and in the United States alike at the time, married women were rarely allowed to own property, so the kitchen—as well as the rest of the house—would have legally belonged to the male head of household. Despite the subtitle, however, the author made clear that he or she was aiming the book at women, and specifically at women who had grown up in comfortable financial circumstances, but who now had husbands with modest incomes that could not cover lavish tables or careless food purchasing. When dealing with the potentially uncomfortable topic of tightened budgets, the author took pains to salvage the readers' pride, assuring them that it was not loss of "position" that made a cost-cutting book about leftovers useful to them. While their income might be reduced, in other words, the author reassured them that their social position was unchanged and that purchasing this book would certainly do nothing to diminish it further.

The author was far from the first to consider the subject of leftovers. Previous cookbook authors had routinely included recipes for using up cooked foods, like Ann Howe's Warmed Over Poultry or recipes for Cottage Cheese that made use of sour milk. Recipes for using up

A typical drawing of an animal with numbers corresponding to cuts of meat. *American Practical Cookery Book, 5.*

to convert leftover cod—a sorrier leftover is hard to imagine—alternatively into Bonne Bouche of Cod, Vol-au-Vent of Cod, or Boulettes of Cod. Or in the recipe for Mayonnaise of Chicken, which educated readers would have pronounced with a French accent, the author transformed a cold boiled bird into an elaborate chicken salad that included lemon juice, herbs, shallots, tarragon vinegar, cream, and a homemade egg yolk emulsion. Meat, in these *réchaufé* recipes, was also physically reshaped to give it new life. Dishes like Calf's Head Fritters called for readers to remove meat from a calf's head, soak it in a lemony marinade for a few hours, and then fry it. In Hashed Calf's Head, the recipe called for a mound of minced veal to be encircled with fried brain patties.

Yet despite the emphasis on economy, it is also clear that this author was by no means aiming at the very poor. Indeed, the fact that the author assumed readers could afford large cuts of meat in the first place—and that they would have meat left from one meal to the next—points to a comfortable economic margin of error. Moreover, he or she made clear that the intended reader of the book should learn about cooking and kitchen management techniques in order to best direct a servant to perform that work efficiently.

For all the emphasis on reinventing leftovers, the book was actually a much more conventional cookbook than it first appeared. The *réchauffé* section occupied only the first third of the book, and the rest was devoted to recipes similar to those found in other general cookbooks of the era. Although the cookbook genre was becoming less comprehensive, that transformation was still far from complete.

old bread abounded, from Cornelius's recipe, To Make Stale Bread, or Cake, Fresh, to Howe's Economy Cakes and Knight's Poverty Pudding. Yet the author of *What to Do with the Cold Mutton* took a truly novel tack, both by putting leftovers front and center and by boldly promising to make leftovers exciting with recipes that would produce more than "the inevitable" boring hash, which the author derided as "the only réchaufé that ever enters the imagination of a plain cook." Instead, the author promised appealing dishes made interesting through imagination. In practice, imagination meant liberal use of sauces, stocks, curry powder, lemon zest, parmesan cheese, vinegars, and spices, which allowed cooks to transform leftover ingredients into wholly new dishes.

In another technique that would grow more popular throughout the late nineteenth century, the author borrowed liberally from French phraseology to make the recipes sound more like haute cuisine than leftover odds and ends. For example, the author offered ways

Preface

It may be thought unnecessary to add another to the already numerous lists of books upon Cookery; books as various in their degrees of excellence as in price. But this little work does not profess to teach "the whole Art of Cookery:" it simply aims at supplying a want often felt by the young and inexperienced mistress of a household, where a moderate income, rather than position, renders economy advisable; and who, accustomed to every luxury and comfort in her father's house, is yet ignorant of the art by which such culinary results are attained, and would gladly see her husband's more modest table as well ordered, though by more simple means. To such persons, the following hints of "What to do with the Cold Mutton" may be of use, as suggesting something more than the only réchauffé that ever enters the imagination of a plain cook—the inevitable "hash."

The recipes that follow the "Book of Réchauffés" have all been long tried and approved, and though some of them may be thought of a more costly character than is compatible with a "moderate income," the expense depends very much upon locality; that which may be procured for possibly one or two shillings in the country, may cost three or four in the city, whilst in other things the reverse may be the case, and what may be dear inland, may be cheap at the sea-coast. When guests are to be entertained, choicer dishes are required than are needed for the daily table, and for such occasions suitable receipts are given. But throughout this little book there is nothing that a plain cook may not manage well, after one or two trials; and if her mistress will only take the trouble of telling her of any error against good taste in matters of arrangement or dishing-up, the result cannot fail to be equally satisfactory to both.

P. K. S.

To Dress Fish a Second Time

To a small quantity of fish, add two handfuls of bread crumbs, two eggs, two ounces of butter, a little essence of anchovy, and a little pepper, salt, and cayenne. Mix these all well with the fish, which should previously be taken from the bones and pounded; butter a plain mould, put in the mixture, and steam it until it is hot through. Any cold boiled fish may be dressed in this way.

Fish and Macaroni

Take the remains of any kind of white boiled fish, remove the bones and skin, and break it in rather small pieces. Boil some macaroni in water till tender, drain it well, and cut it in lengths of about an inch, and mix equal quantities of fish and macaroni.[1] Then put two ounces of butter into a stewpan, add the yolks of two eggs, a little lemon-juice, pepper, and salt, and stir in well half a pint of good melted butter; make the sauce quite smooth, put in the fish and macaroni, and heat it thoroughly in the sauce. Pour it out on a dish, keeping it as high as you can in the centre; cover it thinly with fine bread crumbs, and brown the top with a salamander, or in the oven till of a nice light color.[2]

Bonne Bouche of Cod

Cut the cod into nice slices, removing the skin and bones. Put into a stewpan a small piece of butter, a table-spoonful of flour, a little very finely chopped garlic, some salt, pepper, and nutmeg; moisten with cream or milk and stir the sauce over the fire till well mixed. Put in the fillets of cod, and warm them in the sauce; take them out, and cover each fillet with fine bread crumbs and grated Parmesan cheese; egg them with beaten yolk of egg, and cover again with bread crumbs and Parmesan. Sprinkle well with a little oiled butter, and brown them in a cutlet-pan. Serve very hot.

Vol-au-vent of Cod

Break the cod in small pieces, and free it from skin and bone. Put into a stewpan a small piece of butter and two table-spoonfuls of flour, mix them together, and moisten them with half a pint of good milk; boil fast to reduce the sauce, stirring constantly, that it may not burn or stick to the bottom of the stewpan, and as it becomes thick, add by degrees another half-pint of milk; boil well and strain. Warm the pieces of cod in this sauce, add a little salt, and serve in a vol-au-vent.

A vol-au-vent was a puff pastry that could rise to a height of four or five inches in the oven, surrounding a filling of meat or fish. Acton, *Modern Cookery*, 258.

Boulettes of Cod

Break the cod in very small pieces, warm it in a thick, well-flavored white sauce; make it into small balls, egg and bread-crumb them twice, and fry a light-brown color.

The Epicure's Hash

To about one pound of cold mutton, cut in neat slices, take the following ingredients:—slice two large onions, put them into a stewpan with a small piece of butter, and fry them till they are a good brown color; then add half a pint of good-flavored broth or stock, a dessert-spoonful of Tums or Harvey sauce, three dessert-spoonfuls of tarragon vinegar, a table-spoonful of curry paste, a small lump of sugar, and a little pepper and salt to taste; let this sauce boil up, and then simmer slowly by the fire for half an hour, stirring it occasionally, and thicken it with one table-spoonful of flour, mixed smooth in a little cold water, or half the quantity of corn-starch. Let the thickening boil thoroughly, and when the sauce is ready, put in the slices of meat, let them heat through, but not boil, or the meat will be hard, and serve quite hot, with sippets of toast round the dish.[3]

Mutton Pudding

A very good pudding may be made from cold mutton; boiled is better for the purpose than roast, but either may be used. Cut the mutton in small slices, rather thick; mix well together in a plate some flour, salt and pepper, with a good sized onion finely chopped, and into this mixture dip each piece of mutton; slice three or four potatoes, according to size. Then butter a pudding mould or basin, line it with a light suet crust, lay in lightly the mutton and potatoes in alternate layers, till you have filled up your mould, pour in a tea-cupful or more of good stock, cover the top closely with the rest of the suet crust, and boil or steam it till done. It will not take so long to cook as if made from fresh meat.

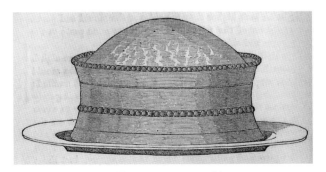

A mould for meat pie or pudding.
Blot, *Hand-Book of Practical Cookery*, 436.

Minced Mutton with Poached Eggs

Mince the mutton small, taking out all skin and sinew. Put into a stewpan a small piece of butter with one or two onions, some parsley, and a sprig of tarragon, all chopped fine, and let them fry well in the butter; then add sufficient stock for the quantity of meat; pepper and salt to taste, a little browning if needed for the color, and a table-spoonful or more of flour mixed in a little stock or water. Stir constantly, and when the stock is smooth and well boiled, add the minced mutton and warm it through, but do not let it boil, or it will be hard. Pour it upon a dish, and serve it with some nicely poached eggs on top.

Hashed Beef

Cut as much cold roast beef as you require for your dish, in neat slices, free from skin and gristle. Put into a stewpan a small piece of butter, a large onion minced, a table-spoonful of flour, and keep stirring over the fire till it browns, but be careful it does not burn. Then stir in by degrees half a pint of good-flavored stock, add salt to taste, and let the sauce boil till it thickens sufficiently, then put in two table-spoonfuls of hot green pickle chopped small, and slices of beef; let them heat through, and serve with sippets of toast round the dish.

Minced Beef au Gratin

Mince small as much cold roast beef as you wish for your dish. Put into a stewpan a small quantity of good brown sauce, together with a shallot chopped small; salt, pepper, and nutmeg; give it a good boil, and warm the meat in this, making it rather thick. Pour it into a deep dish, cover it over thickly with fine bread crumbs, sprinkle over some oiled butter, and put it into the oven to brown nicely, and serve immediately.

Potted Beef

Take some cold boiled beef (the lean half of the round is the best), remove all the skinny parts, mince fine, and then pound in a mortar with some fresh butter till quite smooth. Season with a little nutmeg, a little black pepper, some cayenne, a little mace, and salt if necessary. Press it very firmly into flat pots; clarify some fresh butter, and pour over the top of each pot, and when cold, paper it over, and keep in a cold place.

Larded Cutlets of Veal

Cut some slices from a cold fillet of veal, a third of an inch thick, and divide them into round pieces about the size of a Spanish silver dollar, or rather larger; lard these through with strips of fat bacon, using a large larding-pin for the purpose. Put into a stewpan nearly a pint of good stock, reduce it to half the quantity, add a little salt, a small lump of sugar, and as much coloring as may be needed if the sauce is not dark enough; it should be reduced till it becomes a thinnish transparent glaze; put in the larded rounds of veal, let them stew in this till the bacon is quite cooked and the slices of veal nicely glazed; then take them out of the sauce, moisten it, if too thick, with a little stock, add a small glass of red wine, the juice of a lemon, and a little cayenne pepper; give it a boil, dish the rounds of veal as you would mutton cutlets, pour the sauce in the centre, and serve.

Calf's Head Fritters

Cut the cold calf's head into small round slices, put them in a deep dish, sprinkle on them some chopped parsley, tarragon, and chives, and squeeze over all the juice of a lemon, or two table-spoonfuls of vinegar. Let them remain in this pickle for two or three hours, turning the pieces of calf's head every now and then, so that both sides may imbibe the flavoring; then take them out, drain well from the acid, dip each piece into batter, and fry them in hot fat, a light yellow color; serve very hot.

Hashed Calf's Head

What is left of a boiled calf's head (with the skin on) will make an excellent dish, hashed, if the following directions are carefully attended to:—take the meat, palate, and gelatinous parts from the bones, cutting it in neat slices or pieces; stew down the bones, with a bunch of sweet herbs, in the liquor in which you boiled the head (which should be saved for this purpose), and take as much of this stock, reducing it till strong enough, as may be required for the quantity of meat you hash; to this stock add a little mushroom catchup, the juice of a lemon, one or two anchovies chopped fine, some cayenne pepper, and a little coloring if necessary; boil all these together, then strain, and thicken with a little flour and butter. Then take what remains of the brains, beat them up with two eggs and two table-spoonfuls of flour, a little sage, thyme, and parsley, all chopped very fine, and season with cayenne and salt; make it up into little flat cakes, and fry in butter or good dripping, and drain well on a sieve before the fire. Make, also, some forcemeat balls of fine bread crumbs, a little bit of boiled meat and fat bacon, both minced very small, a little parsley, lemon-peel, and an anchovy, all chopped fine; bind together with yolk of egg, and make into small balls, to be boiled in the gravy, during which time add the pieces of meat to stew a little, and a small glass of port wine. Dish your hash nicely, and garnish round the edge with the brain-cakes, little pieces of bacon rolled and fried, egg balls, and button mushrooms.

Minced Pork with Onions

Mince some cold roast pork, but not too fine. Then slice very thin two large onions; put them into a stewpan with a little bit of butter to brown slightly, add three-quarters of a pint of stock, and let the onions stew well in it; when done, put in three table-spoonfuls of brown sauce, if you have it; if not, a little glaze or browning, salt, pepper, and thicken with a small quantity of flour and butter; boil well, and then add the minced pork; warm it in the sauce, and serve.

Mayonnaise of Chicken

Cut up the remains of a cold boiled fowl into small joints, or you may take the meat from the bones in smallish-sized pieces. Put them into a deep dish with a little oil, vinegar, or lemon-juice, pepper, salt, chopped onion, and parsley, and let them remain in this for a few hours, turning the pieces occasionally, and covering the dish closely over. Make a sauce of the following ingredients:—take the yolks of two hard-boiled eggs, pound them well, and mix with the yolk of a raw egg, a salt-spoonful of very finely chopped shallot, salt, white pepper, a very little pounded sugar, and add some good salad oil by degrees (a drop at a time, or you will curdle the sauce if you pour it in too quickly), stirring it constantly. When getting too thick, moisten with a little tarragon vinegar, then add more oil, and again vinegar, till you have sufficient sauce for your mayonnaise. The proportion of oil to vinegar is three of the former to one of the latter, and you must be guided by taste as to the quantity of salt, pepper, and shallot or onion; also, should the vinegar be weak, a little more than the above proportion may be used, bearing in mind that this sauce must be thick and highly flavored, or when the cream is added it will be sloppy and tasteless. Boil six eggs for ten minutes, throw them into cold water, and when perfectly cold, take off the shells, cut a small slice off the white part at the large end of the eggs, so as to allow them to stand upright, and then cut each into quarters lengthways. Butter thickly a strip an inch wide round the edge of a dish, and on this fix the quarters of egg upright and closely together, the white of the egg being outside, and the butter keeping the border of eggs quite firm. Inside this, put a layer of well dried and shred cabbage lettuce, or if they are very small, as they are early in the season, you may place a row of these little heads inside the egg border; fill in the centre with the pieces of fowl you have drained from the oil, vinegar, etc., keeping them piled high in the dish. Then, the last thing before serving, take a gill of good cream, whip it lightly, and mix carefully with the sauce you have made, pour over the fowl, taking care that it does not touch the egg border, and serve at once. You may place little pieces of very red beet-root, cut out with a steel vegetable cutter, and a leaf of parsley alternately between the quarters of egg, by way of more garnish, if you like it.

Rabbit Fritters

Cut the meat from a cold rabbit in small slices, put them in a deep dish, sprinkle them with parsley, chives, thyme, and a clove of garlic, all chopped together quite fine, a bay-leaf, salt, and pepper, and pour over all a glass of white wine (French or Rhenish if you have it), and the juice of a lemon. Let the pieces of rabbit soak in this, well covered over, for two hours; then take them out, dredge them well over with flour, and plunge them into boiling fat to take a good yellow color; drain them well from the fat, pile them in a dish, and pour the following sauce round. For the sauce, take the wine, lemon-juice, herbs, etc., that the rabbit has been soaking in, add half a pint of stock and a little thickening of flour and butter, and

A carving guide for rabbit.
American Practical Cookery Book, 233.

let it boil well; then strain it through a sieve, put in a tablespoonful of piccalilli chopped fine, give it another boil, and serve.

Venison Sausages

Cut some slices of cold venison, not too much roasted, and mince them very small; take one-third of the quantity of venison of the fat of cold boiled bacon, and mince also very fine; season with salt, pepper, and a little nutmeg; mix all well together, and moisten with some of the gravy from the joint of venison. Fill some fresh sausage-skins with the mixture, making the sausages small; grill them, and serve very hot. Venison sausages make an excellent dish for breakfast.

Game Patties

Make as many patties of a small size as you require for your dish of good light puff paste, egg them over, and bake them a nice light color. Fill the centres with minced venison or hare, or a mince of any kind of game; dish them on a napkin, and send to table quite hot.

Ann Howe, *The American Kitchen Directory and Housewife*

If Americans today think of the 1860s as old-fashioned, people then considered themselves completely modern. They themselves looked back to what they romantically envisioned as simpler times, especially the colonial period. The nostalgia evident in Ann Howe's *American Kitchen Directory and Housewife* may have been amplified by the fact that it came out in 1863 and then again in 1868, as Americans struggled to deal with the war's upheaval and destruction, the deaths of 640,000 men, the assassination of President Lincoln, and the chaos of early Reconstruction. The second edition of the book opened with a new engraving entitled "Our Grandmothers Kitchen," an artist's rendering of an eighteenth-century American kitchen, with a caption instructing readers to notice the old-fashioned woodstove, the spinning wheel, the Johnny cake, and the drying pumpkins, details that would have appeared endearingly quaint to readers accustomed to modern cast-iron cookstoves, factory-produced cloth, and dishes making use of imported ingredients. Deeply uncertain about the future, Americans in the 1860s may have taken comfort in Howe's nostalgic orientation toward the past, the same sort of impulse that led Americans to celebrate Thanksgiving as a national holiday for the first time during and after the Civil War.[1]

Like Mary Cornelius's *The Young Housekeeper's Friend*, Ann Howe's instructions were thorough compared to other cookbooks of the era. Howe began each section with paragraphs of explanation, detailing, for example, the differences between roasting, baking, or broiling meat. She believed she was being so explicit, in fact, that she worried that experienced cooks might "smile at the minuteness of the directions." Her minuteness was appealing, however. The book's 1863 edition, apparently self-published, sold so briskly that Howe felt sales had proved the book to be "a good practical guide to those who are not versed in culinary matters."

Operating the oven was the biggest challenge of any nineteenth-century kitchen. At a time when commercial bakeries were rare—although their presence was growing, especially in urban areas—and when most households produced their own bread and other baked goods

Designed in 1867 by John W. Barber, then in his 70th year. Strobridge & Co. Lith. Cincinnati.

OUR GRANDMOTHERS KITCHEN.

The Mother is preparing for baking bread and pies, the daughter is pounding clothes, the son brings in wood and water. The dinner pot & tea kettle are suspended by hooks & trammels over the fire, before wich corn or jonny-cake is baking. Cut pumpkin is drying in the chimney corner; apples &peaches by the window, You will notice too, the old clock ; spinning wheel , foot stove , bellows, warming pan, The Bible &Hymn Book on the shelf &meeting house out of the window.

"Our Grandmother's Kitchen" was a nostalgic depiction of a colonial kitchen. Frontispiece from Ann Howe,
The American Kitchen Directory and Housewife (Cincinnati: Howe's Subscription Book Concern, 1868),
Michigan State University Special Collections.

on a daily basis, it was crucial to master the oven, which by the 1860s would usually have been a cast-iron stove whose temperature was controlled by heating bricks with a coal fire.[2] But cooking in a coal stove was hardly easier than cooking over a wood fire. Knowing how to build the right kind of fire, how long to keep it burning, and when the temperature was appropriate for baking myriad dishes—sometimes simultaneously—was a complicated task that took long experience. Howe gave detailed instructions on readying the oven for baking: "Keep up a brisk fire for about an hour; it should be in the centre and when burnt down to coals, spread them over the whole surface, and let it remain till they begin to deaden; then sweep them up in a heap, with a broom slightly dampened: remove them with a large shovel. When cleared, throw a little flour into the centre of it;

if it turns black in the course of a minute, put up the lid, and wait a few minutes before putting in the things to be baked; if it merely turns brown, set in immediately. The bricks on the top of the oven should look red before clearing." Inept handling of the oven could be disastrous. If a cook mistimed the heating of the oven, dishes waiting to be cooked could spoil as they sat out, especially in the summer. And food that was burned or undercooked meant wasted money and a hungry night.

Like many nineteenth-century cookbook authors, Howe assumed that her readers would have rudimentary butcher skills and would feel comfortable working with dead animals. Even if readers were not slaughtering the animals themselves, recipes routinely included tasks like disassembling carcasses, skinning, plucking, dehairing, extracting flesh from heads and feet, and making rennet and gelatin. For instance, Howe's recipe for Mock Turtle Soup instructed readers to take a skinned calf's head, then to "remove the brains, and clean the head carefully in hot water." After the skull had boiled she instructed readers to make "forcemeat balls of the brains and tongue, break the bones of the head, put all into the soup, and boil 2 hours more."

While recipes that detailed skinning, plucking, and breaking bones might make it seem like the food coming out of those kitchens would be coarse and crudely served, in fact the opposite was often true. Middle-class eaters in the mid-nineteenth century were deeply concerned with food's appearance and presentation, and Howe provided numerous tips on making food look more attractive. For instance, she instructed readers to boil onions in milk in order to make them look whiter, while she suggested that readers could scorch a little flour and add it to gravy in order to make it look rich and brown. In other recipes like Birds'-Nest Pudding, where hollowed apples were stuffed to resemble birds' nests, or in a Dish of Snow, where a mound of coconut and cream was shaped to resemble snow topped with fallen leaves, she strove for novel, ornamental presentations.

Also like Cornelius, Howe included a long section at the end of her book on household shortcuts, including how to get rid of vermin, clean a mattresses, and make hens lay eggs, as well as recipes for household items like ink, stain removers, and lip salve. In addition, Howe appended a selection of "Simple Remedies" for easing aches, curing illnesses, and healing wounds. Some of her remedies—like blowing in a child's mouth to dislodge an object stuck in its nostril—had nothing to do with food. But many of them did. To cure an asthma attack, for example, she recommended black coffee, and to treat a sprained ankle she counseled elevating the leg and giving up meat for a while. For hoarseness, she suggested eating a variety of mixtures like a sugar-onion syrup or molasses cooked with butter and vinegar. For earache, she advised putting the heart of a warm roasted onion into the ear; if that failed, she said, try laudanum. The prevalence of food in her section of remedies demonstrates both the degree to which nineteenth-century medicine often meant home remedies made with materials at hand, and also the degree to which food and diet themselves were seen to powerfully affect physical health.

Preface

A number of years have elapsed since the first publication of the "American Housewife," and the extensive sale which it has had warrants the conclusion that it is what it claims to be; that is, a good practical guide to those who are not versed in culinary matters. The present edition is much improved, as all the receipts which the writer considered exceptionable have been rejected, and a large number of very superior ones added. A large proportion of the receipts have been procured from experienced housewives, and no efforts have been spared to render each one as correct and good as possible. The mode of cooking is such as is practiced generally by American housekeepers, and the receipts embrace all the various branches of the culinary art, from preparing the most simple broth, to making the most delicate cake, creams, and sweetmeats. The "Housewife" is designed for all classes of society, embracing receipts for rich and plain cooking, and written in such a plain manner that the most unskilled need not err in attempting to follow the directions given. The experienced cook may smile at the minuteness of the directions; but if she has witnessed as much good food spoiled by improper cooking as the writer of these receipts, she will not consider her too explicit. In regard to the seasoning of food, it has been found extremely difficult to give any exact rules, as so much depends upon the quality of the seasoning and food. The cook should be careful not to have the natural flavor of the food disguised by the seasoning and where

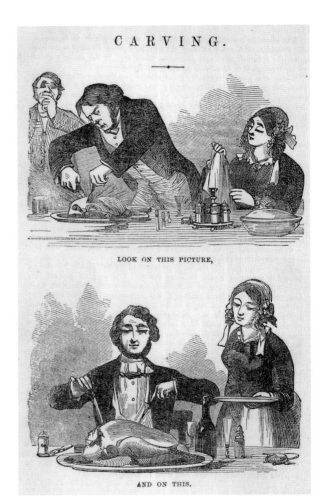

This illustration stressed the social importance of carving skills by contrasting the disorder that arose from unskilled carving with the harmony that came from knowledge and practice.
Lee, *The Cook's Own Book*, xxxvi.

a variety of spices are used, no one of them should predominate. Independent of the receipts for cooking, there are a large number of miscellaneous receipts relative to housewifery, directions for carving, and a few medicinal receipts, which the writer trusts will be found useful to the inexperienced. In conclusion, the writer would give her sincere thanks to those friends who have furnished her with their choice and valuable receipts; and to those into whose hands the book may fall, she would ask a fair trial of the receipts previous to passing judgment.

Meats

OBSERVATIONS RESPECTING MEAT

In cold weather meat is much improved by being kept several days previous to cooking it. Beef and mutton should be kept for at least a week, to render the meat tender, and poultry three or four days. In hot weather meat can be kept sweet but a short time, particularly lamb. It should be kept in a cool, airy place, away from the flies. A little salt rubbed over it tends to preserve it. When meat becomes slightly tainted, it may be restored to its original sweetness by putting it into luke-warm water with live coals, and covering it close for ten or fifteen minutes. When meat is frozen it should be soaked in cold water until the frost is extracted; if not extracted previous to putting it to the fire, it will not cook well. A thick roasting piece of meat requires soaking several hours, in order to extract the frost. Meat packed in snow will keep fresh as long as the snow keeps from melting. Have a thick layer of snow at the bottom of the tub in which the meat is packed, and a thick layer of snow between each layer of meat, over the top, and round the inside of the tub, so that the meat will be completely covered. Poultry should be filled with snow previous to packing it.

Boiled Meat

Meat for boiling should be put in the pot with cool water, heated gradually, and boiled gently. Furious boiling hardens meat. The part that is to be uppermost on the table should be put down in the pot, as the scum is apt to settle on the top of the meat and give it a dark look, unless care is taken to skim it off as soon as the pot boils: fresh meat requiring salt boiled with it, in the proportion of a large spoonful to three or four quarts of water. Allow fifteen minutes boiling for each pound of mutton or lamb that is to be boiled; other kinds require twenty-five minutes, reckoning from the time the water begins to boil. Salt meat should be boiled longer than fresh meat; and if too salt, the water should be changed. The water in which all kinds of fresh meat is boiled, can be made into soup. If the meat is fat, let the liquor remain till cold, in order to remove the grease which will then have all risen to the surface. Boiling is the cheapest method of cooking meat if a soup is made of the liquor; if not, it becomes the dearest, as the gelatine extracted by the process of boiling is the most nourishing part of the meat, and if not used for soup is completely lost.

Beef Smothered in Onions

Fry five or six slices of salt pork, put them, when brown, with tender beef sliced thin, and between each layer of beef put a layer of onions sliced; season with salt and pepper. Stew the whole with sufficient water to just cover it. When tender, take up the meat and onions; thicken the liquor with a little flour and water mixed, turn it over the meat. This is a very savory and acceptable dish to those who are fond of onions.

To Corn Beef

To each gallon of cold water, put a quart of rock salt, an ounce of saltpetre, and quarter of a pound of brown sugar, (some use molasses, but it is not so good for corning beef as sugar.) No boiling is necessary. Put the beef in the brine when perfectly fresh; as long as any salt remains at the bottom of the cask the brine is sufficiently strong. Whenever any scum rises, the brine should be scalded, and more sugar, salt, and saltpetre added. Whenever a piece of beef is put in brine, salt should be rubbed over it, and if the weather is hot, cut a gash to the bone, and fill it with salt. Keep a heavy stone on the top of the beef to make it remain under the brine.

In very hot weather it is difficult to corn beef in cold brine before it spoils. It can be corned when boiled in the following manner: To six or eight lbs. of beef, put a tea cup of salt. After placing the beef in the pot with the salt rubbed over it, turn in cold water and boil it from three to four hours, according to the size of the meat. There should be just sufficient water to cover the beef, and it should boil gently. Keep on a tea-kettle of boiling water to replenish the pot as the water boils away. Skim it well as soon as it boils; if the scum is allowed to settle on the beef, it will make it look dark.

Force Meat Balls

Chop from one to two pounds of veal fine, with a couple of slices of raw salt pork, add a couple of eggs, and pepper to the taste. Do it up into balls of the size of half an egg, and fry them brown.

Calf's Feet

Boil them with the head until tender, then split and lay them round the head. They are nice prepared as follows. After being boiled, dredge with flour, and fry them brown, then take them up and stir a little mixed flour and water into the fat in which they were fried; season the gravy with salt, pepper, and mace. Add, if you like it rich, wine and a little butter, and turn the gravy over the feet.

Plaw

Boil a piece of lean veal tender, then cut it in strips three or four inches long, put it back in the pot with the liquor in which it was boiled, and a tea-cup of rice to three or four pounds of the veal. Season it with salt and pepper, (add sweet herbs, if you like,) put in a piece of butter of the size of a hen's egg. Stew the whole gently until the rice is tender, and the liquor nearly stewed away, taking care that it does not burn. A little curry powder sprinkled in converts it into a curry dish.

Lamb's Fry

The heart and sweet bread are nice fried plainly, or dipped into beaten egg and pounded bread crumbs. They should be fried in lard.

Goose

If a goose is tender under the wings, and you can break the skin easily by running the head of a pin across the breast, you may rely upon its being young and tender. A goose should be prepared in the same manner, and roasted the same length of time, as a turkey of equal size.

Chicken Pie

Joint the chickens, which should be young. Boil them till nearly tender, in just sufficient water to cover them. Take them out of the liquor and lay them in a pudding dish, lined with pie-crust, to each layer of chickens, put three or four thin slices of pork, or a couple of ounces of butter, cut into small bits, season each layer well with pepper and salt, and dredge flour over the top, turn in the liquor in which they were stewed, till you can just see it at the top. Cover it with pie-crust, cut a slit in the centre, and ornament with strips of pastry. Bake it in a quick oven about an hour.

Rabbits

Rabbits are good made into a fricassee, like chicken, or roasted. Fill them with a dressing of soaked bread, seasoned with pepper, and salt, and sweet herbs, mix with a couple of eggs, and a couple of large spoonfuls of melted butter. Sew the bodies up when filled. Cook them about an hour, basting frequently. When well heated they should have a little butter rubbed over them. They are also good made into a pot-pie.

Pigeons

Take out the innards and fill the pigeons when washed, with a dressing prepared like that for turkeys. Lay them in a pot with the breast side down, seasoning them with salt and pepper. Turn in more than sufficient water to cover them. When nearly stewed enough, add a quarter of a pound of butter to each dozen of pigeons. When tender, take them out of the liquor and thicken it with mixed flour and water. If you wish to have them brown, fry them in pork fat after they have stewed till tender. They are very good split open and stewed, and the dressing warmed separately with a little of the gravy. Tough pigeons require a good deal of cooking. If tender, they are nice stuffed and roasted. They should be well buttered before roasting.

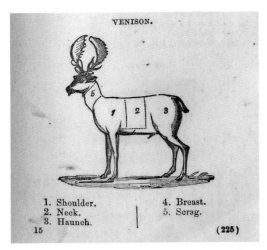

A carving guide for venison. *American Practical Cookery Book*, 225.

Venison

If the weather is cold, venison is much improved by being kept ten or twelve days previous to cooking it. Roast a haunch from three to four hours, according to its size, and baste it frequently, or it will be dry. Sprinkle on salt and pepper. When roasted, add cloves and all-spice, if liked. There should be over a pint of water in the dripping pan when put down to roast. Broil the steaks in the same manner as beef steaks. Venison should have currant jelly as an accompaniment—some cooks put it in the gravy.

To Salt Pork

If salted the day it is killed, before it becomes stiff, it will pack closer. Sprinkle a thick layer of salt at the bottom of a tight barrel. The salt should be coarse; rock salt is the best. Have the pieces of pork as near of a size as possible, so that they will pack closely together. Pack the pork with the rind down, and between each layer, put a layer of salt about half an inch thick. There is no danger of getting too much salt, as the pork will only absorb the requisite quantity; if there is any surplus it need not be wasted, as it will do to use the next time you salt pork. If there is not sufficient brine formed to cover the pork, in the course of two or three days after it is salted, make a strong brine, boil and skim it, turn it, when quite cold, on to the pork. Keep a heavy stone on top of the pork to keep it under the brine. If a white scum or bloody matter appears on the surface, the brine should be scalded, and more salt added. In packing pork, use only fat pieces.

Sweet Bread, Liver, and Heart

They may be fried plain in pork fat; when out of the frying-pan, turn in a little water, mixed with flour, let it boil, then turn it over them. Another method is to par-boil them, and let them get cold, then cut them about an inch thick; season with salt and pepper, dip them into the yolk of an egg, and fine bread crumbs; fry them of a light brown. When removed from the frying pan, make a gravy for them, adding, if you like, spices and wine.

Pressed Head

Pig's head is good baked with beans, or corned and smoked. It is also nice, prepared in the following manner: Boil the cheek, ears, forehead, and rind, till they will almost drop from the bones. Take the whole out of the liquor, chop the meat fine, and warm it in a little of the liquor in which it was boiled, season it highly with salt, pepper, and sweet herbs; or if you like, season with spices, instead of sweet herbs. Put it, while hot, in a strong bag, tie it up tight, and put a heavy weight on it, and let it remain until cold. This will keep a number of weeks in cold weather. It should be cut in slices and eaten cold.

Souse

Clean pig's ears and feet very thoroughly, then soak them in salt and water for a number of days, changing the water every other day. Then boil them tender, and split them. They are good fried, or soused as follows:— after boiling, let them get cold, then turn on boiling vinegar, spiced with mace, pepper-corns, and cloves; add salt. They will keep this way for five or six weeks. When they are to be eaten fry them in lard.

Bologna Sausages

Take equal weights of ham, beef, and veal, chop fine, and season highly with salt, pepper, cloves, and allspice, and fill the skins, which should previously be thoroughly cleaned. To ascertain whether you have sufficient seasoning, before filling the casings, do up a little of the meat into a small cake and fry it; if there is not enough, add more. Put them in brine, and let them remain nine or ten days, then smoke them for a week, or else boil them till tender in the casings, then dry them.

Tongues

Cut off the roots, they are not good smoked, but are nice to make mince pies of. Make a brine for the tongues, as follows:—to each gallon of water, which should be cold, put a quart of rock salt, a couple of large spoonfuls of blown salt. Keep the tongues in the brine a week, then smoke them eight or ten days. They are good boiled, after being in brine, without any smoking. To prepare the roots for pies, take out the pipes and veins, boil the meat till tender, mince it fine, and season it with salt, cloves, mace, and cinnamon, add a little sugar, or molasses, and sufficient brandy to moisten the whole. Keep it in a stone jar covered close, in a cool place. It will keep in this way a number of months in cold weather. Some cooks mix apple with it when they put it in the jar, but it is better to add the apples when the meat is made into pies, as they will have a better flavor when fresh; there should be two-thirds of apple to one of meat.

Curries

Chickens, pigeons, mutton chops, and veal, all make good curries. Boil the meat tender, in just sufficient water to cover it, with a little salt. Chickens should be jointed before boiling. Fry three or four slices of salt pork, take them up and fry the meat in the pork fat, when brown, add part of the liquor in which they were boiled, and the fried pork. Mix a teaspoonful of curry powder with a tea-cup of boiled rice, stir it into the meat, and stew the whole about ten minutes.

Gravies and Sauces

Burnt Butter

Put a couple of ounces of butter into a frying pan; when of a dark brown color, by being heated on a moderate fire, add half a tea cupful of vinegar; season it with salt and pepper. This is nice for fish, salad, or eggs.

Roast Meat Gravy

All meat, when roasted or baked, should have as much as a pint of water in the dripping-pan; if it boils away while the meat is cooking, add more. When the meat is taken up, set the drippings where they will boil, and thicken it with two or three tea-spoonfuls of flour, mixed with water in the same way as for drawn butter. If the gravy is for lamb, or veal, add a little butter. The gravy for pork and geese should have a little of the dressing mixed with it. If you wish your gravies to have a dark, rich look, keep a little flour scorched to thicken them with. This is done by putting a small quantity in a frying-pan, setting it on a moderate fire, and stirring it constantly, till of a dark brown color, taking care that it does not burn.

Oyster Sauce

Separate the oysters from the juice, and if you have not sufficient juice for your sauce, one-third water may be put to it. Set it where it will boil, with a couple of blades of mace, salt and pepper to the taste. Mix a little flour smoothly, with a little milk, and thicken the sauce. When it has boiled several minutes, to a pint of it put half a pint of oysters; as soon as they are scalded through, take the sauce from the fire, or the oysters will shrivel and be hard. Add a piece of butter of the size of a hen's egg, and serve it up immediately with your poultry.

Liver Sauce for Fish

Boil the liver of the fish, then mash it fine, stir it into drawn butter, together with a table spoonful of catsup, a little salt, and pepper. Add, if you like, a little lemon juice, or vinegar.

Cranberry Sauce

Stew the cranberries till soft, with a little water; when tender, add sugar sufficient to sweeten; let it scald in well. Strain it, if you like; it is good without straining.

Pudding Sauce

Stir to a cream, a tea-cup of butter with two of sugar; white is the nicest for sauce, but good brown sugar answers very well. Add the grated rind of a lemon or nutmeg, the juice of the lemon, or sufficient wine or brandy to flavor; cider may be substituted for the wine or brandy. If you wish a liquid sauce, add to the above the following:—heat two-thirds of a pint of water boiling hot, and thicken it with two or three tea spoonfuls of wheat-flour, mix it smooth, with a little cold water; as soon as it boils up well, stir it into the mixed sugar and butter. If lumpy, strain it before mixing it with the sugar and butter.

Tomato Catsup

To each gallon of ripe tomatoes, put four table spoonfuls of salt, five of black pepper, three of ground mustard, half a large spoonful of allspice, the same of cloves, simmer the whole slowly together, with a little water at the bottom of the stewpan, to prevent their burning. Let them stew slowly for three hours, then strain through a sieve. When cold, bottle, and cork, and seal them; keep them in a cool cellar. The catsup should be made in tin, and as late in the season as practicable, in order to have it keep well.

Mushroom Catsup

Put a layer of fresh mushrooms in a deep dish; sprinkle a little salt over them; add successive layers of mushrooms and salt, till you get them all into the dish. Let them remain a number of days, then mash them fine, and to each quart put a table spoonful of vinegar, half a tea spoonful of black pepper, and a quarter of a tea spoonful of cloves. Turn the whole into a stone jar, set it into a pot of hot water, and boil it a couple of hours. Strain without squeezing the mushrooms. Boil the juice a quarter of an hour, and strain it well. When cold, bottle, cork, and seal up tight, and keep it in a cool place.

Walnut Catsup

Procure the walnuts when so tender that a pin will pierce them easily. Keep them in salt and water for a week. Take them out of the salt and water, bruise them, and turn on them sufficient scalding-hot vinegar to cover them. Let them remain several days, stirring them up well each day; then boil them for a quarter of an hour, adding a little more vinegar; strain the whole through a thick cloth, so that none of the coarse particles of the walnuts will run through; season the vinegar highly with pepper, cloves, allspice, and salt. When cold, bottle and seal up tight, and keep it in a cool place.

Curry Powder

Mix an ounce of ginger, one of mustard, one of black pepper, three of coriander seed, the same quantity of turmeric, a quarter of an ounce of cayenne pepper, half an ounce of cardamums, the same of cummin seed and cinnamon.[3] Pound the whole fine, sift, and keep it in a bottle corked tight.

Soups

Mock Turtle, or Calf's Head Soup

Boil the head till very tender, then take it up, strain the liquor, and set it away until the next day. Then skim off the fat, cut up the meat, together with the lights, and put them into the liquor, and stew the whole gently for half an hour. Season the soup with salt, pepper, and sweet herbs; add cloves or curry powder, if you want it seasoned highly, and, just as you take it up, stir in half a pint of white wine. If you wish for force meat balls in the soup, they should be prepared and added to the soup when put on to boil. See the following receipt for making them.

Force Meat Balls

Chop lean veal fine, together with a little raw salt pork; season the meat with salt, pepper, curry powder, or cloves; make it up into balls of the size of half an egg, boil part in the soup fifteen minutes, and fry the remainder, and serve up in a separate dish. For beef soup prepare in the same way, substituting beef for veal.

Oyster Soup

Separate the oysters from the liquor; rinse the oysters in cold water, in order to get off the bits of shell which adhere to them; strain the liquor, and to each quart of it put a pint of milk, or water. Set it where it will boil, and thicken it when it boils with a little flour and water mixed smoothly together; season it with pepper, add a little vinegar, if you like, then put in the oysters, and let them be in just long enough to get scalded through;

otherwise they will be hard. Add salt after taking up the soup; if added before, it will shrink the oysters. Serve up the soup with crackers.

Pea Soup

If dry peas are used for soup, it will be necessary to soak them over night in a warm place, using a quart of water to each quart of the peas. Early the next morning, boil them an hour, putting in a tea-spoonful of saleratus a few minutes before removing them from the fire. Take them up, put them into fresh water, and boil them until tender, which will not be under three or four hours; boil with them a pound of salt pork; it should be taken up as soon as tender. Green peas need no soaking, and only an hour's boiling, together with salt pork.

Portable Soup

Take the liquor in which beef or veal has been boiled, remove all the fat, and boil the liquor till of a thick, glutinous consistency. Season it highly with salt, pepper, cloves, and allspice, add a little brandy, and turn it on to platters, having it not over three quarters of an inch in thickness. When cold, cut in pieces about three inches square, set them in the sun to dry, turning them frequently. When perfectly dry, put them in an earthen vessel, with a piece of white paper between each layer. If the directions are strictly attended to, these cakes will keep good a long time. Whenever you wish to make a soup, take one of them for a quart of water, heat it scalding hot, and it is nice soup. You may add vegetables to it, if you like.

Fish

DIRECTIONS FOR FISH

If fish are fresh, the eyes will be full, the gills red, and the flesh firm and stiff. If the flesh is flabby, the eyes sunken, they are stale. They should be thoroughly cleaned when first procured, and washed in just sufficient water to cleanse them; if much water is used to wash them, the flavor will be diminished. Sprinkle salt in the inside, and if they are to be broiled, add pepper; keep them in a cool place till you wish to cook them. Most fish are the best broiled, or boiled, the day after they are caught. Fresh-water fish are apt to have an earthy taste, which may be removed by soaking them in salt and water after cleaning. Most kinds of salt fish should be soaked in cold water, ten or twelve hours before cooking them.

Chowder

Clean the fish, and cut it up into a number of slices. Fry six, or more, slices of pork, if the chowder is to be a large one; take them up, and put in the pork fat, a layer of the fish, several bits of the fried pork, crackers that have been soaked tender in cold water, season with salt and pepper, and add onions and spices to it, if you like. This process repeat till you get in all the fish required for the chowder; then turn in sufficient cold water to cover the whole, and stew the fish from twenty-five to thirty minutes. When you have taken the fish out of the pot, thicken the gravy with mixed flour and water, add a little butter, and if you want it rich, stir in half a pint of white wine, or a large spoonful of catsup. Bass and cod are the best fish for chowder. Black fish and clams make tolerably good ones; the hard part of the clams should be thrown away.

Cod Sounds and Tongues

Soak them in lukewarm water three or four hours, then scrape off the skin, cut them in two, and stew them in milk.[4] Just before taking them up, stir in a little butter and flour.

Scollops

Boil them, and take them out of the shells; when boiled, pick out the hearts and throw the rest away, as the heart is the only part that is fit to eat.[5] They are good pickled like oysters after boiling, or fried. Dip them in flour, and fry them brown. They are also good stewed, with a little water, salt, and pepper; add butter when you remove from the fire.

Eels

If small, are the best fried; if large, split them open, salt, and pepper, and cut them into pieces of about a finger's length. Let them remain several hours before broiling.

Oyster Pancakes

Mix equal quantities of oyster juice and milk, and to a pint of the mixed liquor put a pint of wheat flour, a couple of beaten eggs, a little salt, and a few of the oysters. Drop by the large spoonful into hot lard.

Oyster Pie

Line a deep pie plate with pie crust, fill it with dry pieces of bread, cover it with nice pastry, and bake it in a quick oven till of a light brown. Have the oysters stewed and seasoned just as the pastry is baked. Take off the upper crust, remove the bread, and put in the oysters; cover with the crust, and serve up while hot.

Pickled Trout

If the trout are large, they should be cut into a number of pieces. Boil them with salt in the water. Lay them in cold vinegar, with whole cloves, allspice, and pepper-corns between each layer of fish. Keep them in a stone jar, in a cool place.

Vegetables

Beets

Beets should not be cut or scraped previous to boiling, as the juice will run out and make them insipid. In summer, when young, they will boil tender in the course of an hour; the tops are good boiled with the roots, when quite small, for greens. In winter they require three hours boiling.

Parsnips

Wash and split them in two, lay them in a pot with the flat side down, turn on sufficient water to cover them. When boiled tender, scrape off the skin and butter them. When boiled whole, the outside gets cooked too much before the inside becomes tender. Boiled parsnips, when cold, are good fried brown.

Onions

Peel and boil them in milk and water, with a little salt. If boiled in water, they will not look white. When tender, take them up and butter them.

Winter Squash

The neck is the best part; cut it in narrow strips, take off the rind, and boil till tender, with salt; then drain off the water, and let the squash steam over a moderate fire a few minutes. It is good not mashed; if mashed, add a small bit of butter. The winter squash makes a much better pie than pumpkins.

Cauliflowers

The white cauliflowers are the best. Take off the outside leaves, and cut the stalk close to the leaves. Let them lie half an hour in salt and water before cooking. Boil them from fifteen to twenty minutes, according to their size. They are the best boiled with milk mixed with water, but water alone will answer. A little salt should be boiled with them.

Slaw

For cold slaw, nothing more is necessary than to cut it into small strips, and let it lie in cold water for half an hour before eating. It should be cut up in the same way for hot slaw, leaving out the stalky part. Melt in a pot a piece of butter of the size of a hen's egg, or beef drippings; when hot, put in the cabbage, and stir it constantly with a spoon over a moderate fire till tender, which will be in the course of twenty minutes; season it with salt and pepper. When tender, add about a cup of vinegar, let it just scald in, then take it out of the pot immediately, or it will turn a dark color.

Peas

Peas are best when fresh gathered, and not shelled till just as they are to be boiled. Cook them with salt, and if not quite young, they are improved by boiling saleratus with them, in the proportion of half a tea spoonful to a peck of peas. Take them out of the water with a skimmer, and butter them.

Green Corn Cakes

Mix a pint of grated sweet corn with three table spoonfuls of milk, a tea cup of flour, a large spoonful of melted butter, a tea spoonful of salt, a little pepper, and one egg. Drop this mixture by the large spoonful into your frying-pan, and fry them till brown: use butter for frying. These are nice served up with meat for dinner.

Hominy

Rinse it thoroughly in cold water; if large ground, boil it about five hours, with a quart of water to a pint of the hominy. Turn off all the water, and add a little salt and butter. The small ground will cook in less time. Hominy is nice when cold, cut in slices and fried.

French, or String Beans

Take off the strings; if old, cut off the edges and through the centre. Boil them with salt, and a little saleratus added preserves their green color, and renders them more digestible; a quarter of a tea spoonful to half a peck will be sufficient. If young and tender, they will boil sufficiently in the course of half an hour. Butter them after taking out of the liquor.

Baked Beans

The small white beans are the best for baking; the large kind answer very well. Pick out the colored and bad ones, wash and soak them over night in lukewarm water, allowing three quarts of water to three pints of the beans. Early the next morning, set them where they will boil, with a tea spoonful of saleratus, to render them healthful. When they have boiled a few minutes, take them out of the water with a skimmer, and put them in an earthen jar or crock; (a tin pan can be used for baking them, but is not so good as earthen.) Gash about a pound of pork in narrow strips, so that it can be sliced when baked; put it with the beans in such a way that all but the rind will be covered. Turn in water till you can just see it at the top. Bake the beans at least three hours in a hot oven: they are better for remaining in four or five hours. The pork should be taken out of the beans when it becomes tender, and the rind crispy. The beans should have considerable salt mixed in with them when put into the baking pot. The white beans are good prepared as for baking, and boiled with pork, and a large proportion of water.

Greens

White mustard, spinach, water cresses, cowslips, young dandelions, and the roots and tops of very small beets, are nice for greens. If not fresh and plump, soak them in salt and water for half an hour previous to cooking. Boil them with a little salt in the water, until they sink to the bottom of the pot.

Salads

To be in perfection, should be fresh gathered, and put in cold water for an hour before eating. Drain off the water, and serve it up without any dressing, letting those who are to partake of it prepare it to suit their own taste. Have on your table sweet oil or melted butter, mustard, vinegar, and sugar. The following sauce is a nice accompaniment to salad: Boil a couple of eggs three minutes, mix them with two tea spoonfuls of made mustard, a tea spoonful of salt, a little black pepper, half a cup of salad oil or melted butter, and a tea cup of vinegar.

Egg Plant

Boil them a few minutes, to extract their bitter flavor, then cut them in thin slices, sprinkle salt between each layer, and let them remain for half an hour. Fry them brown in lard. If you wish to have them particularly nice, dip the slices in the yolk of an egg, sprinkle on pepper and salt, cover them with fine bread crumbs, then fry them.

Ochra

Take an equal quantity of young tender ochra,[6] chopped fine, and ripe tomatoes skinned, two onions cut in slices, and a small lump of butter; stew it till tender with a large spoonful of water. Season, while stewing, with salt and pepper.

Maccaroni

Mix equal quantities of milk and water, and to a quart put a couple of ounces of maccaroni and a tea spoonful of salt.[7] Stew it till tender; then cut it into small pieces, and butter it.

Pickles

DIRECTIONS FOR PICKLING

Vinegar for pickling should be good, but not of the sharpest kind. That made of cider is the best. Brass, copper, and tin utensils only should be used for pickling. The two first should be thoroughly cleaned just before they are used, and the vinegar, when heated, not allowed to cool in them, as the rust formed in consequence is very poisonous. Boil alum and salt in the vinegar, in the proportion of a large spoonful of the first, and half a tea cup of the last, to three gallons of vinegar. Boil part or all of the following spices in the vinegar: pepper corns, cloves, allspice, and mace. If you do not care about spicing all the pickles, a jar of spiced vinegar may be kept, in which you can put a few pickles from one time to another, as required. Vinegar for pickling with spices, should not be allowed to boil but over five or six minutes. Stone and wooden utensils are suitable for pickles; they should not be left in glazed earthenware, as it contains lead, which combines with the vinegar and renders it poisonous. All kinds of pickles should be stirred up occasionally, and if there are any soft ones, pick them out, and throw them away; scald the vinegar, and turn it on the pickles while hot. Whenever any scum rises, the vinegar should be scalded. If it is weak, throw it away, and add fresh, with more salt and alum.

Pepper Vinegar

Cut off the stems of a dozen ripe pepper pods, split and boil them in three pints of vinegar, until reduced to one quart, then strain it through a sieve. A little of this mixed with the vinegar used for pickling, imparts a fine flavor to the pickles, being much superior to black pepper. It is also very nice to season salads, sauces, and catsups.

Butternuts and Black Walnuts

Nuts for pickling should be so tender as to admit of being pierced easily with a pin. Soak them in salt and water for a week, changing the water several times. Drain off the water, wipe them with a coarse cloth, till they become smooth. To each gallon of vinegar to be used for pickling the nuts, put a tea cup of salt, a large spoonful of powdered cloves and mace mixed, half an ounce of allspice, and pepper-corns. Scald the whole together, then turn it while hot on to the nuts. In the course of a week, turn the vinegar from them, and scald and turn it back on them boiling hot. They will be fit to eat in the course of a fortnight. The vinegar in which they are pickled makes a nice catsup.

Cabbage and Cauliflowers

The purple cabbage makes the best pickle. Pull off the loose leaves, quarter the cabbages, put them in a keg, with a layer of salt to each layer of cabbage, and let them remain for nearly a week. Then scald some vinegar with peppercorns, cinnamon, and mace, in the proportion of an ounce each to a gallon of the vinegar; add a little alum, and turn it over the cabbages, in the brine which should remain with them. Cloves and allspice improve the taste of the cabbages, but turn them a dark color. The vinegar should be turned from them four or five times, scalded and turned on to them while hot, to make them tender. If the cabbage is sliced up, less scalding will be necessary. Cauliflowers are pickled in the same manner as cabbages. If cut into bunches, and pickled with beet roots to color them, they have a very pretty appearance.

East India Pickle

Chop cabbage, leaving out the stalk, together with three onions, a couple of green peppers, a root of horse-radish to each cabbage. Soak the whole in salt and water for three days, then turn off the brine, and turn on scalding-hot vinegar, spiced with cloves, allspice, and cinnamon.

Nasturtions

Take those that are small and green, put them in salt and water, changing it twice in the course of a week.[8] When you have done collecting them, turn off the brine, and turn on scalding vinegar, with a little alum in, to turn them a good color.

Cucumbers

They should be small, green, and of a quick growth, and pickled soon after they are picked, to be very nice. A very good and easy way of pickling, is to put them down with salt, having a layer of the salt to each layer of cucumbers; they should be covered with the salt on the top; let them remain till you are through collecting them, and the weather has become cool. They will have a shrivelled appearance when taken out of the salt, but will swell out to their original size by being soaked in cold water four or five days. The water should be changed every day to freshen them. When freshened, turn off all the water, and scald them in spiced vinegar, with alum to green them; do not let them boil. They should be scalded a number of times to be made brittle. The following method is more troublesome, but it makes more delicate pickles: Turn on boiling water, with a spoonful of salt in it, when fresh picked; let them remain in it four or five hours, then put them in cold vinegar, with alum and salt, in the proportion of a large spoonful of the former and a tea cup of the latter to each gallon of vinegar. When you have finished collecting the cucumbers, turn the vinegar from them, scald and skim it, until clear, then scald the cucumbers in it, without boiling, adding pepper-corns, and ginger-root, sufficient to spice the pickles. A few pickled peppers put in the jar with the cucumbers give them a fine flavor. Whenever any scum rises on the pickles, turn it from them, scald and turn it while hot on to them; if weak, throw it away, and add fresh, with more alum and salt; if there are any soft ones, pick them out and throw them away. Pickled cucumbers need close watching during the warm weather, as they are very liable to spoil.

Pickled Peaches

Take those that are ripe, but not very mellow; put them in scalding hot water for one minute, then wipe them immediately with a dry cloth, in order to remove the down of the peach-skin. Take good vinegar, but not of the sharpest kind, spice it with cinnamon and mace, and to each gallon of vinegar put three pounds of brown sugar. Put with it the beaten whites of two or three eggs, scald and skim it till clear, taking the kettle from the fire each time it is skimmed. When partly cooled, turn it over the peaches, having them just covered with the vinegar. A gallon of vinegar with three pounds of sugar is sufficient for about a peck of peaches.

Plums and Cherries

Allow a pound of white sugar to one of fruit. Put them in alternate layers in a jar, with a little cinnamon or cloves; cover the whole with good vinegar, and set the jar into a pot of cold water; put the pot over the fire, and let the cherries remain until the water boils for a few minutes, and the fruit begins to cook. They are also good pickled in the same manner as the peaches, with the exception of scalding in hot water previous to pickling. Keep them in a cool place, covered up tight.

Directions for Baking

DIRECTIONS FOR HEATING OVENS, AND BAKING

Brick ovens are the best for baking most things, particularly those things which require a long time for baking. Bread is much sweeter baked in them. But as it is a good deal of extra trouble and expense to heat a brick oven, when you have a good one attached to your cooking-stove it will generally be found preferable to use the latter, and, with care and attention, most things can be baked very well in them. It should be well heated, particularly at the bottom, before setting in the articles to be baked. A new brick oven, before used for baking, should have a fire kept in it for half a day: on removing the fire, shut up the oven, and do not use it till it has been heated again. If not treated in this way, it will not retain its heat well. Light, dry wood, split fine, should be used for heating ovens. Pine and ash mixed are the best. Keep up a brisk fire for about an hour; it should be in the centre, and when burnt down to coals, spread them over the whole surface, and let it remain till they begin to deaden; then sweep them up in a heap, with a broom slightly dampened: remove them with a large shovel. When cleared, throw a little flour into the centre of it; if it turns black in the course of a minute, put up the lid, and wait a few minutes before putting in the things to be baked; if it merely turns brown, set in immediately. The bricks on the top of the oven should look red before clearing. In cold weather, the doors of the kitchen should be kept closed while the oven is being heated. Care must be used to have your oven ready at the right time, particularly in warm weather, when bread is apt to get sour from a little delay in baking it, when light.

Hop Yeast

Boil a handful of hops in two quarts of water, till reduced to three pints. Then strain the liquor, and put it back in the pot, and thicken it with a cup of wheat flour, previously mixed smooth with a little cold water. Let it boil three or four minutes, then mix it with about six medium-sized potatoes, that have just been boiled, peeled, and mashed; let the whole stand till lukewarm, then strain it, and put to it a cup of good yeast, and set it where it will keep just lukewarm. When of a frothy appearance, add a table spoonful of salt. Turn it immediately into a jar, keep it covered up, and set it in a cool place. The potatoes may be omitted in making the yeast, but the yeast will not be so lively, nor the bread so delicate. Scald your yeast jar thoroughly, before putting in fresh yeast. If your yeast gets sour, on using it, put a tea spoonful of saleratus in, before mixing it with your bread. If it does not foam up well, it is too stale to use. This kind of yeast will keep well for a fortnight, excepting in quite hot weather. Yeast cakes are the best to use in summer, as they will keep well for a long time.

Indian Bread

Sift the meal; and if the meal is not fresh and sweet, it is improved by scalding it, either with milk or water. When just lukewarm, add the yeast, and about the same quantity of wheat or rye flour as Indian meal; use the same proportion of yeast and salt as for wheat bread, and add a little melted lard. Knead it up stiff and bake in the same manner as wheat bread. It will take about two hours to bake it, if the loaves are of the size you would make wheat bread, if the loaves are larger, more time for baking them will be required.

Potato Bread

Boil mealy potatoes very soft, peel and mash them, rub them with sifted flour, in the proportion of one-third of potatoes to two-thirds of the flour.[9] Wet up the whole with lukewarm water, add the yeast, and flour to make it sufficiently stiff to mould up. Keep it warm till risen; it will rise quicker than unmixed wheat bread, and should be baked as soon as risen, as it sours very quick. If sour, add a tea spoonful of saleratus, dissolved in a little cold water; it should be strained before mixing it with bread of any kind, or it will settle in yellow spots in the bread.

Drop Biscuit

Mix a pint of sweet cream with a pint of milk that is also sweet, a tea spoonful of salt, three beaten eggs, and sufficient sifted wheat flour to make the dough of the consistency of unbaked pound-cake. Drop the mixture by the large spoonful into buttered tins, and bake them immediately in a quick oven. They can be made of sour milk and sour cream, substituting a couple of tea spoonfuls of saleratus for the eggs.

Hard Biscuit

Weigh out four pounds of flour, and rub three pounds and a half of it with four ounces of butter, two tea spoonfuls of salt, four beaten eggs, and add just enough sweet milk to moisten the whole. Pound the dough out thin with a rolling-pin, sprinkle over lightly part of the reserved flour, then roll it up, continue to pound the dough out thin, sprinkling on the flour until the whole is used. Pound it out about half an inch thick, cut into small cakes, lay them on buttered tins, and cover them over with a damp cloth, to keep them from drying, till you are ready to bake them. They should bake, in a moderately-hot oven, about three-quarters of an hour.

Butter Crackers

Rub six ounces of butter with two pounds of flour; dissolve a couple of tea spoonfuls of saleratus in a little milk, strain it on to the dough, add a tea spoonful of salt, and just milk sufficient to enable you to roll it out. Beat it out thin with a rolling-pin, sprinkle on flour, and roll up. This repeat three times, then have it rolled out thin, and cut it into small crackers. Bake them in a moderately-hot oven till hard and crispy. If the oven is too hot, remove them till cooled, then set in again.

Economy Cakes

Bread that is sour can be made into good breakfast cakes. Cut it up into small pieces, and if not wanted for immediate use, it can be kept a number of weeks by drying the pieces in a very moderately-hot oven, taking care that it does not burn. When you wish to make cakes for breakfast, soak it over night in cold water; the next morning, drain off all the water, mash the bread fine, and to three pints of it put a tea spoonful of salt, three eggs, a tea spoonful of saleratus dissolved in milk, and a pint of wheat or rye flour. Add just sufficient milk to enable you to fry them, in the same manner as buckwheat cakes. If the flour which is used for them is mixed over night, with a spoonful of yeast, the eggs may be omitted.

Indian Griddle Cakes

Mix a quart of Indian meal with two thirds of a pint of wheat or buckwheat flour, a tea spoonful of salt, half of a cup of lard, and sufficient milk to make a thick batter: if you have not milk, water may be substituted. Then add half a cup of yeast, and fry, when light, in considerable fat, having it quite hot when they are dropped into it. Indian cakes, when raised, are very liable to be sour;

if so, add a little saleratus. They are better raised with three or four eggs than yeast, and can be fried as soon as mixed. They are also good mixed with sour milk, substituting saleratus for eggs. If Indian meal is not sweet, it should be scalded; but if fresh, it is better without. Tolerable good cakes may be made of Indian meal, with water mixed with milk.

Corn Dodgers

Scald a quart of Indian meal, when sifted, with just sufficient water to moisten the whole, add a tea spoonful of salt, and mould them up into cakes of the size of large biscuit, having them nearly an inch in thickness. Rub flour on the hands when moulding them up, to keep them from sticking. Fry them in sufficient fat to nearly cover them; it should be hot enough to boil up around them on putting them in. When quite brown on the under side, turn them. It takes from twelve to fifteen minutes to cook them so that they will not be moist in the centre. When about to be eaten, split open and butter them. Another way is, to wet the Indian meal with cold milk, adding salt, and a large spoonful of lard melted to a pint of the milk, and then mould them up into small cakes and bake them.

Hoe Cakes

Scald a pint of Indian meal with just sufficient water to make a thick batter, stir in a little salt, and two large spoonfuls of butter, and bake in square buttered pans, having the batter about an inch and a half in thickness.

Raised Waffles

Mix sifted flour with sufficient warm sweet milk to make a thick batter. The milk should be added gradually, so that the batter may be free from lumps. To two quarts of flour put two large spoonfuls of melted butter, a tea spoonful of salt, and one-third of a cup of domestic yeast; sprinkle flour over the top. When well mixed together, set the batter where it will keep just lukewarm till risen. When cracks appear on the top, it is light; add two or three beaten eggs, and bake in waffle-irons well greased, previous to filling them with the batter.

Waffle Gravy

As waffles are rather hard and dry when baked, they are improved by the following sauce: Boil a pint of milk, take it from the fire, and stir in a tea spoonful of salt and half a cup of butter. When the butter is melted, and stirred in with the milk, it is ready to serve up with the waffles.

SWEET CAKES

Ginger Snaps

Melt half a cup of lard, the same quantity of butter, mix the melted shortening with a cup of sugar, a cup of molasses, a large spoonful of ginger, and a little flour; dissolve a tea spoonful of saleratus in a cup of water, and stir it to the above ingredients, adding flour till sufficiently stiff to roll out. Cut it into small circular cakes, after rolling it out half an inch thick. Bake them in buttered tins, in an oven moderately hot. They should be baked slow, or they will not be hard and crispy.

Sponge Gingerbread

Mix with a pint of molasses two large spoonfuls of butter melted, one spoonful of ginger, and a quart of flour. Dissolve a table spoonful of saleratus in about a third of a cup of water, and strain it into the mixture. Stir it in well, then add a cup of milk—sour is the best—and flour sufficiently to enable you to roll it out easily. Flour your board and rolling-pin, then roll out a part of it at one time, half an inch thick, and lay it on buttered tins, and bake it in a very hot oven, taking care not to burn it. It will be very light and spongy if made according to the directions, provided the molasses is good. The New Orleans molasses is the best for this, as well as all other kinds of gingerbread. Good gingerbread cannot be made of dark-colored molasses. This kind of gingerbread will not keep well over two days.

Strawberry or Raspberry Cake

Mix a pint of sour milk with a cup of butter melted, or a cup of sour cream. Stir in sifted wheat flour to make a thick batter, then add to it a tea spoonful of salt, and one of soda, dissolved in a third of a cup of water. Stir it in well, then add more flour to render it stiff, so that it can be rolled out. It should be two thirds of an inch in thickness, and baked in a quick oven. Split it open when baked, and put in a thick layer of strawberries or raspberries; sprinkle over thick, white powdered sugar; close it up, and eat it while hot.

A strawberry. *American Practical Cookery Book*, 176.

Rich Cookies

One tea cup of butter, two of sugar, a couple of eggs, a tea spoonful of saleratus, dissolved in a cup of milk or water, a grated nutmeg, or two table spoonfuls of carraway seed, and sufficient flour to make them stiff enough to roll out easily.[10] Mix and bake in the same manner as plain cookies.

Rusk

One pint of warm milk, half a pint of yeast, and flour to make a thick batter. When light, add three quarters of a pound of sugar, half a pound of butter or lard; add cinnamon or nutmeg to the taste, and flour to make them as stiff as biscuit dough. Let them remain till of a spongy lightness. Then mould them into cakes of the size you would make biscuits, lay them on buttered tins, and let them remain from twenty to twenty-five minutes before setting them in the oven. They should be baked quick. Mix a cup of milk with a large spoonful of sugar, and rub it over the top of the rusk as soon as baked, with a cloth tied on a stick.

Raised Doughnuts

Heat a pint of milk just lukewarm, and stir into it a small cup of melted lard, and sifted flour till it is a thick batter; add a small cup of domestic yeast, and keep it warm till the batter is light, then work into it four beaten eggs, two cups of sugar, rolled free from lumps, a tea spoonful of salt, and two of cinnamon. When the whole is well mixed, knead in wheat flour till about as stiff as biscuit dough. Set it where it will keep warm, till of a spongy lightness, then roll the dough out half an inch thick, and cut it into cakes two inches wide and two or three in length. Let them remain a few minutes after rolling out, then fry them in a pot, with about a couple of pounds of lard; the fat should be so hot that it will boil up around them as they are dropped into it. Only a few should be boiled at once; if crowded, they will not fry well. When brown on the under side, turn them, and let them fry till perfectly done, which is ascertained by breaking one open. It takes about four or five minutes to cook them; the more eggs the less time will be required. They can be made good without any eggs, but they will require more fat, as they absorb it, and are more greasy than when made with eggs. The fat which remains after frying a batch of doughnuts, may be used again for the same purpose, adding a little more if necessary.

Quick Doughnuts

Melt your lard for frying, take three table spoonfuls of it, and mix with a pint of sour milk, a couple of quarts of flour, two cups of sugar, rolled free from lumps, a tea spoonful of salt, and half a nutmeg. When the ingredients are well mixed, add a couple of tea spoonfuls of saleratus, dissolved in about one-third of a cup of luke-warm water. Knead them up stiff, with additional flour. Roll and fry them immediately in the same manner as raised doughnuts; they should be of about half the thickness, and will fry much quicker. They can be made of sweet milk instead of sour, if a couple of tea spoonfuls of cream of tartar is added.

Crollers

Dissolve a tea spoonful of soda in half a cup of milk, and strain it on to half a pint of flour. Mix four large spoonfuls of melted butter, or lard, with six spoonfuls of sugar that has been rolled smooth, four beaten eggs, and one nutmeg. When stirred well together, add the mixed flour and milk, and additional flour to render them just stiff enough to roll out easily. When rolled about a third of an inch in thickness, cut them into strips, not over half an inch in width, with a jagging iron—if you have not one, a knife may be substituted. Cut and twist them into any fanciful form you please. Heat about a pound of lard in a pot; some use a frying pan, but the crollers are apt to burn when fried in the latter. The fat should boil up as the crollers are put in; as soon as brown on the under side, they should be carefully turned over. When a light brown on both sides, they are sufficiently cooked. If you wish to have your crollers very rich, omit the saleratus and milk.

Whistles

Half a pound of white sugar, quarter of a pound of butter, and six eggs, the whites and yelks beaten separately.[11] Stir the sugar and butter to a cream, then add the eggs previously beaten, and sifted flour to make a thick batter; flavor it with rosewater, if you like. Drop the mixture by the large spoonful on to buttered paper. The mixture should be dropped several inches apart, and spread out thin. Bake them till of a light brown, on a board, which will not take over five minutes. Lay them on a moulding-board that has white sugar sprinkled on it; roll them on a stick while warm. When cold, fill them with any kind of jelly that is thick.

Trifles

A Dish of Snow

Grate a cocoanut, leaving out the brown part, heap it up in the centre of a dessert dish, ornament it with myrtle, or box; served it up with snow cream, or cream and white sugar.

Ice Currants

Take large bunches of ripe currants, wash and drain them dry, then dip them into the whites of eggs previously beaten to a stiff froth. Lay them on a sieve at such a distance from each other that they will not touch, sift double-refined sugar over them thick, and set them in a warm place till dry.

Ice-Creams

DIRECTIONS FOR FREEZING CREAMS

Turn the cream into the freezer when sweetened and flavored, and set the freezer in a tub or keg of about the same depth as the freezer; if a hole is made in the bottom of the keg it will be found a convenience in order to let the water drain off from the ice while melting. The keg should be much larger than the freezer, so that considerable ice may be strewed around it; it should be crushed fine and put round the keg with alternate lays of coarse salt, having it reach almost to the lid of the freezer: the ice should be the last layer, in order to keep the salt from getting into the freezer when opened. (Snow, when it can be procured, is better than ice for freezing creams, as the cold produced by it when mixed with salt is more intense.) Cover the whole with a flannel cloth to keep the ice from melting rapidly; let it remain for half an hour, then open the lid of the freezer, scrape off what adheres to the side of the freezer, and mix it with the rest, then shake it constantly for half an hour, which is done by turning it half way round, then back, opening the freezer every ten minutes to scrape off what adheres to the sides, and mixing it with the rest. This process of turning the freezer half way round, then back, and mixing the cream as it freezes with that in the centre, which freezes less rapidly, is necessary to render it of a smooth consistency. A pudding-stick should be used to scrape the cream from the sides of the freezer, if there is any acid fruit in the cream, as the action of the acid on an iron spoon will impart a disagreeable flavor to the cream. In the course of an hour the cream will be of the consistency of snow, if the weather is dry; if damp, a longer time will be required to freeze it. It should then be put into moulds, if you wish to have the cream in handsome shape, and the moulds placed in the keg with fresh ice and salt, which should cover them, and a blanket thrown over the whole; keep it in a cool place until wanted for use. It usually takes a couple of hours for the cream to freeze sufficiently for eating. If you have no forms let the ice-cream remain in the freezer, packing it in fresh ice and salt. When the cream is to be eaten, wrap cloths around the sides and bottom of the forms or freezer for a couple of minutes, having previously wrung them out of very hot water. The forms should be wiped on taking from the keg, so that no salt will adhere and get into the cream.

Vanilla Ice-Cream

When cream alone is used, flavor it with the extract of vanilla, and mix with the cream powdered white sugar in the proportion of six ounces of sugar to a quart of cream. When well mixed, freeze it according to the preceding directions. If preferred, the cream may be flavored with the extract of lemon or peach. A vanilla bean may be substituted for the extract; it should be boiled in a little milk to extract the flavor. Mix the milk, when cold, with the cream.

Arrowroot Ice-Cream

Allow one large spoonful of arrowroot to a quart of milk, and two quarts of cream. Mix the arrowroot smooth with a little of the milk, and stir it into the remainder while boiling. When the whole boils thick like starch, remove it from the fire, flavor it with extract of lemon, strain it, and let it remain till cold before mixing it with the cream. Use the same proportion of sugar as for vanilla cream.

Syllabub, or Whip Cream

Take good sweet cream; to a pint of it put a large spoonful of white wine; sweeten it to the taste with powdered white sugar, and flavor it, if you like, with extract of lemon, or vanilla. Beat it up well with a large spoon, unless you have a whisk. As fast as the froth rises, take it off, and put it in a whip bowl, or cover jelly in glasses with it. If the weather is hot, it will be necessary to cool the cream, by placing it on ice, before attempting to beat it, or the froth will not rise.

To Ice Coffee

Make coffee very strong; turn it off from the grounds, so that it will be perfectly clear. Make it very sweet with white sugar, and to each quart put a pint of cream, and freeze it in the same manner as ice cream.

Pastry and Pies

Pastry

For good plain pastry, allow half a pound of shortening to a pound of flour; for rich pastry, allow three-quarters of a pound of shortening to a pound of flour. Half a pint of shortening to a quart of flour, is a good rule for common pastry. Lard alone makes the most delicate looking pie-crust, but the crust will taste better to have some butter used with the lard. Rub half of the shortening with two-thirds of the flour; add a little salt, unless very salt butter is used. When the shortening and flour are thoroughly rubbed together, add just sufficient cold water to moisten, so that it can be roiled out easily. Divide the crust into two equal portions, reserving one for the upper crust; roll out that for the under crust very thin, using considerable flour on the roller and moulding-board, to prevent it from sticking to them. Grease your pie-plates, and line them with the pastry. Roll out that reserved for the upper crust quite thin, spread on the shortening with a knife, sprinkle over the remainder of the flour, roll it up, and use it to cover the pies. The crust should be rolled from you, and it will be more delicate and flaky if rolled out several times, and the reserved shortening spread on, and the flour sprinkled over. The upper crust should be rolled about half an inch thick for the pie; trim off the edges with a knife after covering the pie, press the crust down with a jagging iron or your fingers, to keep the juices of the fruit from running out, while baking. Make small gashes in the centre of juicy fruit pies. Pastry, to be nice, should be baked in a quick, but not furiously-hot oven. In cold weather it will be necessary to have the shortening warmed, so as to soften it when used, but care must be taken not to have it melt, or the pastry will not be flaky.

Rhubarb Pie

Take good-sized tender stalks of rhubarb, cut them into small bits without stripping off the skin; if old and tough, it will be necessary to remove the skins previous to cutting them. Bake them in deep plates with a thick layer of sugar to each layer of rhubarb; an ordinary-sized pie requires half a pint of sugar. A lemon cut into small bits improves the pies; one lemon will answer for two

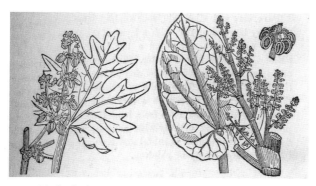

Rhubarb plants. *American Practical Cookery Book*, 137.

pies. Cover the pies with a thick crust, make apertures in the centre of the crust, press the edges down tight. Bake it slowly for about one hour. Rhubarb makes a good tart stewed tender and strained. To a quart of the strained rhubarb put a pint of milk, three beaten eggs, three ounces of pounded crackers, the grated rind of a lemon with the juice; sweeten to the taste.

Lemon Pies

Allow for each pie you wish to make, two good-sized lemons. Squeeze out the juice, chop the rind fine, mix them with a couple of crackers that have been soaked soft in cold water and mashed, add the juice, and a half a pint of molasses or sugar; the molasses is the best. Bake the pies with an under and upper crust. Another method is to grate the rind, squeeze out the juice of two medium-sized lemons, mix the grated rind and juice (leaving out the white part) with a quart of milk, a couple of large spoonfuls of powdered crackers, one spoonful of melted butter, six large spoonfuls of rolled white sugar, and six beaten eggs. Bake the mixture in deep pie-plates, with a lining and rim of nice pastry. It will take about twenty-five minutes to bake the pies in a quick oven. They should be eaten cold, and are very delicate made by the last rule; the first makes a good plain pie.

Grape Pie

Grapes are the best for pies when tender and green; if not very small they require stewing and straining to get rid of the seeds; sweeten to the taste when strained. If the pies are made of whole grapes, allow half a pint of sugar to a medium-sized pie; put in the sugar and grapes in alternate layers, in deep pie-plates, add a table spoonful of water to each pie.

Pumpkin and Squash Pies

The common round pumpkin is most used for pies, but the butter pumpkin, the winter squash, and Valparaiso squash, make more delicate pies. Cut them up into small pieces, taking out the seed, and stew them over a moderate fire, with just sufficient water to keep them from burning at the bottom of the pot. When stewed soft, turn off the water, and let it steam over a slow fire for fifteen or twenty minutes, taking care that it does not burn; then remove it from the fire, strain it through a colander, when cool. If the rind is cut off before boiling, there will be no necessity for straining it; but it should be mashed free from lumps. If you wish the pies very rich, to a quart of the strained pumpkin put two quarts of milk and ten eggs; if plain, use a quart only of milk to one of the pumpkins, and three or four eggs. The thicker the pie is of the pumpkin, the less will be the number of eggs required. They can be made without any; but they will not be very good. Add sugar, salt, and ginger, to the taste. Mace, and the grated rind of a lemon, make them very nice; they are also improved by cream in the proportion of a pint to a quart of pumpkin, and three pints of milk. Pumpkin pies require a very hot oven, and long baking, without a good many eggs are put in them. The rim of the pies are apt to get baked too hard before the pumpkin is sufficiently baked; on this account, it is best to heat the mixture when prepared for the pies, previous to filling them. Bake the pies as soon as filled, or the under crust will be clammy. Stewed pumpkin can be kept a number of weeks, by sweetening, and adding salt and ginger to the taste, then scalding the whole in well; keep it in a cool place.[12] When you wish to make pies of a portion of it, add milk and eggs.

Puddings

DIRECTIONS FOR PUDDINGS

A bag that is used for boiling puddings should be made of thick cotton cloth, and previous to filling it with a pudding, it should be wrung out of hot water, and floured on the inside. Do not fill it entirely with the pudding, as it will swell when boiling. Indian and batter pudding require a great deal of room, as they swell more than other kinds. Have an old plate at the bottom of the pot in which you boil the pudding, to keep the bag from sticking to it and burning. The water should boil when the pudding is put in, and in the course of a few minutes turn the bag over, or else the pudding will settle, and be heavy. The pot should boil without any cessation, and there should be sufficient water to cover the pudding all the time it is boiling. Keep a tea kettle of hot water to fill up the pot, as the water boils away. When you wish to turn out the pudding, dip the bag into cold water for a minute, and it will slip out easily. When puddings are baked, raisins or other kinds of fruit should not be put in till they have been in the oven long enough to thicken, so that they will not sink to the bottom. If dredged with flour previous to adding them, they will be less liable to fall to the bottom.

Hasty Pudding

This pudding is very improperly named, as it takes a long time to cook it well. Wet up sifted Indian meal with cold water, to make a thick batter; stir it into a pot of boiling water gradually. Boil it an hour, then add dry Indian meal gradually, till it becomes so thick that the pudding stick will remain stationary in the centre of the pot, taking care not to get it too stiff or lumpy; add salt to the taste. Boil it over a very moderate fire, and stir it frequently, so that it will not burn to the bottom of the pot, and the whole have a disagreeable taste. If it is to be eaten without frying, it will boil sufficiently in the course of an hour and a half. It will be necessary to boil it an hour longer for frying. Just before removing it from the fire, stir in half a pint of wheat, or rye flour, to make it adhere, so that it can be fried well; when it has scalded in, turn the

pudding into pans, having it nearly two inches deep in them. It must remain till cold before it can be fried. Cut it into slices half an inch thick, flour the slices, and fry them till brown in a good deal of fat; it should be very hot when the pudding is put in, or it will not brown well.

Green Corn Pudding

Grate sweet green corn; to three cups of it when grated put a couple of quarts of milk, two tea spoonfuls of salt, half a cup of melted butter, and six beaten eggs. Bake it an hour, and serve it up with meat. It can be used for dessert if accompanied with pudding sauce.

Bread and Butter Pudding

Cut about a pound of light good bread into thin slices, spread them with butter, as for eating, lay them in a pudding-dish, and strew between each layer of bread seeded raisins. Beat six eggs with three or four large spoonfuls of sugar, mix them with three pints of sweet milk, and a grated nutmeg. Turn the whole over the bread, let it remain until full one-half of the milk is absorbed by the bread, then bake it three quarters of an hour. No sauce will be required for the pudding.

Birds'-Nest Pudding

Pare and halve tart mellow apples, scoop out the cores, mix a little flour and water to form a thick paste, and put a little of it on each apple so that the Zante currants, which are added, will stick to the apples, there should be three or four in each one. Line a buttered pudding-dish with pastry, have a rim of pastry on the dish, put in the apples with the hollow side up, and lay long narrow strips of citron round the apples. Stir to a cream half a pound each of butter and fine white sugar, add eight eggs, the whites and yelks beaten separately, flavor it with mace or nutmeg, set it on a few coals, and stir till quite hot; take it from the fire, continue to stir it till just lukewarm, then turn it over the apples, and bake the pudding immediately.

Fritters and Dumplings

Apple Dumplings

Pare tart mellow apples, take out the cores with a small knife or apple-corer, and fill the holes with sugar. Make a good plain pie-crust, roll it two-thirds of an inch thick, cut it into pieces just large enough to enclose one apple, lay the apples in them, close the crust tight over the apples, and tie the dumplings, each one separately, in a piece of cloth that has been wrung out of hot water and floured. Put them into boiling water, and boil them without intermission for an hour: if allowed to stop boiling, they will be heavy. Serve them up with butter and sugar.

Another method of making them is, to line a large quart or three-pint bowl with a crust made of sour milk, flour, and a tea spoonful of soda; fill it with sliced tart apples, adding a little sugar to them. Cover them with a thick crust, cover it over with a plate, tie the bowl up tight in a cloth, and place the bowl in a pot of boiling water. Boil it between two and three hours. Then turn the dumpling on to a platter. If done right, it will be a nice brown. The bowl should be buttered before lining it with the crust. Peaches are nice in the same way.

Sweetmeats

Peaches in Brandy

Peel the peaches, which should be of a nice kind and mellow, but not very ripe; the freestone is the best. Make a syrup of nice white sugar, allowing half a pound of sugar to a pound of the peaches, and boil them in the syrup till they become tender, but not so much so as to break. Take the peaches out of the syrup, and lay them on platters. Mix the syrup with peach brandy, putting a pint of it to a pint or the syrup, and turn it, while hot, on to the peaches. When cold, put them in jars that can be sealed up, and keep them in a cool place. It is advisable to put them in small jars, as they will not keep long after they are opened. Pears, plums, quinces, and cherries, are all of them nice preserved in the same way. They will be less likely to ferment if the jars are kept in dry sand.

Hartell's Self-Sealing Jar.

An ad for Hartell's self-sealing jars was inserted into the text of one cookbook, like an early version of product placement. The copy assured readers that the jars made home canning so easy that a servant would have to be extremely stupid to use them incorrectly. Elizabeth Nicholson, *What I Know; or, The Economical Cook and House-Book* (Philadelphia, J. W. Bradley, 1860), 77, Michigan State University Special Collections.

Tomato Figs

Allow three pounds of sugar to six pounds of tomatoes. Take those that are fully ripe, and the pear-shaped or single tomatoe.[13] Scald them, and take off the skins; stew them slowly with part of the sugar, not using any water, as the juice of the tomatoes will form a syrup. When the sugar appears to have penetrated them, spread them on dishes, and dry them in the sun; sprinkle over the reserved sugar while drying. When perfectly dry, pack them in jars, with a layer of sugar between each layer of tomatoes. Preserved in this way, they will keep well for a year, and resemble figs in flavor. Care should be taken not to have the rain or dew fall on them while drying. The syrup that remains after they have been stewed, boiled down so that it will be rich, is nice to sweeten pies.

Watermelon Rinds

Take a thick rind of a ripe watermelon. Cut it into small strips, cut off all the red part, and scrape off the outsides. Boil the rinds with peach leaves and saleratus, in the proportion of a dozen leaves and a tea spoonful of saleratus to a couple of quarts of water. These will turn them of a fine green color; when tender, take them out of the water, and put them in cold water that has half a large spoonful of alum dissolved in it, in order to make them brittle and green. Let them soak for an hour, then rinse them in clear water, and boil them in a syrup made of an equal weight of white sugar. Boil with them lemons cut into small pieces, allowing one lemon to two pounds of the rinds. Boil them fifteen or twenty minutes; when a little cool, add a little essence of ginger to flavor them. If you have not the essence, boil in the syrup with the rinds a few slips of green ginger, or powdered ginger, tied up in small bits of cloth. In the course of three or four days, turn the syrup from the rinds, boil it to a rich syrup, that will just cover the rinds; turn it on them scalding hot. These make a very delicate sweetmeat, and will keep without any trouble.

Pumpkin Chips

The butter pumpkin is the nicest for preserving; the winter squash is also better than the common round pumpkin. Halve the pumpkin, take out the seeds, cut off the rind, and cut the pumpkin into chips of the size of a dollar. For each pound of the chips to be preserved, allow a pound of nice white sugar, and a gill of lemon juice. Put the chips in a deep dish, and sprinkle on each layer the sugar, which should be powdered. Let the whole remain till the succeeding day, then boil it with half a pint of water, and a large spoonful of ginger, tied up in cloths, to three pounds of the chips; add the rinds of the lemons, cut into small pieces, leaving out the white part. Boil the whole together, till the chips become tender. The syrup should be boiled again in the course of a few days, and turned, while hot, on to the chips.

Preserved Fruit

TO PRESERVE FRUIT IN THE SUN

Strawberries, raspberries, and blackberries, are said to retain their natural flavor more perfectly when preserved by the heat of the sun, instead of being scalded over the fire. This method is as follows: Place them on shallow dishes, covering them entirely with powdered double-refined sugar, using the same quantity of sugar as in the ordinary way of boiling. Expose them to the sun on the roof of your house for several days, having them where the sun will shine on them through the day, and taking them in as soon as the dew falls, or if the weather becomes damp. Keep the berries in small jars, corked and sealed tight, and pack the jars in boxes of dry sand.

Jellies

Bags for straining jelly are usually made of flannel, but after using several times they shrink up so thick, that the jelly will not run through them readily; on this account, those made of thick white cotton cloth are preferable, and will answer just as well. The bags should taper down to a point, and have a hole at the top, so that they can be suspended on a nail while the jelly is draining through into a pitcher or mug placed under them. It should be wrung out of hot water previous to using it for straining jelly, and not squeezed, while the jelly is passing through it; if squeezed, the jelly will not be clear. If not clear the first time, jelly should be turned back into the bag, and drained through again. If not wanted for immediate use, put the jelly into small jars or tumblers. To ascertain when jelly is sufficiently boiled, put a spoonful of it in a tumbler of cold water; if it sinks in a solid mass to the bottom, it is sufficiently cooked.

Calf's-Feet Jelly

Take four feet that have been previously cleaned, boil them in four quarts of water till very soft, and the water is reduced to one quart. Take it from the fire and let it remain till perfectly cool, then scrape off the dregs which adhere to the bottom of the jelly. Put it in a preserving kettle, and set it where it will melt, slowly. When melted, take it from the fire, mix with it half a pint of white wine, the juice and grated rind of a couple of fresh lemons, and a stick of cinnamon. Wash and wipe dry six eggs, take the whites of them and beat to a froth, stir them into the jelly when it becomes cool; bruise the shells and mix them with the jelly. Set it on a moderate fire; when hot, sweeten it to the taste. White sugar is the best, but brown will answer very well. It should boil slowly for fifteen minutes, then strain it; if not clear the first time, let it pass through the jelly-bag till it becomes so, taking care not to squeeze the bag. When transparent, turn it into glasses and put them in a cool place. If the weather is hot, set them in a pan of ice water. This kind of jelly will keep well only two or three days in hot weather. A knuckle of veal and sheep's-feet make a nice jelly prepared in the same manner as calf's-feet.

Common Drinks

Hop Beer

Put to five quarts of water six ounces of hops, and boil them three hours; then strain off the liquor and put to the hops four more quarts of water, four or five raw potatoes pared and sliced, a half pint of ginger, and boil the hops two hours longer. Then strain and mix it with the rest of the liquor, stirring in a couple of quarts of molasses. Take half a pound of rusked bread, pound it fine, and brown it in a pot over the fire, stirring it constantly. Slices of bread toasted very brown will do, but are not as good as the rusked bread to enrich the beer. Add it to the liquor, and when cool, so as to be just lukewarm, stir in a pint of fresh made yeast, that has no salt in it, as the salt keeps it from fermenting readily. Keep the beer covered in a temperate situation till the fermentation ceases, which is ascertained by the subsiding of the froth. Then turn it off carefully into a beer-keg, jugs, or bottles. The bottles should not be corked tight, as the beer will be apt to burst them. Keep the beer in a cool place.

Spring Beer

Take a small bunch of part or all of the following roots: Sweet-fern, sarsaparilla, winter-green, sassafras, prince's-pine, and spicewood. Boil with them a couple of ounces of hops, three or four raw potatoes sliced and pared, to three gallons of water; let the whole boil for three hours, then strain off the liquor, and put to the roots and hops three gallons of fresh water, and boil three hours longer.

The strength of the roots is obtained more thoroughly by changing the water, as, when strongly saturated with the hops, it will bind up the juices of the roots. Strain the liquor when boiled sufficiently, add to it molasses in the proportion of a quart to three gallons of beer, and a couple of slices of bread toasted very brown. When it becomes just lukewarm, stir in a pint of lively new yeast that has no salt in it. If the liquor seems too thick, dilute it with lukewarm water. Keep it in a temperate situation, cover it over, but not so high as to exclude the air entirely, or it will not work. When fermented, keep it in a tight keg or bottles.

Ginger Beer, or Wine

Boil gently in a gallon of water, three large spoonfuls of ginger, three of cream of tartar, two lemons cut in slices. When the whole has boiled an hour, strain and sweeten to the taste with sugar, which is the best. When just lukewarm, add half a pint of fresh lively yeast, that has no salt in it. When fermented, turn it off carefully, bottle and cork it, and keep it in a cool place. It will be fit to drink in the course of seven or eight days. This beer resembles champagne. A simple ginger beer may be made as follows: Turn a gallon of boiling water on to three or four large spoonfuls of ginger, let it steep for half an hour, then set it where it will cool. When just lukewarm, add half a pint of molasses, and a cup of lively yeast. It will be fit to drink as soon as fermented.

Cherry Bounce

Procure the wild black cherries, pound them, in order to break the pits, then mix with them sugar, good whiskey or rum, in the proportion of a gallon of spirits and two pounds of the sugar to a couple of quarts of cherries; put the whole in a tight cask, shake it up once every day for three months, then let the liquor run through a thick cloth twice to clear it. Keep it, when strained, in casks or bottles. This is very good for bowel complaints, and a fine tonic.

Mead

Put to each pound of honey three pints of warm water, stir it up well, and let it remain until the honey is held in complete solution, then turn it into a cask, leaving the bung out. Let it ferment in a temperate situation, and bottle it as soon as fermented.

Effervescing Drink

Put a tea spoonful of tartaric acid in half a tumbler of cold water, and sweeten it to the taste with any nice fruit syrup you please, or white sugar. Dissolve half a tea spoonful of soda in one-third of a tumbler of cold water, and mix it with the tartaric acid in the other tumbler; a little essence of ginger added to the above, makes a very healthy, and pleasant drink. Vinegar of berries may be substituted for the tartaric acid, using a large spoonful of it to a tumbler of the drink.

Cookery for the Sick

Wheat Gruel

Tie up a small quantity of wheat flour in a thick cotton cloth, and boil it five hours, and then dry it perfectly. To make the gruel, grate off a dessert spoonful and mix it into a thin paste with water, and then stir it into half a pint of boiling milk, and add salt to the taste. This is excellent food for children who have a bowel complaint.

Beef Tea

Boil a pound of fresh lean beef ten minutes, then cut it into small bits, turn on a pint of lukewarm water and set it where it will keep warm for half an hour, then strain and season it with salt and pepper to the taste. This is a quick method of obtaining the juices of the meat, but the tea is not so nourishing and good, when the stomach is unable to bear a small quantity of liquid on it, as the following method: Cut lean beef into small bits, fill a junk bottle with them, cork it tight, put it in a pot of lukewarm water, and set the pot where the water will boil for four or five hours.[14] A table spoonful of this is as nourishing as half a pint of the tea made by boiling the meat.

Wine Whey

Stir a couple of wine glasses of wine into a pint of boiling milk, take it from the fire, and let it remain till the curd separates from the whey and settles; then turn off the whey and sweeten it with white sugar.

Miscellaneous Receipts

To Keep Various Vegetables in Winter

Cabbages, celery, salsify, and parsnips, keep best when covered with earth. Turnips, potatoes, and similar vegetables, should be protected from the air and frost; a linen cloth thrown over in severely cold weather is good to keep them from freezing. It is said that the dust of charcoal will keep potatoes from sprouting in the spring. Onions, pumpkins, and squashes, should not be kept in cellars, as the dampness makes them decay.

To Keep Eggs for Five Months

It is advisable to buy eggs for family use, when cheap, and preserve them as follows: Mix half a pint of unslacked lime with the same quantity of salt, and a couple of gallons of water. The water should be turned on the lime boiling hot. When it becomes cold, put in the eggs carefully, so as not to crack the shells; if cracked they will spoil very soon. The eggs should be perfectly fresh when put in, and the lime water no stronger than the above mixture; if too strong the lime will eat the shells.

Another good way, is to grease the shells, and pack them in salt. Early in the fall is a good time to put them down for winter use.

Cottage Cheese

Take sour milk, but not that which is so old as to have disagreeable taste, set it in a warm place, but not very hot. When the curd and whey separate, drain off the whey, put the curd in a strong bag, squeeze out the whey, mash the curd fine, and mix it with a little fresh cream or butter; add salt to the taste, and do it up into small cakes.

To Make Good Food of Poor Bread

If dry or sour bread is cut into small pieces and put in a pan, and set in a very moderately warm oven till of a light brown, and hard and dry in the centre, it can be kept for weeks. Whenever you wish to use a portion of them for puddings or griddle-cakes, soak them soft in cold water or milk. If the bread is sour, use sufficient saleratus or soda to destroy the acidity of it in making the pudding or cakes. With proper care, there need be no waste of even poor bread.

Vinegar

Vinegar made of cider is the best; that of wine or sour beer is good. Much of the vinegar sold is not good, being made of poor, and often unwholesome materials; on this account it is advisable for housekeepers to manufacture their own vinegar; it is also much more economical. Procure a barrel, or a half a one of cider, put to it a piece of paper dipped in molasses, keep the barrel in a warm place, in a situation exposed to the influence of the sun, until it becomes vinegar. Tea, coffee, and sour beer, which you have left after meals, may be added to the vinegar without injury to it, if not added in large quantities at once, so as to weaken the vinegar. Very good vinegar may be made of fair, good apple parings, by putting to them rather more than sufficient water to cover them, in an unglazed earthen pot, with a paper dipped in molasses put in it. Keep it in a warm situation; in the course of several weeks it will ferment, and become good vinegar.

Lip Salve

Dissolve a small lump of white sugar in a large spoonful of rose water; common water may be substituted; mix it with a couple of large spoonfuls of sweet oil, a piece of spermaceti of half of the size of a butter-nut.[15] Simmer the whole eight or ten minutes.

Stains from the Hands

Vinegar or lemon juice are good to remove stains from the hands. The following will be found a great convenience to keep, for those who are liable to get stained hands with ink, fruit, or dye stuffs: Mix equal proportions of oxalic acid and cream of tartar, and keep it in a covered box, out of the reach of children, as it is poisonous if swallowed. When it is to be used, dip the fingers in warm water, rub on a small portion of the powder. When the stains disappear wash the hands, using fine soap.

To Clean Beds and Mattresses

When feather beds or pillows become soiled or heavy they can be cleaned and made fresh and light, if treated in the following manner: Rub them over with a stiff brush dipped in warm soap suds. When rubbed clean put them on a clean shed, where the rain will fall on them. When thoroughly soaked through, let it remain in a hot sun for a week, to dry through, shaking it up well each day, and turning it over. They should be covered with a thick cloth at night, or they will become damp and mildew. The above mode of cleaning feather beds is quite as effectual in restoring them to their original lightness as the old tedious process of emptying them and washing the feathers separately; but care must be taken to dry the beds perfectly previous to sleeping on them. Hair mattresses that have become hard and dirty can be rendered as good as new by ripping them, washing the ticking, and picking the hair free from bunches, and keeping it in a dry, airy place for a number of days. The ticking should be dry when the hair is put back into it.

To Destroy Various Household Vermin

Hellebore, rubbed over with molasses, and put in places that cockroaches frequent, will destroy them very soon. Arsenic spread on bread and butter, and placed round rat or mice holes, will put a stop to their ravages; but as they are apt to die in the walls when poisoned, and cause a disagreeable smell for a long time, it is not, perhaps, advisable to use it in a dwelling house. It can be used to clear barns of them without incommoding any one. To kill flies, when so numerous as to be troublesome, keep cobalt mixed with spirits and sugar, on a shallow plate. The spirits will attract the flies and the cobalt will poison them, so that they will die very soon. Bedsteads that have bugs in them should be taken apart and washed thoroughly with cold water, which is better than scalding them; then beat up the white of an egg with quicksilver, and put it round the crevices of the bedsteads with a feather; it should also be applied to the holes of the sacking, where the cord is put through. The quicksilver may be mixed with lard instead of the egg. When the bugs get into the cracks of walls they should be filled with verdigris paint; if under the paper, it will be necessary to pull it off and wash the walls and repaper them. Camphor, in small bits, or the flour of sulphur, sprinkled round the places that ants frequent, it is said, will drive them away; sage is also good. Much care is necessary to keep the above articles from children, as they are poisonous, excepting those which are used to kill ants.

To Make Hens Lay

Let them have a wide range, as they will not do well if confined for any length of time. In winter give them a coop, with sand to roll in, and plenty of pure water to drink.

Feed them well on corn, buckwheat, and warm boiled potatoes. In winter, when they cannot procure worms, it will be necessary to give them a little meat occasionally; also to mix a little lime with their food, as without it they cannot lay, however well fed they may be. The lime is necessary to form the shell. Some pound up egg shells and give it to them, but it is apt to learn them to eat their eggs. Young chickens should be fed on Indian meal or pieces of bread soaked soft.

Soap from Ashes

To prepare a lye for soap, take a barrel without a bottom and place it on a board that has a trough to convey the water into another vessel; cover the bottom of the barrel with straw, then sprinkle over a couple of quarts of lime; fill the barrel with ashes; turn on cold water (well-water will answer), a pail only at one time, and turn it on slowly. Continue to turn on water, at intervals of three or four hours the first, the third, and fifth days. When the lye becomes strong enough to bear up an egg, put to fifteen gallons of it eleven pounds of grease, heated to the boiling point. Stir it for five minutes every day, till it forms soap. If it does not come in the course of a week, add a pailful of soft water.

Simple Remedies

Earache

The heart of a roasted onion put, when warm, into the ear, when aching, will generally relieve it; when this fails, apply cotton with a few drops of laudanum on it. A strong decoction of tobacco is very efficacious. A little sweet oil is good for a slight pain in the ear.

For Hoarseness

Slice up raw onions, sprinkle over loaf-sugar thick, and let it remain till a syrup is formed, then take a tea spoonful of it frequently. Molasses, warmed with a little butter and vinegar, will often afford relief, if taken freely. The following is a good remedy in cases of obstinate hoarseness: Make a strong decoction of horse-radish, sweeten it with honey or white sugar, and add a little vinegar to it. Take a tea spoonful occasionally.

To Extract Substances from the Nostrils

When a child has any substance wedged in its nostrils, press the vacant nostril so as to close it, and apply your lips close to the child's mouth, and blow very hard. This method will generally force the substance out of the nostril.

To Cure the Bites of Spiders or Mosquitos

Make a bread and milk poultice, and mix with it twenty drops of laudanum, and bind it on the place that is bitten; if a severe bite, apply leeches. For mosquito bites apply salt, moistened with water. Camphor is also good.

Treatment for a Sprained Ankle

Wash the sprain frequently in cold salt and water. It should be kept cool, and the ankle elevated, to prevent inflammation. The patient should walk as little as possible. Take cooling medicine, and live on vegetable food.

Asthma

A cup of very strong coffee, without milk or sugar, will often afford relief. The following is said to help the most obstinate cases: Dissolve a pint of saltpetre in a pint of water, dip sheets of fine brown paper in the solution until saturated, and dry the paper. For a fit of asthma, burn a strip of it in a close room, having the patient exhaling the fumes of it.

What Shall We Eat? A Manual for Housekeepers, Comprising a Bill of Fare for Breakfast, Dinner, and Tea, for Every Day in the Year

What Shall We Eat, published in 1868, leans toward the Gilded Age in its brevity and its exclusive focus on recipes and menus. Unlike earlier cookbooks, which generally organized their recipes in categories like puddings, vegetables, and meats, the unnamed author of *What Shall We Eat* used the recipes to create a complete menu for one week out of each month in the year. By providing menus, the book offers intriguing hints about when Americans would have eaten certain foods, how they would have paired dishes together, and how much they ate—at least those who could afford to eat the costly dishes and large quantities the author suggested they should.

Modern readers may be surprised by what seems like the gargantuan size of the meals suggested here. For instance, one dinner menu called for roast turkey with stewed potatoes, canned sweet corn, baked sweet potatoes, cranberry jelly, and apple pie. So far, the meal sounds like a Thanksgiving feast. However, this was only

a casual dinner suggested for a Friday in January, and it *also* included pea soup with ham, boiled whitefish, a beef ragout, chocolate cream, oranges, raisins, and almonds. One reason for these big meals may have been that people then had bigger calorie needs and bigger families. Mid-nineteenth-century Americans, even financially comfortable ones, were on average much more physically active in their daily lives than Americans today, and women generally spent many more years pregnant and breastfeeding. For both reasons, their calorie needs were high. Furthermore, not only were nineteenth-century families bigger than families today, on average, but they may also have been providing food for boarders or servants.

Beyond these pragmatic explanations, another important reason for the large meals suggested by the author may have been a kind of conspicuous consumption.[1] When households followed menus like these, they demonstrated that they could afford not only to purchase

Oranges with Jelly was a showy dish valued more for presentation than flavor, typical of the ornate food presentations becoming more fashionable throughout the Civil War era. This particular dish was made by carefully filling emptied orange peels with stripes of different colored gelatin, arranging them in a pyramid, and decorating the result with myrtle leaves. Acton, *Modern Cookery*, 312.

the costly ingredients, but also to pay servants—almost certainly more than one—to prepare a range of complicated recipes, meal after meal after meal. Indeed, the very fact that the book presents these extensive menus casually and as a matter of course would have amplified the author's own status as an authority on matters of taste.

At the same time, of course, it's important to remember that not everyone who bought this cookbook necessarily followed it. While practical cooking instructions were valuable, cookbooks also served less pragmatic functions, especially as a form of leisure reading. Readers who could rarely afford the time or money to prepare the meals the book described may still have enjoyed the visions it provided of long, sumptuous meals, exotic ingredients, and intricate preparations. Thinking about the ways people may have read cookbooks for fun—rather than reading them only as a source of information—is a good reminder that cookbooks only offer us hints about how people ate, and that, by themselves, they are never reliable descriptions of reality.

Yet some people did of course eat big, lengthy meals like the ones suggested here. One thing that *What Shall We Eat* shows vividly is that some nineteenth-century Americans ate an incredible variety of foods, many of which are only rarely eaten in the United States today. Modern meat eating, in particular, feels impoverished compared to the variety of cuts and species consumed then. In addition to familiar forms of poultry, beef, and pork, the recipes here called for turtle, mutton, lamb, veal, rabbit, venison and other game, plus a variety of game birds and songbirds, including snipe, partridge, lark, grouse, woodcock, quail, prairie chicken, pigeon, duck, and goose. The author also called for meat from *parts* of animals many Americans today consider inedible or off-putting, like tongue, kidney, heart, tripe, liver, heads, brains, feet, cheeks, tails, glands, and giblets. And all of this was in addition to a wide variety of fish and shellfish, including scallops, oysters, crabs, clams, shrimp, lobster, eels, bass, cod, salmon, black fish, whitefish, pike, perch, sardines, anchovies, halibut, herring, mackerel, smelts, porgies, flounder, shad, bluefish, trout, sole, frostfish, and a variety of fish eggs.

Meals were organized around meat, with side dishes and vegetables generally playing supporting roles to the meaty main course. On the first day of the book, suggested for a Monday in January, breakfast consisted of cold roast beef, potatoes and sauce, chopped sausages on buttered toast, potted fish, rolls and butter, and tea and coffee. Dinner, presumably eaten in the early afternoon, was oyster soup, boiled halibut, roast pork served with applesauce, potatoes, and tomatoes, pastries filled with ground beef, and a plain pudding and sauce for dessert, with fruit and nuts. The light evening meal, which the author called lunch or tea, was cold pickled salmon and tongue with bread and butter, canned peaches, teacakes, cream cake, and tea and coffee. Not a single meal in the book appeared without meat, breakfasts very much included.

Indeed, the author was emphatic about the importance of breakfast, arguing that the first meal of the day should be as thoughtfully prepared—and as ample—as the other meals. Besides warning readers against serving wine for breakfast, the author also instructed them not to start the day with hefty foods like omelets, sardines, fish eggs, or hot cakes, which the author believed made people feel heavy and slow. Of course, these prohibitions offer another good hint about people actually *were* eating. Yet the suggested breakfasts here could hardly be called light. One typical breakfast called for

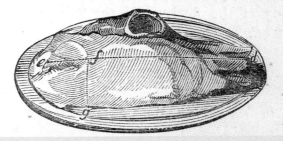

HALF A CALF'S HEAD.—FIG 20.

Recipes for calf's head appeared regularly in mid-nineteenth-century cookbooks. *American Practical Cookery Book*, 238.

fresh salmon, beefsteak, potted tongue, and a variety of breads, while another suggested broiled kidneys, cold veal, scrambled eggs, and radishes, among other items. Breakfasts suggested in *What Shall We Eat* regularly included items like liver, game birds, shellfish, lamb chops, and steak, along with a variety of vegetables.

In contrast to the humbler introductions in most of the other cookbooks here, this author's introduction was brisk and unapologetic. The author noted proudly that the recipes had "all been tested by actual experience," which was not always the case in nineteenth-century cookbooks. In fact, nineteenth-century cookbook authors—like Mary Cornelius, for instance—often readily admitted that they had not tried all the recipes they were recommending. The author also praised the book's menu format, writing that the book was designed "to suggest to ladies, without the trouble of *thinking*, what is seasonable for the table, each day in the week, and how it shall be cooked."

Seasonality was in truth a major motivation for organizing the menus into months of the year. While preserved foods were legion in this era and certain foods were increasingly transported long distances by rail and ship, it was still imperative to consider the seasonal availability of ingredients when planning meals. In this book, as a result, lobster, asparagus, and lamb all featured heavily in April, while June recipes were filled with cherries, radishes, cucumbers, and strawberries. Likewise, the August menus called for fresh tomatoes, peaches, melons, blackberries, huckleberries, and eggplant. By November, the meals leaned heavily on pears, apples, and oysters. Sometimes, when an item did appear out of season, as when an April menu suggested blueberry pie, the author instructed readers to use canned fruit. These monthly menus serve as a useful reminder that much more so than Americans today, Americans in the 1860s ate differently at different times of the year.

Preface

What Shall We Eat?

The design of this Manual is to suggest to ladies, without the trouble of *thinking*, what is seasonable for the table, each day in the week, and how it shall be cooked. Also to present to the community of housekeepers, who sigh over the responsibility of providing for the daily wants of life, an agreeable variety, which may be varied to suit the income of the reader. The receipts have all been tested by actual experience. A daily "bill of fare" for breakfast, dinner, and tea is given, for one week in each month, which will present to the reader at once what is wanted, without the trouble of looking over a cookbook. A collection of Pickles and Sauces of rare merit form a desirable addition at the end.

Breakfast

A word on this early meal. It should be what will best fortify a man for the labor of a long day, and should consist of palatable solids. In a chilly climate like America, wine is a mistake, even with French cookery; if strong, it diminishes business keenness; if weak, it imparts no warmth. Instinct points to hot beverages, either coffee, tea, or chocolate. Every variety of cold meats, game, potted meats, and fish, tongue, boar's head, pickled poultry, etc., are suitable, and with bread form a desirable meal. Omelets, sardines, and roes of different fish, hot buttered cakes, etc., make the eater heavy for the day. There is really no time when one needs so good a supply of food as at breakfast, when one has not eaten for twelve or fourteen hours, and fuel is needed for active existence; yet no meal is so much neglected, and people well informed fritter an appetite away on toast and tea. Fruit is a good digester, dried mango-fish from India, cranberry jam, etc., are all good. A breakfast should be as carefully composed as a dinner. Secure by art what is due to the dignity of the meal, and give it its true position.

January

MONDAY

Breakfast.—Cold roast beef. Potatoes à la maître d'Hotel. (Boil the potatoes, and cut in thin slices. Take a pint of milk, and when scalding hot, stir in a tablespoonful of butter and flour, rubbed together. Add a small bunch of parsley, chopped fine. When well mixed, throw in the potatoes, shaking carefully without a knife or spoon, to avoid breaking. Salt to taste.) Sausage toast. (Scald the sausages in boiling water, fry to a light brown, chop fine, and spread on buttered toast.) Potted fish. Rolls and butter. Tea and coffee.

Dinner

Oyster Soup.—Take fifty oysters, strain through a sieve, and put the liquor on the fire. When scalding hot, take ¼ lb. of butter, and beat with 6 oz. of flour; roll ½ doz. butter crackers to powder, and add all to the liquor, with salt and pepper to the taste, and a small punch of powdered mace. Then add the oysters with a quart of milk (and a gill of cream if you have it), and stir with a silver spoon for ten minutes. Do not let them *boil*, but thoroughly scald.

Boiled Halibut.

Roast Pork.—Serve with apple-sauce, potatoes, and tomatoes. Baste with a little butter and flour, and rub with dried sage crumbled.

Beef Patties.—Chop fine rare roast beef, season with pepper, salt, and a little onion. Make a plain paste, cut into shapes like an apple puff, fill with the mince, and bake quickly.

Dessert

Flour Pudding.—Five eggs, 1 qt. milk, 4 tablespoonfuls of flour, well stirred together. Bake in a quick oven, and eat with cold sauce.

Fruit and nuts.

Tea, or Lunch, If the Dinner Is Late

Cold pickled salmon, tongue, bread and butter, canned peaches, tea and coffee, Benton tea-cakes (1 qt. of flour mixed with milk to a paste, 1 tablespoonful of melted butter. Roll very thin, and bake on hot hearth).

Cream cake (1 lb. flour, 1 lb. sugar, ½ lb. of butter, ½ pt. milk, 4 eggs, citron, raisins, and spice to taste).

TUESDAY

Breakfast.—Breaded veal cutlet. Fried potatoes. Pickled tripe. Waffles. (Put 2 pints of milk into *separate* pans; warm one slightly, melt in it ¼ lb. of butter, and set it away to cool. Beat 8 eggs, and mix with the other pan, stirring in gradually ½ lb. of flour, and a little salt. Then mix the contents of both pans together, and add a large tablespoonful of yeast. Set near the fire to rise. When quite light, heat the waffle-iron and butter it, pour in the batter, and when done one side, turn. Send to the table hot, six on a plate, buttered, and strewn with powdered sugar if desired.) Hot brown bread. Cold bread. Tea and coffee.

Dinner

Beef Soup.—Take a shank bone, with part of the leg, and put in a kettle with soft water to cover it, with a small piece of butter to keep from burning, while the juices are extracting. Set on the back of the range, and cook slowly for six hours, then strain, and when *cold*, remove every particle of fat. Place in another pot 5 carrots, 5 onions, 1 cup of rice, ½ a bunch of celery, and a small bunch of parsley. In this pot may be placed any bones, or pieces of *cooked* meat. Let them also stew slowly for six hours, then strain through a colander, and add to the soup, with ½ a cup of tomato catsup. Let *all* come to a boil together, then serve. Use a wooden spoon in stirring. This quantity of soup will suffice a small family for a week, and should be kept in a cool place, in an earthen vessel.

Fresh Cod, boiled, with melted butter.

Roast Chickens, with mashed potatoes, cauliflower, and stewed celery.

Cold Tongue.

Dessert

Squash Pie.—One qt. of pulp strained through a sieve; boil 1 qt. of milk, and stir the squash into it, with 2 spoonfuls of flour shaken in. Add 2 eggs, and a piece of butter size of an egg. Season to the taste with sugar, cinnamon, and a little salt.

Coffee Custard.—Boil a pint of milk, and pour upon it, while boiling, 2 tablespoonfuls of *whole* coffee, warmed by the fire. Let it cool for an hour, then sweeten, add the yolks of 4 eggs, thicken over the fire (stirring all the time). When thick enough, strain, and fill the glasses.

Grapes, apples, and hickory nuts.

Tea, or Lunch

Cold roast meat, raw oysters, apple-sauce, French bread and butter. Crackers. Scotch cake. (Stir to a cream 1 lb. of sugar and ¾ lb. of butter, add the juice and grated rind of a lemon, with a wine-glass of brandy. Beat separately the whites and yolks of 9 eggs, and stir into cake. Add 1 lb. of sifted flour, and just as it goes into the pan, 1 lb. of stoned raisins.)[2]

Breakfast.—Hashed chicken on toast. Cold snipe. Mutton chops. Graham rolls. Dry toast. French bread and butter. Chocolate and coffee.

Dinner

Barley Broth.—Boil gently, for half an hour, ½ pt. of pearl barley in a gallon of water. Take 3 lbs. lamb chops, with fat cut off, and put in a stewpan, with water to cover them. Add any kind of vegetables, carrots, turnips, onions, and celery cut fine. When tender, add to the barley water, and boil slowly 2 hours. Salt and pepper to taste.

Fried Scallops.

Roast Ducks, (scald, to prevent being oily,) with baked potatoes, onions, canned sweet corn, and celery.

Chicken Patties.—Chop fine and season well, and serve in puff paste.

Dessert

Arrowroot Pudding.—Simmer a pint of milk with a little cinnamon, take a tablespoonful of arrowroot, mix with cold water, and pour into the milk, stirring all the time. When cold, add 3 eggs well beaten, and stir all together. Bake ½ an hour in a dish lined with puff paste, and grate a little nutmeg on the top.

Delicate Dish.—Beat the whites of 6 eggs, with 2 spoonfuls of currant jelly, to a *solid* froth, so that it will not fall. Serve with cream and powdered sugar.

Grapes, apples, and pecan nuts.

Tea, or Lunch

Stewed oysters, cold game, French bread. Strawberry jam, sponge cake.

THURSDAY

Breakfast.—Cold boiled ham. Cold roast duck. Omelet, with parsley. Stewed potatoes, with cream. Steamed toast. Corn bread (3 cups of meal, 1 cup of flour, 1 tablespoonful of butter, do. sugar, 1 teaspoonful of soda, 1 qt. of buttermilk, or sour milk, 2 eggs). Tea and coffee.

Dinner

Giblet Soup.—Scald and clean a set of giblets, stew in a little gravy with 2 onions, a bunch of sweet herbs. 2 glasses of white wine, pepper, and salt. When tender, take them out and strain the broth. Make a stock with 2 lbs. of beef, and 5 pints of water. Skin 2 onions, slice thin, and fry in butter. Add flour to thicken the broth, with majoram and parsley, and stir all into the boiling stock.[3] Boil ½ an hour, pass through a sieve, and put again on the fire, skimming carefully. Add the giblets, 2 glasses of wine, and a little lemon-juice. Season well.

Boiled Striped Bass, melted butter.

Roast Leg of Mutton, with boiled potatoes, fried parsnips, boiled hominy, and baked tomatoes.

Scalloped Oysters.—Scald the oysters in their own liquor, take them out with a fork, lay in a deep dish, sprinkling over each one rolled cracker crumbs, pepper and salt, and small pieces of butter. Stir a little butter and flour together, and stir into the liquor; then fill up the dish with it, and brown in the oven.

Dessert

Baked Quince Pudding.—Scald some quinces till tender, pare, and scrape off the pulp; then strew it with ginger, cinnamon, and sugar. To a pint of milk, or cream, put the yolks of 4 eggs and stir in the quince to a proper consistency. Bake in a dish lined with paste. *Canned* quinces can be used if necessary.

Caramel Custard.—Melt ¼ lb. of pounded sugar over a slow fire till it begins to tint, stirring all the time. Boil 1 oz. of isinglass in a pint of milk, and pour it on the caramel, stirring till quite dissolved. Beat 4 eggs and add; then stir over the fire to thicken. Put in a mould, and then set on the ice.

Fruit and nuts.

Tea, or Lunch

Cold Ham Cake. (Take ham that may be getting dry, pound finely, with the fat, in a mortar, season with pepper and mixed spice; add clarified butter sufficient to moisten, and place ½ an hour in the oven. Put the mould in warm water a few minutes, that it may turn out well.) Pickled oysters, dry toast, French bread, griddle-cakes, brandy peaches, cup-cake (4 eggs, 4 cups flour, 3 cups powdered sugar, 1 cup butter, 1 cup milk, 1 glass white wine, spices, and a teaspoonful soda). Tea.

FRIDAY

Breakfast.—Cold roast mutton, pickled pigs' feet, rolls, brown bread cream toast, boiled samp. Tea and coffee.

Dinner

Pea Soup.—Put 1 qt. split peas into 3 qts. boiling water (first soak the peas over night); boil gently till dissolved, strain through a sieve, and add thyme, sweet marjoram, and some mushroom catsup. A small piece of ham will improve the flavor. Serve with small pieces of fried bread.

Boiled Whitefish.

Roast Turkey.—With stewed potatoes, canned sweet corn, baked sweet potatoes, and cranberry jelly.

Beef Ragout.—Fry 2 lbs. of beef till quite brown, put it into a stewpan with 6 onions, pepper it well, and stew slowly 4 hours. Serve it up with pickled walnuts, gherkins, and capers, just warmed in the gravy.

Dessert

Apple Pie.

Chocolate Cream.—Scrape into 1 qt. of milk (or cream) 1 oz. of best French chocolate, and add ¼ lb. of sugar. Boil and mill it. When smooth, take it off, and add the whites of 6 eggs, beaten to a froth. Strain through a sieve, and put in glasses.

Oranges, raisins, and almonds.

Tea, or Lunch

Cold turkey, roast oysters, cheese, Graham crackers, preserved ginger, tea and chocolate, almond cake (2 oz. blanched bitter almonds, pounded fine; 7 oz. flour, sifted and dried; 10 eggs; 1 pound loaf sugar, powdered and sifted, and a wine-glass of rose-water).

SATURDAY

Breakfast.—Broiled ham, potted game, chipped potatoes, milk toast, corn bread, tea and coffee.

Dinner

Fish Soup.—Take one pound each of any fresh water fish—pike, perch, eels, &c.; wash in salt and water, and then stew with carrots, leeks, sweet herbs, and onions, in as much water as will cover them. Stew until all is reduced to a pulp, then strain, and boil an hour, with a little mace, celery, and mushroom catsup, or any high-seasoned sauce.

Fried Clams.

Broiled Beefsteak, with celery, potatoes, and stewed tomatoes.

Broiled Snipe.

Dessert

Cranberry Tarts.

Rice Pudding, with Fruit.—Swell the rice in milk, over the fire, and add pared and quartered apples, with a little currant jelly.

Pears and dates.

Tea, or Lunch

Cold corn beef, hashed chicken, fried hominy, hot biscuit, raised, cranberry sauce, chocolate, New Year's cake (3 lbs. flour, 1½ lbs. powdered sugar, 1 lb. butter, 1 pt. milk, with a teaspoonful of soda dissolved in it, juice of a lemon. Cut into shapes to bake).

Breakfast.—Corn beef hash, cold snipe, corn meal griddle-cakes (scald half a pint of Indian meal, half a pint dry, do. flour, and stir all into a pint of milk, with a table-spoonful of butter, and one egg. Spread very thin on the griddle). Rolls, dry toast, tea and coffee.

Dinner

Celery Soup.—Blanch the heads of two bunches of celery in warm water, and put them in a stewpan of broth made from boiled chicken, with a lump of sugar. Boil an hour, until soft enough to pass through a sieve; add a cup of milk, and season to taste.

Roast Beef, with potatoes, beans, tomatoes, and spiced currants.

Oyster Pie.

Cold Boiled Ham.

Dessert

Apple Puffs.—Pare and core apples, stew until tender, and when cold mix with sugar, grated lemon, and a little quince marmalade. Put in thin paste, and bake ¼ of an hour.

Soft Boiled Custard.

Macaroons, grapes, apples, and figs.

Tea, or Lunch

Broiled smoked salmon, sliced ham, steam toast, Graham crackers, assorted cakes, currant jelly, bread and butter, tea and chocolate.

MONDAY

Breakfast.—Beefsteak broiled, cold tongue, baked potatoes, cracker toast (made of Boston hard crackers dipped in boiling milk, thickened with butter and flour), corn pone. (Take a pint of meal and scald it, and when cold, add 2 eggs, salt, and a cup of milk. Heat a round cake-pan, and butter well; then put the pone in, and bake ½ an hour with a quick fire). Tea and coffee.

Dinner

Chicken Soup with Tomato.—Boil an old fowl slowly until it falls to pieces, season with salt, whole pepper, and 2 onions. Strain it, add two cups of tomato, and boil well together.

Frost Fish Fried.

Roast Turkey, with currant jelly, mashed potatoes, and stewed celery.

Sweetbreads.—Parboil them slightly, and fry a light brown, with some mushroom catsup in the gravy.

Dessert

Custard Cream of Chocolate.—Grate 2 oz. of spiced chocolate into a pint of milk; put into a stewpan, and add the yolks of 6 eggs. Stir over the fire until it thickens.

Bread Pudding.—1 qt. of bread crumbs, covered with milk, cinnamon, and nutmeg. Stir in, when hot, ¼ lb. of butter, ¼ lb. of sugar, and mix well together. When cool, add 6 eggs, and bake one hour in a deep dish.

Oranges, nuts, and raisins.

Cold roast veal, sardines, Graham bread, French rolls, preserved pears, tea and chocolate, ginger cup-cake (5 eggs, 2 teacups of molasses, 2 do. brown sugar rolled fine, 2 do. butter, 1 cup of milk, 5 cups flour, ½ cup of powdered allspice and cloves, ½ cup ginger, ½ teaspoonful soda melted in vinegar).

TUESDAY

Breakfast.—Codfish balls, cold turkey, muffins (1 qt. milk, 2 eggs, 2 spoonfuls of yeast, do. flour, butter size of an egg, melted in the milk, and a little salt. Warm the milk and add the rest; let it rise, and bake on a griddle). Corn bread, rolls, tea and coffee.

Dinner

Sago Soup.—Take 2 qts. of gravy soup, made of beef, thicken with sago to the consistency of pea soup, and season with catsup.

Codfish, with oyster sauce.

Chicken Pillau, with potatoes, fried parsnips, and stewed celery. (Put a large fat chicken, old or young, into a pot, with 1 carrot, onion, and a sprig of sweet herbs. Boil and skim. When the chicken is half cooked add a pint of tomatoes, cut up (fresh or canned), and a little broken mace. When it is done enough to eat as boiled fowl, take it up; take out the carrot and onion, and measure the liquor. There should be about 3 pints. To each 2½ cups of soup, put 1 of rice, and when it has boiled ten minutes, stir in a piece of butter, size of an egg. Before putting in the rice, pepper and salt the broth, and when it is tender (but not too soft) take it up. Serve in an oval dish, the fowl in the middle of the rice).

Croquettes of Calf's Brains.—Blanch the brains, and beat them up with one or two chopped sage leaves, pepper, salt, a few bread crumbs soaked in milk, and 1 egg. Roll them into balls, and fry a light brown.

Dessert

Apple Pie.—Pare and quarter apples, scald in sugar and water, and grate the rind of a lemon over them. Add the juice of the lemon, ½ doz. whole cloves, butter size of a walnut, and fill up the dish with the syrup. Use puff paste.

Almond Custard.—One pt. of cream, do. milk, ½ lb. shelled sweet almonds, 2 oz. bitter almonds, 4 tablespoonfuls rose-water, ¼ lb. white sugar, the yolks of 8 eggs, ½ teaspoon oil of lemon. Blanch the almonds, and pound to a paste, mixing the rose-water with it. Beat the eggs very light, and add with the sugar. Stir all gradually into the cream and milk, and beat well together. Stir on the fire till thick, and when cold, add the whites beaten to a froth.

Figs and pecan nuts.

Tea, or Lunch

Cold ham, potted fish, Indian griddle-cakes, cheese, brown biscuit (3 quarts Graham flour, put into one of milk and water, with a tablespoonful of butter, a teaspoonful of soda, and a little salt). Preserved pine-apple, tea. Harrison cake (5 cups flour, 1½ butter, 2½ sugar, 1 molasses, 1 cream, 4 eggs, 1 lb. raisins, citron, and mixed spice. Bake 3 hours).

Breakfast.—Broiled liver, cold venison, potato cakes fried, milk toast of Graham bread, rolls, tea and coffee.

Dinner

Mock Turtle Soup.—Take half a calf's head, fresh, and unstripped of skin, remove the brains, and clean the head carefully in hot water, leaving it in cold water for an hour. Then put it into 6 qts. warm water, with 2 lbs. veal, do. pork, a roasted onion stuck with cloves, a rind of lemon, 2 sliced carrots, a bunch of herbs, and a head of celery. Let it boil slowly 2 hours; then take out the head and pork. Make forcemeat balls of the brains and tongue, break the bones of the head, put all into the soup, and boil 2 hours more. Put into a small stewpan a piece of butter, onions sliced thin, with parsley, thyme, mace, and allspice. Add flour to thicken, and stir into the soup slowly. Boil gently 1 hour more, pass through a sieve, season with salt, cayenne, lemon-juice, and a pint of Madeira wine. Add mushrooms if desired, and serve with lemons cut in quarters.

Fried Eels.

Broiled Woodcock, with squash, sweet potatoes, and hominy.

Boiled Corn Beef.

Woodcock.

A woodcock, skewered through the eye and ready for broiling or roasting. Acton, *Modern Cookery*, 220.

Dessert

Cranberry Pie.

Burnt Cream.—Make a rich custard without sugar, flavor with lemon, and when cold, sift white sugar thickly over it, and brown in the oven.

Oranges and grapes.

Tea, or Lunch

Fried oysters, ham cake, hominy, dry toast, preserved damsons, bread and butter, chocolate, pound cake (1 lb. flour, do. powdered sugar, 1 lb. butter, 10 eggs, ½ glass of wine, do. brandy, do. rose-water, mixed; 12 drops essence lemon, 1 tablespoonful mixed spice).

Breakfast.—Turkey hash, pickled tripe, fried potatoes, buckwheat cakes, brown and white bread, tea and coffee.

Dinner

Rice Soup.—Make a beef soup, boil 5 hours, then strain and add a cup of rice, same of tomato, pepper, and salt.

Fried Halibut.

Boiled Mutton, caper sauce, with baked potatoes, canned sweet corn, and turnips.

Calf's Liver Stewed.—Cut the liver in pieces, lard nicely, and spread chopped parsley, pepper, and salt over them. Put a small piece of butter well mixed with flour in the bottom of a stewpan, put in the liver, and let it cook gently in its own juices until done.

Dessert

College Pudding.—Take ½ lb. of grated bread crumbs, suet (chopped fine), and currants; mix with 4 oz. of flour and 1 egg. Beat in a glass of brandy, season with nutmeg, and boil 3 hours in a mould. Serve with cold sauce.

Lemon Jelly.—One qt. calf's foot stock, ½ pt. lemon juice, ¾ lb. of sugar, the rind of 2 lemons cut *thin*, and the whites and shells of 5 eggs. Boil 20 minutes, and throw in a teacup of cold water; then let it boil 5 minutes longer. Take from the fire and let it stand ½ an hour covered close. Then run through a bag till clear.

Apples, nuts, and dates.

Tea, or Lunch

Cold woodcock, broiled herring, cracker toast, French bread and butter, currant jelly, tea, Turk's cap (1 pint cream, 7 eggs, ½ lb. flour, and salt; bake quickly).

FRIDAY

Breakfast.—Mutton chops, minced codfish, with egg, stewed potatoes, rice cakes, gems (wheat flour, unbolted, mixed with water and salt, baked in a roll pan on the top of the range), cold bread, tea, and coffee.[4]

Dinner

Clam Soup.—Strain the clams, and put on the liquor to boil; beat a spoonful of butter and 1 of flour together, with pepper, and stir into cold water; add to the soup with the clams chopped fine, and when nearly done, add a little milk.

Baked Whitefish.

Boiled Turkey, oyster sauce, with potatoes, squash, and sweet corn.

Ris de Veau.—Blanch 3 sweetbreads, and simmer in a well-flavored gravy till quite done. Have ready 3 round trays of oiled paper, and lay them in, lightly wetted with gravy, fine crumbs of bread, pepper, salt, and a little nutmeg. Do slowly on a gridiron, and serve in the cases.

Dessert

Peach Pie.

Fancy Cakes

Figs, nuts, and prunes.

Tea, or Lunch

Veal cake. (Bone a breast of veal, and cut in slices. Cut also slices of ham, and boil 6 eggs hard; butter a deep pan, and place all in layers, one over the other, cutting the eggs in slices, and seasoning with cayenne, chopped herbs, anchovy, or any high-flavored sauce. Cover, and bake 4 hours, and when taken from the oven lay a weight upon it; when cold, turn it out.) Cold roast beef, English pickles, crackers assorted, strawberry jam, rolls, plain cake (4 lbs. flour, 2 lbs. currants, and ½ lb. of butter, with clove, caraway seeds, and lemon peel, grated to the taste. Wet with milk, and ½ pt. yeast).

A relatively intricate mould for cake or blancmange, a popular gelled custard. Acton, *Modern Cookery*, 319.

SATURDAY

Breakfast.—Venison steak, cold boiled mutton, waffles, Indian banock,[5] bread and butter, cocoa and coffee.

Dinner

Vermicelli Soup.—Plain beef, without vegetables; when strained, add vermicelli.

Striped Bass, Broiled.

Boiled Beef, sauce piquant, with tomatoes, potatoes, and parsnips, boiled.

Boil the *rump* slowly for 5 hours; make a strong gravy of veal, ham, 2 spoonfuls of vinegar, parsley, cloves, onions, and herbs. Strain, and add mushrooms, capers, and a glass of brandy.

Grouse Roasted.

Dessert

Mince Pie.—Take 2 lbs. of beef chopped fine, 2 lbs. stoned raisins, 2 lbs. currants, 1 lb. sultana raisins, 2 lbs. apples, ¾ lb. sugar, 2 lbs. suet, the juice of 2 lemons, and the rind of 1 chopped fine, ¼ lb. of mixed spice, 2 glasses of brandy, 2 oz. of citron, and 2 of candied lemon peel. Mix well together in a jar. It will improve by lying a few days. Use puff paste.

Blanc Mange.—Boil 1½ oz. of isinglass, 3 oz. of sweet and 6 oz. of bitter almonds, (well pounded,) in a quart of milk. Sweeten, strain through a napkin, and put in the mould.

Fruit and nuts.

Tea, or Lunch

Cold boiled turkey, scalloped oysters. (Dry the oysters with a cloth, and spread in layers in a deep dish, sprinkling each layer with pepper and salt, butter, and bread crumbs or rolled cracker. Bake 20 minutes.) Muffins, bread and butter, raspberry jam, Madeira buns (beat 8 oz. of butter to a cream, and add 2 eggs; take 14 oz. of flour, 6 of white sugar, ½ nutmeg, one teaspoonful ginger, and a spoonful of caraway seeds. Mix and work into the butter, and beat ½ an hour. Add a wineglass of sherry, and bake quick in patty pans). Tea.

SUNDAY

Breakfast.—Liver hash, cold grouse, chipped potatoes, gems of cornmeal, brown bread milk toast, buckwheat cakes. (To 3 pts. of buckwheat flour mixed into a batter, add one teaspoonful of carbonate of soda, and one of tartaric acid dissolved in water. Bake at once.) Tea and coffee.

Dinner

Bean Soup.—Soak a pint of small white beans over night, boil slowly 3 hours, adding a small piece of ham when half done. Season well, and strain.

Hard-shell Crabs.

Roast Beef, with rice, sweet potatoes, and baked tomatoes.

Potted Pigeons.—Stew the gizzards and livers, chopped fine; add grated ham, bread crumbs, and herbs. Make into a forcemeat, rolling it round the yolk of a hard-boiled egg, and stuff the pigeons. Put into a stew-pan with water and a little butter; add gravy of the gizzards, a little flour, and an onion. Stew gently until done, adding a glass of wine.

Dessert

German Puffs.—Put ½ lb. of butter into ½ a pt. of milk, and when it boils add a cup of flour; beat well together, and when cold add 6 eggs well beaten, with ½ cup of sugar, and grated lemon. Bake in a moderate oven.

Pomme Mange.—Peel and core 1 lb. of apples, and add to ½ lb. of sugar and ½ pt. of water. Boil till quite stiff, with some lemon peel. Put in a mould.

Oranges, bananas, and nuts.

Tea, or Lunch

Cold lamb, smoked salmon, broiled. Graham dry toast, cheese, milk biscuit, preserved grapes, rice cake (1 lb. ground rice, do. lump sugar sifted, 8 eggs well beaten, the rind of a lemon. Beat all half an hour; and bake 1½ hours). Tea.

April

MONDAY

Breakfast.—Fresh shad broiled, poached eggs, corn bannock, cold roast veal, dry toast, rice cakes, rolls and bread. Tea and coffee.

Dinner

Soup à la Bisque.—¼ lb. rice, and 12 crabs, (soft shell); boil in good broth, and when done pound, and rub through a sieve. Fill the heads of the crabs with fish stuffing, and add a little butter.

Bluefish Broiled.

Roast Veal, stuffed, with Bermuda potatoes, raw tomatoes dressed, and asparagus.

Lobster Plain.

Dessert

Jelly Tarts of Puff Paste.

Cocoanut Pudding.—Grate a cocoanut after taking off the brown skin, mix with 3 oz. white powdered sugar, and ½ peel of a lemon; mix well with milk, put in a tin lined with paste, and bake not too brown.

Bananas, and nuts.

Tea, or Lunch

Veal cake, cold tongue, Graham dry toast, preserved pears, rolls, crackers and cheese, cup cake with almonds.

TUESDAY

Breakfast.—Veal hash, omelet, stewed potatoes, wheat gems, brown bread cream toast, rolls. Tea and coffee, potted fish.

Dinner

Black Bean Soup.—Thicken a strong beef broth, strained, with black beans.

Baked Shad.

Roast Lamb, mint sauce, with baked potatoes, asparagus, and spinach.

Pigeon Pie.—Cut a nice rump steak into small pieces, and cover the bottom of a dish, add seasoning, and sweet herbs. Boil 2 eggs hard, chop the livers fine, add bread crumbs, butter, and seasoning, and stuff the pigeons. Put in with the steak, cover with water or gravy, and bake with a paste.

Dessert

Apple Dumplings.—1 large apple, quartered, cored, and put together, covered with a thin paste, and boiled till done. As many as are needed, serve with hot sauce.

Chocolate Pudding.—Boil 1 pt. milk, dissolve in it 1 oz. of chocolate, sweeten with loaf sugar, add the yolks of 8, and the whites of 4 eggs well beaten; strain, and pour into a mould, buttered and papered; steam for ½ an hour; let it settle for 10 minutes, and serve with the following sauce: boil ½ stick vanilla in 1 pt. milk till it is reduced one half; strain, sweeten, and thicken with arrowroot.

Figs, and nuts.

Tea, or Lunch

Ham sandwiches, (chop the ham fine, and season with mustard, pepper, and salt, spread between thin slices buttered bread,) cold game, minced codfish, rolls, toast, stewed prunes, kringles. (Beat well yolks of 8, and whites of 2 eggs, mix with 4 oz. butter, warmed, 1 lb. flour, and 4 oz. sugar to a paste. Roll into thick biscuits, and bake on tin plates.)

Breakfast.—Blue fish, scrambled eggs, baked potatoes, cold chicken, Indian griddle-cakes, rolls, tea and coffee.

Dinner

Turnip Soup.—Scrape fine 6 large turnips into 2 qts. strong beef soup, with 2 onions fried in butter. Let it simmer slowly, then rub through a sieve till smooth.

Boiled Halibut, oyster sauce.

Roast Beef, with Yorkshire pudding, and vegetables. 1 pt. boiling milk to a small loaf of bread, crumbed fine, 4 eggs, a little salt and flour. Bake in a tin under the drippings of the beef.

Matelote of Fish.—Cut into small pieces any white fish, put into a stewpan with 1 oz. of butter to brown, adding ½ pt. wine, do. good gravy, spice, and seasoning, a sliced carrot and turnip. Take the fish out carefully, keep hot, and thicken the gravy with butter and flour, adding 6 button onions which have been scalded, the same of mushrooms and oysters, lemon-juice, and cayenne. Pour boiling hot on the fish.

Dessert

Dried Apple Pie.

Rice Custards.—Sweeten a pint of milk, and boil, sifting in ground rice till thick; take off the fire, and add 3 eggs, beaten; stir again over the fire for three minutes, and put into cups that have lain in cold water without wiping. When cold turn out, and pour soft custard around them, with currant jelly on the top of each one.

Prunes, oranges, and candied fruits.

Tea, or Lunch

Mutton kidneys, fried. (Cut in thin slices, flour and fry quickly, serve in good gravy). Roast beef deviled, sardines, apple fritters, (yolks of 6 eggs, whites of 3; beat well and strain, then add 1 pt. milk, a little salt, ½ nutmeg grated, and a glass of brandy. Mix into a thick batter with flour, slice the apples in round, taking out the core, dust with sugar, (let them stand an hour or two) and dip each slice in batter, frying in boiling lard.) Rolls, toast, grape jelly, chocolate.

Breakfast.—Codfish balls, fried Indian pudding, boiled eggs, cold lamb, milk toast, rolls, tea, and coffee.

Dinner

Chicken Soup.—Boiled, strained, with rice and seasoning.

Spanish Mackerel.

Roast Ducks, with asparagus, lettuce, and tomatoes, currant jelly.

Breaded Veal Cutlets.

Dessert

Brandy Pudding.—Line a mould with stoned raisins or dried cherries, then with thin slices of French roll, next to which put macaroons, then again fruit, rolls, and cakes, till the mould be full, sprinkling in by degrees 2 wine-glasses of brandy. Beat 4 eggs, put to a pint of milk or cream, lightly sweetened, ½ a nutmeg, and the rind of ½ a lemon grated. Let the liquid sink into the solid part, then tie tight with a floured cloth, and boil 1 hour. Keep the mould right side up. Serve with sauce.

Cream Fritters.—One and a half pts. of flour to 1 pt. of milk; beat to a froth with 6 eggs; add 1 pt. cream, ½ nutmeg, a teaspoonful salt, mix well, and fry in small cakes.

Bananas and nuts.

Tea, or Lunch

Roast oysters, cold miroton of veal,[6] minced fresh fish, Boston crackers, with anchovy sauce, (soak the crackers split in cold water, butter and spread on the sauce thickly.) Muffins, bread, quince marmalade, sponge cake, (1 coffee-cup sugar, do. flour, 4 eggs.) Tea and cocoa.

FRIDAY

Breakfast.—Shad roes fried brown, omelet with parsley, lamb chops, chipped potatoes, brown bread, rolls, tea and coffee.

Dinner

New England Clam Chowder.—Fry thin slices of pork in a deep pot; lay in the head and shoulders of a fresh cod, cut in pieces, put in layers, the pork between; season with pepper, salt, and a few cloves; fill up with water and boil; when nearly done add a pint of milk, and 6 Boston crackers split open.

Broiled Shad.

Roast Chickens, with potatoes, asparagus, and tomatoes.

Ragout of Veal.—Fry 2 lbs. of veal till brown, then put into a stew-pan with 6 onions, pepper, and mixed spice, add boiling water, and let it stew slowly for 4 hours. Serve with pickled walnuts, or capers, in the gravy.

Dessert

Almond Pudding.—Two and-a-half oz. white bread crumbs, steeped in a pint of cream, (or milk) ½ pt. blanched almonds pounded to a paste, with a little water, yolks of 6 eggs and whites of 3, beaten; mix all together, and add 3 oz sugar, and 1 oz. beaten butter. Stir over the fire till thick, and bake in a puff paste.

Blueberry Pie.—Use canned fruit.

Oranges, almonds, and raisins.

Tea, or Lunch

Clam fritters, cold tongue, potted fish, stewed potatoes, hot brown bread, steam toast, preserved plums, buns.

SATURDAY

Breakfast.—Fresh trout, fried chicken, with cream, water cresses, scrambled eggs, Graham biscuit, corn bread, rolls, tea and coffee.

Dinner

Mullagatawnee Soup.—Six onions, and ½ lb. butter, pound well, and add 3 spoonfuls curry powder, a little cayenne and salt. Beat all together with some India pickle and flour,[7] and stir into 3 qts. of strong beef soup. Let it boil half an hour, rub through a sieve, and serve with rice.

Baked Bluefish.

Beef à la Mode, with turnips, carrots and potatoes. A round of beef, weighing 20 lbs., rub with salt, and tie with tape; chop the marrow from the bone, ¼ lb. suet, herbs, thyme, and parsley; add 2 grated nutmegs, ½ oz. cloves, do. mace, tablespoon pepper, do. salt, and 2 glasses Madeira wine; cut 1 lb. pork in small pieces, make incisions in the beef and slip in, then lay in a deep dish, and cover with the seasoning. Bake or stew slowly (with water in the dish) 12 hours. If to be eaten hot, begin the night before. Add wine and a beaten egg in the gravy.

Sweetbreads, Fried.

Dessert

Bread Pudding.—One pt. bread-crumbs, covered with milk, add cinnamon, lemon-peel, and grated nutmeg; put them on a gentle fire until the crumbs are well soaked. Take out the cinnamon, and lemon-peel, beat the milk and crumbs together, add 4 eggs well beaten, 1 oz. butter, 2 oz. sugar, ½ lb. currants, and boil it one hour.

Pine-apples, and macaroons.

Oranges, and nuts.

Tea, or Lunch

Oyster pie, cold corned beef, eggs on toast, cranberry jelly, biscuit, Turk's cap, sponge cake.

SUNDAY

Breakfast.—Veal chops, with tomato sauce, fried potatoes, cold ham, poached eggs, corn bannock, bread, tea and coffee.

Dinner

Oyster Soup.

Fried Perch.

Boiled Chicken, with potatoes, asparagus, macaroni, and rice.

Broiled Pigeons.—Cut the pigeons down the back, flatten, and truss. Egg them both sides, season, dip in chopped herbs and crumbs, a little warmed butter sprinkled over them, and broil a light brown.

Dessert

Tipsy Pudding.—Lay in a dish slices of sponge or pound cake, well soaked in brandy, and pour over them a rich soft custard.

Jam Tarts.

Pine-apples and oranges.

Tea, or Lunch

Cold à la mode beef, broiled ham, mashed potato cakes fried, cheese, crackers, preserves, pound cake with fruit.

MONDAY

Breakfast.—Fried trout, pickled tongue, potted game, steam toast, Graham biscuit, boiled eggs, cucumbers. Tea and coffee.

Dinner

Green Pea Soup.—Boil 1 qt. fresh peas in salt water, with a handful of parsley and sorrel, until perfectly tender. Drain, and pound in a mortar, and mix gradually into veal or beef broth. Season with pepper and salt, fry some boiled onions and lettuce, with bread cut into dice, and put into the soup before serving, also a few heads of boiled asparagus.

Boiled Salmon, melted butter.

Broiled Chicken, with peas, string beans, and potatoes.

Fricandels of Veal.—Chop the fat and lean of 3 lbs. of a loin of veal very fine; then soak a French roll in some milk; beat 3 eggs; add pepper, salt, and mace. Make the mixture somewhat in the shape of a small chicken, rub it with egg and bread-crumbs, fry until brown, pour off the fat, boil water in the pan, and stew the fricandels in this gravy; two will make a handsome dish; thicken the gravy.

Dessert

Macaroni Pudding.—Simmer 1 or 2 oz. of pipe macaroni in a pint of milk, with a bit of lemon and cinnamon, till tender; put it into a dish with milk, 2 or 3 yolks of eggs, but only 1 white; sugar, nutmeg, a spoonful of peach water, and ½ glass raisin wine. Bake with paste around the edges.

Bohemian Cream.—Rub a pint of fresh strawberries through a sieve, add 6 oz. powdered sugar, the juice of a lemon, 1½ oz. isinglass dissolved in ½ pt. water. Mix all together, and set on the ice, stirring till it begins to set. Whip a pint of cream to a froth, and stir into the strawberries, letting the mould remain on ice till wanted. Then put it into warm water for an instant, and turn out.

Cherries and nuts.

Tea, or Lunch

Radishes, cucumbers, cold veal, potted fish, broiled smoked salmon, muffins, rolls, sponge cake, strawberries. Tea.

TUESDAY

Breakfast.—Cold birds, omelet, minced salt fish, cream toast, radishes, water-cresses, rolls, tea and coffee, strawberries.

Skewered songbirds. Blot, *Hand-Book of Practical Cookery*, 278.

Dinner

Gumbo Soup.

Trout.

Roast Veal, with asparagus, lettuce, peas, and potatoes.

Pigeons, with Peas.—Put the pigeons into a stewpan with a little butter, just to stiffen; then take them out, put some small slices of bacon into the pan, give a fine color, draw them, and add a spoonful of flour to the butter; then put in the pigeons and bacon, moisten by degrees with gravy, and bring it to the consistency of sauce; boil it; season with parsley, young onions, and let it simmer; when half done put in a quart of peas; shake them often; and when ready thicken the peas with flour and butter. There should be no gravy left.

Dessert

Quaking Pudding.—Scald 1 qt. cream (or milk); and when almost cold add 4 eggs well beaten, 1½ spoonfuls flour, some nutmeg, and sugar; tie it close in a buttered cloth; boil 1 hour, and serve with wine sauce.

Crème au Marasquin.—Whip a pint of cream until it thickens, add powdered sugar, a glass of maraschino, and 1 oz. isinglass dissolved in water. The latter must be liquid, but cold.

Strawberries and cream, nuts.

Tea, or Lunch

Cold boiled ham, cucumbers, dried beef with cream, biscuit, rolls, strawberries, bread, cake. Tea and chocolate.

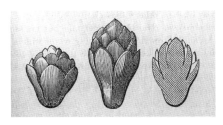

Radishes like these, cut in decorative shapes with a small knife, were meant to be served with butter. Blot, *Hand-Book of Practical Cookery*, 341.

WEDNESDAY

Breakfast.—Minced veal, pickled shad roes, potted game, corn muffins, dry toast, radishes, rolls, scrambled eggs. Tea and coffee.

Dinner

Mutton Broth.

Baked Pike, caper sauce.

Mutton Pillan, with peas, beans, and potatoes. Take ½ lb. neck of mutton, boil it well, then cut it into small pieces, and fry it in butter; then let it simmer ½ an hour with 2 cups boiled rice, a few cloves, a little cinnamon, and some cardamoms.

Squabs, Roasted.

Dessert

Plum Pudding, not rich.—Four oz. each of grated bread, suet, and stoned raisins, mix with 2 well-beaten eggs, 4 spoonfuls of milk, and a little salt. Boil 4 hours. A spoonful of brandy, sugar, and nutmeg, in melted butter, may be used as sauce.

Raspberry Cream.—Boil 1 oz. isinglass in 1½ pts. milk; strain through a hair sieve; boil 1½ pts. cream; when cool add ½ pt. raspberry juice to it; then add the milk, stir well, sweeten, and add a glass of brandy. Whisk it till nearly cold, then put in a mould.

Strawberries and nuts.

Tea, or Lunch

Cold tongue, miroton of veal, cucumbers, radishes, strawberries, pound cake, waffles, toast, rolls, tea and chocolate.

THURSDAY

Breakfast.—Boiled chicken, clam fritters, muffins, steam toast, hot brown bread, cucumbers, strawberries, tea and coffee, boiled eggs.

Dinner

Tomato Soup.

Lobster.

Roast Beef, with peas, lima beans, and potatoes.

Rissoles.—Pound cold meat, season, and mix with a little good gravy and butter. Roll paste into oval pieces, lay a spoonful on one end, double it over, press the edges together, and scallop them. Brush over with yolk of egg, and fry brown.

Dessert

Cherry Pie.

Orange Butter.—Boil 6 eggs hard, beat them in a mortar with 2 oz. fine sugar, 3 oz. butter, and 2 oz. blanched almonds, beaten to a paste; moisten with orange-flower water, and when all is mixed rub it through a colander on a dish. Served with sweet biscuits.

Strawberries, pine-apple, and nuts.

Tea, or Lunch

Potted shrimps, dried chipped beef, milk toast, rolls, corn pone, strawberries, radishes, chocolate.

FRIDAY

Breakfast.—Cold roast beef, smelts, omelet, chipped potatoes, rice cakes, Graham bread, water cresses, radishes, cucumbers, tea and coffee.

Dinner

Soup à la Bisque.

Fresh Mackerel.

Roast Lamb, with peas, asparagus, tomatoes, and lettuce.

Sweetbreads.

Lobster Pie.—Cut 2 boiled lobsters in pieces, and lay in a dish; beat the spawn in the mortar; put the shells on to boil in some water, with 3 spoonfuls of vinegar, pepper, salt, and some mace. A large piece of butter rolled in flour must be added when the good is obtained. Pour into the dish strained, stew in some crumbs, and put a paste over all. Bake only till the paste is done.

Dessert

Rhubarb Pie.

Lemon Syllabub.—Grate the peel of a lemon with *lump sugar*, and dissolve the sugar in ¾ pt. of wine; add the juice of half a lemon, and ¼ pt. cream. Whisk the whole until properly thick, and put into glasses.

Strawberries, cherries, and bonbons.

Tea, or Lunch

Kidney Toast.—(Take cold veal kidneys, cut in small pieces; pound the fat in a mortar, with salt, pepper, and a boiled onion. Bind all together with beaten whites of eggs, heap it on toast, cover with yolks beaten, sprinkle with bread crumbs, and bake in the oven.) Salt fish broiled, cold ham, raised biscuit, corn-bread, fruit, cucumbers, and radishes. Lemon cheese-cakes.—(Mix 4 oz. sifted lump sugar, with 4 oz. butter; then add yolks of 2 and white of 1 egg, the rind of 3 lemons chopped fine and the juice of 1½, 1 Savoy biscuit,[8] some blanched almonds, and 3 spoonfuls of brandy. Bake in patty pans.) Tea and cocoa.

SATURDAY

Breakfast.—Broiled fresh salmon, beef-steak, fried potatoes, cream toast, Graham biscuit, potted tongue, rolls, tea and coffee.

Dinner

Bean Soup.

Soles, Fried.

Boiled Leg of Mutton, with lettuce, peas, spinach, and potatoes.

Beefsteaks, with Mushrooms.

Chicken Patties.

Dessert

Sweetmeat Pudding.—Cover a dish with thin puff paste, and lay in it 1 oz. each of candied lemon, orange, and citron, sliced thin. Beat the yolks of 8 and whites of 2 eggs, and mix with 8 oz. butter warmed, and some white sugar. Pour all over the sweetmeats, and bake 1 hour in a moderate oven.

Flemish Cream.—Dissolve ½ oz. isinglass in 1 pt. water, strain it to ¼ pt. cream; add 1 glass brandy, and whisk to a light froth. Put in a mould.

Cherries and candied fruits.

Tea, or Lunch

Cold lamb, sandwiches of ham, sardines, waffles, dry toast, rolls, cucumbers, strawberries, small pound-cakes, tea.

SUNDAY

Breakfast.—Broiled kidneys, with tomato sauce, cold veal, scrambled eggs, Graham bread, gems, rolls, bread, tea and coffee, radishes.

Dinner

Asparagus Soup.—To 2 qts. of good beef or veal broth, put 4 onions, 2 turnips, and some sweet herbs, with the white parts of a hundred young asparagus. If large, half the quantity will do. Let them simmer till tender enough to rub through a tammy,[9] then strain and season, adding boiled tops of asparagus.

Boiled Salmon.

Chickens à la Carmelite, with peas, beans, and potatoes. Put a piece of butter, size of a walnut, in a stewpan; as it melts dredge in flour, and when well mixed add a teacup of milk. Cut up the chickens and add them, with pepper, an onion, and mace. Stew till tender, adding milk and water, if too dry. Take out the chickens, and cover with chopped parsley and lemon-juice mixed; thicken the sauce, and add a glass of white-wine.

Beefsteak, Broiled.

Dessert

Mother Eve's Pudding.—Grate ¾ lb. bread; mix with same quantity chopped suet, the same of apples and currants; mix with these 4 eggs, and the rind of half a lemon shred fine. Boil in a shape 3 hours, and serve with sauce.

French Flummery.—Boil slowly 2 oz. isinglass shavings in a quart of cream, 15 minutes. Stir, and sweeten with loaf sugar; add a spoonful of rose-water, and one of orange-flower water. Strain into a form.

Cherries, strawberries, and nuts.

Tea, or Lunch

Ham cake, cold corned beef, minced salt fish, crackers and cheese, toast, corn bannock, biscuit, macaroons, strawberries, cucumbers, tea.

MONDAY

Breakfast.—Broiled halibut, cold tongue, stewed potatoes, raw sliced tomatoes, omelet, rolls, dry toast, cucumbers, fruit, tea and coffee.

Dinner

Vegetable Marrow Soup.—Boil the marrow and strain, then add to beef or veal broth, thicken with 2 spoonfuls of arrowroot, and a little cream. Do not allow it to boil after the latter is added.

Stewed Codfish.—Cut in slices an inch thick, lay in a large stewpan, and season with salt, pepper, a bunch of herbs, an onion, ½ pt. white-wine, and ¼ pt. water. Cover close, and let it simmer five minutes, then squeeze in the juice of a lemon, a piece of butter size of an egg, rolled in flour, and a blade of mace. Let it stew slowly till done, and take out the herbs and onions.

Chicken Pillan, with squash, corn, beans, and potatoes.

Baked Calves' Head.—Wash the head, and place in a large earthen dish, on large iron skewers, laid across the top of the dish; cover it with bread crumbs, grated nutmeg, chopped sweet herbs, a little fine-cut lemon, and flour; thick pieces of butter in the eyes, and all over the head, then flour it again; put in the dish a piece of beef, cut small; herbs, an onion, pepper, mace, cloves, a pint of water, and bake the head a fine brown. Boil the brains with sage, separately. When the head is done enough take it out, and set by the fire to keep warm, then stir all in the dish together, and boil in a stewpan; strain it off, put it in the saucepan again with a piece of butter rolled in flour, the brains and sage chopped fine, a spoonful of catsup, and two spoonfuls of wine. Beat well together, and serve in the dish with the head. Leave the tongue in the head.

Dessert

Baked Custard.

Whipt Cream.—A qt. cream, the whites of 4 eggs, ½ pt. white-wine, ¼ lb. powdered sugar, 12 drops essence of lemon. Beat to a froth, and put in glasses with a little jelly in the bottom.

Peaches and melons.

Tea, or Lunch

Cold tongue, minced beef on toast, peaches and cream, cucumbers, corn pone, boiled rice, dry toast, tea, lemonade.

TUESDAY

Breakfast.—Corned beef hash, cold roast chicken, boiled eggs, steam toast, raised biscuit, lettuce, huckleberries, rolls, coffee and tea.

Dinner

Giblet Soup.

Baked Pike.—Stuff the pike with grated bread, 2 hard boiled eggs chopped fine, a little nutmeg, lemon peel, and the roe or liver chopped; then lay it in the dish, with the tail in the mouth; put pieces of butter all over it, and sprinkle with flour. Garnish with toast and lemon, and serve with melted butter.

Boiled Corned Beef, with corn, squash, beans, and baked potatoes.

Duck, with Peas.—Put the duck in a deep stewpan, with a piece of butter, (singe it first,) flour it, and turn it two or three times, then pour out all the fat. Put to the duck a pint of good gravy, do. peas, 2 lettuces cut small, sweet herbs, pepper and salt; cover close and stew half an hour. When well done thicken with a little butter and flour, shake all together three or four minutes, and serve in a dish, the duck with the sauce poured over it.

Dessert

Cream Pudding.—Boil 1 qt. of cream with a blade of mace, and half a nutmeg, grated; let it cool; beat the yolks of 8 eggs, and whites of 3, and mix them with a spoonful of flour, ¼ lb. blanched almonds, beaten with rose-water, and by degrees mix in the cream. Tie in a thick cloth well floured, boil half an hour, and when done throw fine sugar and melted butter over it.

Peaches and Cream.

Melons, plums, and bonbons.

Tea, or Lunch

Broiled smoked salmon, lobster salad, corn pone, Graham biscuit, blackberries, peaches and cream, macaroons, and small sponge cakes, dry toast, tea and chocolate.

A blackberry. *American Practical Cookery Book*, 166.

WEDNESDAY

Breakfast.—Broiled spring chicken, brown bread, cream toast, cold ham, potted fish, rolls, scrambled eggs, blackberries, cucumbers, tea and coffee.

Dinner

Codling Soup.—Take the meat from a young cod, pound it in a mortar, with some shred parsley, and bread crumbs soaked in milk; make the mixture up into balls with an egg, seasoned well. Stew down 2 or 3 codlings or haddocks into broth, strain it, pulp the meat through a sieve, boil it with parsley roots, thicken, and serve with the forcemeat balls.

Broiled Bluefish.

Roast Beef, with corn, egg plant, squash, and rice.

Pigeon Fricassée.—Cut 8 pigeons into small pieces, and put in a stewpan with 1 pt. water and same of claret. Season with salt, pepper, mace, an onion, a bunch of herbs, a piece of butter rolled in flour; cover close, and

let them stew till there is just enough for sauce; then take out the onion and herbs, beat up the yolks of 3 eggs, push the meat to one side, and stir them into the gravy. Keep stirring till sauce is thick, then put the meat in a dish, and pour over it.

Dessert

Charlotte Russe.

Ice Cream.—Newport receipt.—1 qt. new milk, with cream to suit, 2 tablespoonfuls cornstarch, yolk of 1 egg, sugar, and flavoring to taste. Wet the starch in a little of the milk, mix with the egg, and stir into the milk boiling hot. When cool, it is ready for the freezer.

Peaches, plums, and hot-house grapes.

Tea, or Lunch

Cold veal, sardines, Boston crackers, with tomato catsup, cream toast, rice cakes, blackberries and huckleberries, pound-cake, rolls, gems. Tea.

THURSDAY

Breakfast.—Cold roast beef, sweetbreads fried, raw tomatoes, muffins, potted tongue, rolls and bread, berries, cucumbers. Tea and coffee.

Dinner

Green Corn Soup.

Baked Cod's Head.—Lay the head in a buttered pan, with a bundle of herbs, an onion stuck with cloves, 3 or 4 blades of mace, ½ spoonful black pepper, a small piece of lemon-peel, a bruised nutmeg, a small bit of horserad-

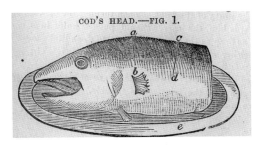

A guide to carving cod's head, a common dish of the era.
American Practical Cookery Book, 227.

ish, and a quart of water. Flour the head, and stick butter and bread crumbs over it. Bake it well, and lay it in the dish it is to be served in, covered close, and placed over hot water. Boil the liquor 3 or 4 minutes, strain it, and add a gill of wine, 2 spoonfuls of catsup, 1 of mushrooms pickled, and ¼ lb. butter rolled in flour. Stir till it is thick, and pour into the dish. Stick pieces of fried bread round the dish, and in the head.

Boiled Lamb, with baked tomatoes, corn, lima beans, and potatoes.

Brown Fricassée.—Cut chickens in small pieces, and rub with yolks of eggs; then roll them in grated bread and nutmeg, and fry a fine brown with butter. Pour off the butter, and add ½ pt. brown gravy, 1 glass white wine, a few mushrooms, salt and pepper, and a little butter rolled in flour. When thick, dish it for the table.

Dessert

Blackberry Pudding.—A good batter mixed with the fruit, boiled 1 hour, and served with wine sauce.

Kisses.—Beat the whites of 4 eggs till stiff, then stir in gradually (one spoonful at a time) 1 lb. powdered sugar, and add 12 drops essence of lemon. Lay a wet sheet of paper on a square pan, and drop at equal distances a teaspoon of stiff currant jelly with a little sugar and egg *under* each one. Then pile the froth so as to cover each lump of jelly, as round as possible. Set in a cool oven, and when colored they are done. Place the two bottoms together, lay them lightly on a sieve, and dry in a cool oven till they stick together.

Apples, peaches, and melons.

Tea, or Lunch

Cold miroton of veal, dried beef stewed in cream, waffles, crackers and cheese, bread and toast, berries and radishes, Indian pound-cake. Tea and chocolate.

FRIDAY

Breakfast.—Codfish fried, chipped potatoes, cold tongue, minced lamb, omelet, corn bread, brown bread, berries, rolls. Tea and coffee.

Dinner

Lobster Soup.—Make a stock of small fish, take the meat from 1 or 2 lobsters, and cut in small pieces; lay it aside, and break the shell, boiling it gently several hours with the stock. Make the coral into forcemeat balls, with a small piece of stock fish, bread crumbs, parsley, and egg. When the stock is done, strain, and thicken with butter and flour. Warm the lobster in it, and serve with the balls. It may be seasoned delicately with any sauce.

Boiled Soles, melted butter.

Roast Veal, with peas, beans, and potatoes à la maître d'hôtel.

Neat's Tongue Fricassée.—Boil the tongues till tender, peel, and cut in thin slices; fry them in fresh butter; then pour it out, add enough gravy for sauce, herbs, an onion, pepper, salt, mace, and a glass of white-wine; simmer all ½ an hour; take out the tongue, and strain the gravy; then put both into the pan again with yolks of 2 eggs beaten, a piece of butter size of a walnut, rolled in flour, and a little nutmeg. Shake together 5 minutes, and serve.

Dessert

Huckleberry Pie.

Apple Soufflé.—Scald and sweeten the fruit, beat through a sieve, and put in a dish. Pour a rich custard 2 inches deep over it; when cold, whip the whites of the eggs to a froth, and lay in rough pieces on the custard; sift fine sugar over it, and put in a slack oven for a short time.

Peaches and melons.

Tea, or Lunch

Ham sandwiches, salad, tongue, potted game, corn muffins, biscuit, jelly tarts, berries, cup cake. Tea.

SATURDAY

Breakfast.—Beefsteak, cold snipe, raw tomatoes, dropped eggs on toast, milk toast, berries, cucumbers, tea and coffee, rolls.

Dinner

Oxcheek Soup.—Take the meat from half an ox-head, and put in a pan with 3 sliced, fried onions, herbs, allspice, pepper, and salt, a large spoonful each. Lay the bones close on the meat, and put 1 qt. water to every pound cut meat. Cover the pan with coarse brown paper, tied closely, and let it stand in the oven 4 hours. When done, take out the bones, and pour the soup and meat into a pan. When it is to be used, take off the fat, warm the soup, and cut the meat into pieces not larger than a mouthful. Make the brains into forcemeat balls, and season highly with walnut catsup and cayenne.

Stewed Terrapin.—Boil them 10 minutes, and then take them out, remove the outer shells, and put back again. Then boil till the claws are tender. Take them out of the inner shell, taking care not to break the gall, which must be separated from the liver and thrown away; also the spongy part. Cut them into small pieces, put in a stewpan with salt, pepper, and some butter. After they have stewed a few minutes, put in a wineglass of water to each terrapin. When they have stewed 10 minutes add butter rolled in flour, and 1 glass white-wine to each one. Stew 5 minutes more, and take off. Add beaten yolks of eggs (1 yolk to 2 terrapins) well stirred in, cover tightly, let it stand 5 minutes, and serve in a deep dish.

Lamb Chops, breaded; with succotash (corn and beans), squash, and potatoes.

Lamb's Head, Stewed.—Wash, and lay in water 1 hour; take out the brains, and with a sharp penknife take out the tongue and bones, so as to leave the meat whole; chop together 2 lbs. veal, 2 lbs. beef-suet, thyme, lemon peel; nutmeg grated, 2 rolls grated and yolks of 4 eggs. Tie the head with thread, stew 2 hours in 2 qts. gravy. Make the mixture into balls, and fry in dripping; beat the brains with parsley, and fry in little cakes; strain the gravy, and season with catsup, and serve the head with the fried balls and brains around it.

Dessert

Soft Boiled Custard, frozen; with sliced peaches, curds, and whey.—Wash very clean in cold water a piece of rennet 2 inches square; wipe it dry, and pour on it lukewarm water enough to cover it. Let it stand all night, then take it out, and stir the water into a quart of warm milk. Set the milk in a warm place till it becomes a firm curd—then on the ice. Eat with wine, sugar, and nutmeg.

Melons, plums, and nuts.

Tea, or Lunch

Ham cake, cold beef, sardines, pâté de foie gras, wine jelly, sponge cake, berries, steamed toast, rolls, Indian bannock. Tea.

SUNDAY

Breakfast.—Broiled salmon, cold corned beef, mutton chops, raw tomatoes, gems, rolls, bread, berries, Indian griddle-cakes.

Dinner

Tomato Soup.—Chicken or veal broth thickened, with tomato pulp in it.

Perch.

Broiled Quail, with egg-plant, squash, corn, and tomatoes.

Ragout of Veal.—Cut a neck of veal into steaks, flatten with a rolling-pin, season with salt, pepper, and spice, lard them with bacon, lemon-peel, thyme, and dip them in yolks of eggs. Put in a pan with ½ pt. strong gravy, and stew leisurely; season high, and add mushrooms and pickles, also add a glass of wine.

Dessert

Blackberry Pie.

Lemon Pudding.—Grate the rind of a fresh lemon, and squeeze in the juice. Stir together ¼ lb. powdered sugar, and ¼ lb. butter to a cream; beat 3 eggs well and add; mix all together with a tablespoonful of wine and brandy, and a teaspoonful of rose-water; beat all very hard. Make a paste of 5 oz. flour, and ¼ lb. butter; cover a buttered soup-plate, put in the pudding, and bake a light brown.

Peaches and grapes.

Tea, or Lunch

Boiled ham, cold birds, crackers, raw tomatoes, waffles, dry toast, peaches and cream, berries, German cake—from a Hungarian Countess (1 lb. sugar, 1 lb. beaten almonds, 1 lb. citron beaten, 1 oz. mace, cinnamon and cloves mixed. Make as stiff as pie-crust, roll out an inch thick, cut in shapes, and glaze with sugar and water. It will keep a year.) Tea and chocolate.

A brand name coffee pot, a luxury few
Americans would have possessed in the 1860s.
American Practical Cookery Book, 293.

November

MONDAY

Breakfast.—Pork steak, cold quail, pickled scallops, baked potatoes, milk toast of brown bread, rolls. Tea and coffee.

Dinner

Harrico Soup.—Take mutton cutlets, trim, and fry to light brown; then stew in 3 qts. of brown gravy soup till tender. Take 2 carrots, 2 onions, celery cut fine, a glass of port wine, and one of mushroom catsup, and add to the soup, after straining. Cook till all is tender, and thicken with a little butter and flour.

Blackfish, Boiled.

Roast Beef, with lima beans, squash, and potatoes.

Spiced Veal.—Two and a half lbs. of veal well chopped, 4 crackers pounded fine, 2 eggs, 2 slices of pork chopped fine, a piece of butter size of an egg, ½ teaspoonful pepper, and same of salt. Put into a shape, cover with bread crumbs, and bake 2 hours.

Dessert

Carrot Pie.—Boil and strain 6 carrots to a pulp, add 3 pts. milk, 6 eggs, 2 tablespoonfuls butter melted, juice of ½ a lemon, and grated rind of a whole one. Sweeten and bake in a deep dish.

Sponge Pudding.—Butter a mould thickly, and fill it three parts full of small sponge cakes soaked in wine, then fill up the mould with a rich cold custard. Put a buttered paper over the mould, and bake it. Serve with wine sauce.

Plums, pears, and chestnuts.

Tea, or Lunch

Rice Cakes. (Soak ½ lb. rice over night, boil soft, drain dry, mix ¼ lb. butter with it, and set away to cool. Then stir it into a qt. of milk, stir in ½ pt. flour, and add 6 eggs with salt. Fry thin on a griddle). Cold tongue.

Potted Fish. (Boil lobsters, shrimps, or any shell-fish, pick out the meat, and put in a stew-pan with a little butter, chopped mushrooms, and a little salt. Simmer gently, then add the yolks of 2 eggs beaten with a cupful of milk or cream, and a little chopped parsley. Let all stew till of the consistency of paste, then put into a pot, and press down. When cold cover with melted butter, and tie on an oil-skin cover). French rolls, Graham bread, stewed quinces. Tea and coffee.

Cup-cake, with hickory nuts.

TUESDAY

Breakfast.—Cold turkey, sweetbreads, stewed with mushrooms, buckwheat cakes, wheaten grits with cream, rolls and bread. Coffee.

Dinner

White Soup.—Take broth made of veal, or white poultry, cut the meat off, and put the bone back, adding 2 or 3 shank-bones of mutton, and ¼ lb. fine lean bacon, with a bunch of sweet herbs, a piece of fresh lemon-peel, 2 or 3 onions, 3 blades of mace, and a dessertspoonful of white pepper. Boil all till the meat falls quite to pieces, and strain.

Trout.

Roast Prairie Chickens, with sweet potatoes, rice, and beets, spiced currants.

Hock.—One lb. rump steak, do. pork steak, ½ loaf of bread. Chop together like sausage-meat, add 2 eggs, and season with salt, pepper, and sage. Bake like bread, and cut in slices.

Dessert

Quaking Pudding.—Scald 1 qt. of cream (or milk), and when almost cold add 4 eggs well beaten, 1½ spoonfuls of flour, nutmeg, and sugar. Tie it close in a buttered cloth, boil one hour, turn it out with care, and serve with wine sauce.

Cranberry Tarts.
Pears and hickory nuts.

Tea, or Lunch

Cold lamb with tomato catsup.

Kidney Fritters. (4 eggs well beaten, with a teacup of cream or milk, pepper and salt, pounded mace, chopped parsley, and mushrooms, or mushroom catsup. Chop the kidneys fine, and mix together; pour into a buttered pan, and stir over the fire.) Muffins, Graham crackers, bread, quince jelly, macaroons. Tea.

WEDNESDAY

Breakfast.—Beef hash, salt mackerel broiled, cold duck, buckwheat cakes, rolls, boiled hominy. Tea and coffee.

Dinner

A Cheap Soup.—Two lbs. lean beef, 6 potatoes, 6 onions parboiled, a carrot, turnip, head of celery, ½ pt. split peas, 4 qts. water, some whole pepper, and a red herring. Boil well, and rub through a coarse sieve. Serve with fried bread.

Boiled Perch.—Boil quickly with salt, then simmer slowly 10 minutes; melted butter and parsley sauce.

Boiled Mutton, butter sauce, with potatoes, onions, turnips, and carrots.

A French Pie.—Lay a puff paste on the edge of a dish, put veal in slices with forcemeat balls, and sweetbreads cut fine. Add mushrooms, seasoning, cover with gravy, a crust, and bake 1 hour.

Dessert

Hasty Pudding.—One qt. milk, while boiling shake in 2 tablespoonfuls of flour, and stir till it thickens. Put in a deep dish, stir in an oz. of butter, do. sugar, and add grated nutmeg. Sugar sauce.

Floating Island.

Pears, apples, and dates.

Tea, or Lunch

Cold roast veal, birds stewed and spiced, cold.

Potato fritters. (Boil 2 large potatoes, scraped fine, 4 eggs, 1 large spoon of cream, do. wine, a squeeze of lemon, and a little nutmeg. Beat the batter ½ an hour, and fry in boiling lard.) Corn pone, crackers, and cheese, stewed pears, dry toast, bread, tea.

Seed Cake. (1½ lbs. flour, 1 lb. sugar, 8 eggs, 1 oz. seeds, 2 spoonfuls yeast, and same of milk.)

THURSDAY

Breakfast.—Cold rabbit, minced mutton, poached eggs, corn muffins, rice cake, rolls. Tea and coffee.

Dinner

Spanish Soup.—Three lbs. beef, 1 lb. ham, cover well with water, boil and skim. Add a teaspoonful pepper, simmer 2 hours; cook separately a cup of rice, onions cut small, and cabbage. Eat them separate from the soup if desired.

Roast Oysters.

Roast Veal, with corn, tomatoes, and baked mashed potatoes.

Beef Steak Broiled.

Dessert

Peach Pie.

Matrimony.—Make ice cream, after the Newport receipt, (1 qt. milk, 1 pt. cream, 2 tablespoons corn starch, and the yolk of one egg, sweeten and flavor to taste; mix the corn starch in part of the milk, and add the egg, then add to the milk, boiling hot. When cool it is ready for the freezer,—and mix with fresh, or canned peaches; freeze all together.)

Grapes, chestnuts, and pears.

A pear. *American Practical Cookery Book*, 167.

Tea, or Lunch

Cold roast beef, pickled tripe, crackers with anchovy paste spread on them; raspberry jam, corn bread, dry toast.

Sponge Cake. (Break 10 eggs into a deep pan, with 1 lb. sifted sugar, set the pan into warm water, and beat ¼ of an hour, till the batter is thick and warm. Then take out of the water, and whisk till cold. Stir in lightly 1 lb. flour, and flavor with essence of lemon.) Tea and chocolate.

FRIDAY

Breakfast.—Turkey hash on toast, cold ham, sardines, scallops fried, cream toast, rolls. Tea and coffee.

Dinner

Game Soup.—Take 2 old birds, or pieces left from the table, cut fine, with 2 slices of ham, 3 lbs. of beef, a piece of celery, and 2 large onions. Put on the fire with 5 pts. of boiling water, and stew gently for 2 hours. Then strain, and put back into the pot with some stewed celery, and fried bread, season well, skim, and serve hot.

Lobster.

Roast Lamb, with cauliflower, oyster plant, and potatoes.

Chicken Pie.—Half boil a large fowl, and cut in pieces; put the broth rich into a deep dish with a handful of parsley scalded in milk, and season well. Add the fowl, and bake with a raised crust. When done, lift the crust, and add ½ pt. cream, scalded, with a little butter and flour in it; mix well with the gravy.

Dessert

Apple Pie.

Boiled Rice, in cups, with cream and sugar.

Apples, pears, and nuts.

Tea, or Lunch

Dutch herring, raw oysters, cold hock, milk toast, Graham bread, stewed apples.

Spanish Fritters. (Cut French rolls into pieces length of a finger, mix together one egg, cream, sugar, and cinnamon, and soak them in it. When well soaked, fry a light brown, and serve with wine and sugar sauce.) Chocolate, cheese.

SATURDAY

Breakfast.—Beefsteak with mushrooms, cold potted game, fried Indian pudding, sausage, toast, rolls. Tea and coffee.

Dinner

Venison Soup.—4 lbs. venison cut in small pieces, and stewed gently in brown gravy soup. Strain, and serve with French beans cut in diamonds, adding 2 glasses of port wine; separate from the soup if desired.

Fried Perch.

Roast Turkey, cranberry sauce, with potatoes, beets, and squash.

Irish Stew.—5 thick mutton chops, 2 lbs. potatoes, peeled and cut in halves, 6 onions sliced, and seasoning. Put a layer of potatoes at the bottom of the pan, then a couple of chops, and some onions; then another similar.

Add 3 gills of gravy, and 2 teaspoonfuls mushroom catsup. Cover close, and stew 1½ hours. A small slice of ham is an addition.

Dessert

Baked Apple Dumplings.

Blancmange.

Fruit and nuts.

Tea, or Lunch

Cold tongue, pickled fish, French bread, boiled rice, stewed prunes. *Ginger Pound-cake.* (1 lb. butter, do. sugar, do. flour, 8 eggs, and 2 tablespoons yellow ginger.) Tea and coffee.

SUNDAY

Breakfast.—Cold roast turkey, ham cake, anchovy, toast, fried samp, buckwheat cakes, brown bread, gems. Tea and coffee.

Dinner

Tomato Soup.—Plain beef soup, with 2 cups of fresh or canned tomatoes, well seasoned.

Boiled Cod, oyster sauce.

Roast Ducks, with currant jelly, sweet potatoes, cauliflower, spinach, and stewed potatoes.

Boiled Ham.

Dessert

Minced Pie.

Delicate Dish.

Grapes, apples, and almonds.

Tea, or Lunch

Broiled salmon, cold corned beef, Boston crackers, with tomato catsup, waffles, dry toast, preserved grapes, assorted cakes. Tea.

Feeding the North

1. Andrew F. Smith, *Starving the South: How the North Won the Civil War* (New York: St. Martin's Press, 2011), 9–10.

2. "What Do People Eat?" *Frank Leslie's Illustrated Newspaper* August 29, 1857, col. A., accessed via Thomson-Gale 19th Century U.S. Newspapers, March 2011.

3. Alan Taylor, *William Cooper's Town: Power and Persuasion on the Frontier of the Early American Republic* (New York: Knopf, 1995). Ted Steinberg, *Down to Earth: Nature's Role in American History* (New York: Oxford University Press, 2009), 50–53.

4. William Cronon, *Changes in the Land: Indians, Colonists, and the Ecology of New England* (New York: Hill and Wang, 1983); Steven Stoll, *Larding the Lean Earth: Soil and Society in Nineteenth-Century America* (New York: Hill and Wang, 2002); Virginia DeJohn Anderson, *Creatures of Empire: How Domestic Animals Transformed Early America* (New York: Oxford University Press, 2004)

5. Early American cookbooks contain many calls for such uses for lard, as do handwritten "receipts" or recipes. For published cookbooks, see Amelia Simmons, *American Cookery, or the art of dressing viands, fish, poultry, and vegetables, and the best modes of making pastes, puffs, pies, tarts, puddings, custards, and preserves, and all kinds of cakes, from the imperial plum to plain cake: Adapted to this country, and all grades of life* (Hart-

ford: Printed for Simeon Butler, Northampton, [1798]); Lucy Emerson, *The New-England cookery, or the art of dressing all kinds of flesh, fish, and vegetables, and the best modes of making pastes, puffs, pies, tarts, puddings, custards and preserves, and all kinds of cakes, from the imperial plumb to the plain cake. Particularly adapted to this part of our country* (Montpelier, VT: Printed for Josiah Parks, 1808); Lydia Maria Francis Child, *The Frugal Housewife, Dedicated to Those Who Are Not Ashamed of Economy* (Boston: Carter and Hendee, 1830); Eliza Leslie, *Seventy-five Receipts For Pastry, Cakes, And Sweetmeats* (Boston: Munroe and Francis, 1832). Michigan State University has made these four sample texts (and many others) digitized and text-searchable on its "Feeding America" website. Good archival repositories for handwritten receipts directing the processing and use of animal products include the Winterthur Library (in Delaware), the Houghton Library (at Harvard), and the Clements Library (at the University of Michigan). For a larger discussion of lard production and consumption in nineteenth-century American foodways, see Kelly J. Sisson Lessens, "Master of Millions: King Corn in American Culture," Ph.D. diss., University of Michigan, 2011.

6. Stoll, *Larding the Lean Earth*, 47, 80–85.

7. Ann Vileisis, *Kitchen Literacy: How We Lost Knowledge of Where Food Comes From and Why We Need to Get It Back* (Washington, DC: Island Press, 2008), 38.

8. Ibid., 38, 256 n. 236.

9. Cronon, *Changes in the Land,* especially 119–120 and 126–128.

10. William Cronon, *Nature's Metropolis: Chicago and the Great West* (New York: Norton, 1991), 102.

11. John C. Hudson, *Making the Corn Belt: A Geographical History of Middle-Western Agriculture* (Bloomington: Indiana University Press, 1994), 3.

12. Ibid., 6.

13. Ibid., 43–44.

14. Ibid., 68, 80–81.

15. Ibid., 10.

16. Cronon, *Nature's Metropolis*, 103.

17. Hudson, *Making the Corn Belt*, 93–95. See also John Mack Faragher, *Sugar Creek: Life on the Illinois Prairie* (New Haven: Yale University Press, 1986).

18. Jeremy Atack and Fred Bateman, *To Own Their Soil: Agriculture in the Antebellum North* (Ames: Iowa State University Press, 1987), 10.

19. Cronon, *Nature's Metropolis*, 103–104.

20. Charles E. Orser, "Corn-Belt Agriculture during the Civil War Period, 1850–1870," in *Look to the Earth: Historical Archaeology and the American Civil War*, ed. Clarence R. Geier and Susan E. Winter (Knoxville: University of Tennessee Press, 1994), 181–182.

21. William Woys Weaver, *Sauerkraut Yankees: Pennsylvania Dutch Foods and Foodways*, 2nd ed. (Mechanicsburg, PA: Stackpole Books, 2002), 172.

22. On gender and the trope of virgin land, see Annette Kolodny, *The Lay of the Land: Metaphor as Experience and History in American Life and Letters* (Durham: University of North Carolina Press, 1984).

23. Stoll, *Larding the Lean Earth*, 191–193.

24. Andrew F. Smith, *Eating History: Thirty Turning Points in the Making of American Cuisine* (New York: Columbia University Press, 2009), 40.

25. Smith, *Starving the South*, 84–86; Smith, *Eating History*, 37–42.

26. Smith, *Eating History*, 41.

27. Frieda Knobloch, *The Culture of Wilderness: Agriculture as Colonization in the American West* (Chapel Hill: University of North Carolina Press, 1996), 54.

28. Knobloch, *The Culture of Wilderness*, 57. On corn, wheat, and hay production during this time, see Atack and Bateman, *To Own Their Soil*, 182–183. On the 1850s' increase in wheat values, see Cronon, *Nature's Metropolis*, 115.

29. Orser, "Corn-Belt Agriculture," 179.

30. Cronon, *Nature's Metropolis*, 228–229; Hudson, *Making the Corn Belt*, 81–82.

31. Vileisis, *Kitchen Literacy*, 33, 42. See also Daniel Walker Howe, *What Hath God Wrought: The Transformation of America, 1815–1848* (New York: Oxford University Press, 2007), 526.

32. Alfred Chandler Jr., *The Visible Hand: The Managerial Revolution in American Business* (Cambridge: Belknap Press of Harvard University Press, 1977), 81–87.

33. Vileisis, *Kitchen Literacy*, 38.

34. Ibid., 59–63.

35. Vileisis, *Kitchen Literacy*, 61. On passenger pigeons, see also Jennifer Price, *Flight Maps: Adventures with Nature in Modern America* (New York: Basic Books, 1999).

36. X., "What Shall We Eat?" (Boston) *Chronotype,* reprinted in (Rochester) *North Star*, July 27, 1849, col. A; "How to Eat Pineapple," (Bellows Falls) *Vermont Chronicle*, July 30, 1850, col. C; both accessed via Thomson-Gale 19th Century U.S. Newspapers, March 2011.

37. "What Do People Eat?" *Frank Leslie's Illustrated Newspaper*, August 29, 1857, col. A., accessed via Thomson-Gale 19th Century U.S. Newspapers, March 2011.

38. Harriet Robinson, *Loom and Spindle, or Life Amongst the Mill Girls with a Sketch of "The Lowell Offering"* (New York: Thomas Y. Crowell, 1898), 195.

39. Literature on "separate" or "women's" spheres includes Kathryn Kish Sklar, *Catharine Beecher: A Study in American Domesticity* (New Haven: Yale University Press, 1973); Carroll Smith-Rosenberg, "The Female World of Love and Ritual: Relations between Women in Nineteenth-Century America," *Signs* 1, no. 1 (1975): 1–29; Nancy Cott, *The Bonds of Womanhood: "Woman's sphere" in New England, 1780–1835* (New Haven: Yale University Press, 1977); Carl N. Degler, *At Odds: Women and the Family in America from the Revolution to the Present* (New York: Oxford University Press, 1980); Mary P. Ryan, *Cradle of the Middle Class: The Family in Oneida County, New York, 1790–1865* (New York: Cambridge University Press, 1981); Linda K. Kerber, "Separate Spheres, Female Worlds, Woman's Place: The Rhetoric of Women's History," *Journal of American History* 75, no. 1 (1988): 9–39.

40. On urban dwellers' growing ignorance of foods and of running a house, see Vileisis, *Kitchen Literacy*, 41, 46–47.

41. Ibid., 44.

42. Weaver, *Sauerkraut Yankees*, 19–22.

43. Hasia Diner, *Hungering for America: Italian, Irish, and Jewish Foodways in the Age of Migration* (Cambridge: Harvard University Press, 2001), 126, 128, 103–106.

44. On regional preferences, see Steven Mintz, "Food in America," http://www.digitalhistory.uh.edu/historyonline/food.cfm, accessed March 11, 2011.

45. Child, *The Frugal Housewife*.

46. On Hale and Beecher as literary domestics, see Mary Kelley, *Private Woman, Public Stage: Literary Domesticity in Nineteenth-Century America* (New York: Oxford University Press, 1984); Beecher and Hale quoted in Harvey Levenstein, *Revolution at the Table: The Transformation of the American Diet* (Berkeley: University of California Press, 2003), 13–14.

47. Diner, *Hungering for America*, 126, 128.

48. Donna R. Gabaccia, *We Are What We Eat: Ethnic Food and the Making of Americans* (Cambridge: Harvard University Press, 1998), especially 134.

49. *Cleveland Daily Herald*, December 4, 1841, col. B.; *Charleston* (S.C.) *Mercury*, August 2, 1859; both accessed via Thomson-Gale 19th Century U.S. Newspapers, March 2011.

50. Paul Ruschmann, "Beer Gardens," in *The Oxford Companion to American Food and Drink*, ed. Andrew F. Smith (Cambridge: Oxford University Press, 2007), 45.

51. Gabaccia, *We Are What We Eat*, 134.

52. Ruschmann, "Beer Gardens" and "Beer Halls," in Smith, *Oxford Companion*, 45–46.

53. See "Five Points, 1827," *Valentine's Manual*, 1855. Lithographers: McSpedon & Baker, in W. T. Lhamon, *Raising Cain: Blackface Performance from Jim Crow to Hip Hop* (Cambridge: Harvard University Press, 1998), 14.

54. Ibid., 20, 25.

55. Mark Kurlansky, *The Big Oyster: History on the Half Shell* (New York: Random House, 2007), 124–128.

56. Ibid., 184–197.

57. For a comparative look at the place of sugar in the diets of the British working poor, see Sidney Mintz, *Sweetness and Power: The Place of Sugar in Modern History* (New York: Penguin, 1986).

58. Seth Rockman, *Scraping By: Wage Labor, Slavery, and Survival in Early Baltimore* (Baltimore: Johns Hopkins University Press, 2009), 178–179. On sugar's price decrease, see Levenstein, *Revolution at the Table*, 32.

59. Levenstein, *Revolution at the Table*, 23.

60. Kurlansky, *The Big Oyster*, 157–159.

61. Ibid., 160–162.

62. John Mack Faragher, *Women and Men on the Overland Trail*, 2nd ed. (New Haven: Yale University Press, 2001), 11.

63. John D. Unruh, *The Plains Across: The Overland Emigrants and the Trans-Mississippi West, 1840–60* (Urbana: University of Illinois Press, 1993), 145–155. See also Jacqueline B. Williams, *Wagon Wheel Kitchens: Food on the Oregon Trail* (Lawrence: University Press of Kansas, 1993).

64. Susan Lee Johnson, *Roaring Camp: The Social World of the California Gold Rush* (New York: Norton, 2000), 99–122.

65. Ibid..

66. Reginald Horsman, *Feast or Famine: Food and Drink in American Westward Expansion* (Columbia: University of Missouri Press, 2008), 196; Joseph R. Conlin, *Bacon, Beans, and Galantines: Food and Foodways on the Western Mining Frontier* (Reno: University of Nevada Press, 1986), 90–95.

67. Johnson, *Roaring Camp*, 120; Horsman, *Feast or Famine*, 197–198.

68. Arthur Ignatius Judge, ed., *A History of the Canning Industry* (Baltimore: Canning Trade, 1914), 10–14.

69. Ibid., 7–8.

70. On early canning, see also Vileisis, *Kitchen Literacy*, 76.

71. Smith, *Starving the South*, and Steinberg, *Down to Earth*, 95.

72. Douglas V. Meed, *Essential Histories: The Mexican War, 1846–1848* (Oxford: Osprey, 2002), 21, 55–56.

73. Cronon, *Nature's Metropolis*, 230.

74. Ibid., 231.

75. See Gavin Weightman, *The Frozen Water Trade: A True Story* (New York: Hyperion, 2003).

76. Cronon, *Nature's Metropolis*, 218, 230.

77. Ibid., 209.

78. Ibid., 210.

79. Smith, *Starving the South*, 80–81; Steinberg, *Down to Earth* 95; Smith, *Eating History*, 69.

80. Judge., *History of the Canning Industry*, 43, 19, 41.

81. Ibid., 8–10; Smith, *Starving the South*, 80.

82. Smith, *Eating History*, 68–72.

83. Letter quoted in Mrs. P. A. Hanaford, *The Young Captain: A Memorial of Capt. Richard C. Derby, Fifteenth Regt., Mass. volunteers, who fell at Antietam* (Boston: Degen, Estes, 1865), 131; Edward H. Underhill, "Campaigning with the Light Artillery," 3:1221, and John M. Farrington, "137th Regiment Infantry: Historical Sketch," 3:940, in New York Monuments Commission for the Battlefields of Gettysburg and Chattanooga et al., *Final Report on the Battlefield of Gettysburg* (Albany: J. B. Lyon Company, Printers, 1900). All three sources are also discussed in Jim Rupp, "Food in the American Civil War," http://www.articlesbase.com/history-articles/food-in-the-american-civil-war-3287769.html#ixzz1HGZiwU6h, accessed March 2011.

84. *The Ripley* (OH) *Bee*, August 8, 1861, accessed via Thomson-Gale 19th Century U.S. Newspapers, March 2011.

85. "What the Soldiers Eat," (Philadelphia) *North American and United States Gazette* July 14, 1862, accessed via Thomson-Gale 19th Century U.S. Newspapers, March 2011.

86. Knobloch, *The Culture of Wilderness*, 55; Smith, *Eating History*, 78–80.

87. Smith, *Eating History*, 80.

Seeing the Civil War Era through Its Cookbooks

1. Some Americans had celebrated a Thanksgiving holiday for years, especially after Sarah Josepha Hale, the editor of the popular *Godey's Lady's Book* and author of the Thanksgiving poem, "Over the River and through the Woods," launched a campaign in its support in the mid-1840s. Thanksgiving was only the third official national holiday, after Washington's Birthday and Independence Day. Andrew F. Smith, *Starving the South: How the North Won the Civil War* (New York: St. Martin's Press, 2011), 145–162.

2. Nancy Siegel, "Cooking Up American Politics," *Gastronomica: The Journal of Food and Culture* 8, no. 3 (2008): 53–61.

3. In the North, the United States Sanitary Commission supported the growing network of military hospitals with diet kitchens. Barbara Haber, "Pretty Much of a Muchness: Civil War Nurses and Diet Kitchens," in *From Hardtack to Homefries: An Uncommon History of American Cooks and Meals* (New York: Free Press, 2002), 34–60.

4. Hasia Diner, *Hungering for America: Italian, Irish, and Jewish Foodways in the Age of Migration* (Cambridge: Harvard University Press, 2001); and Donna R. Gabaccia, *We Are What We Eat: Ethnic Food and the Making of Americans* (Cambridge: Harvard University Press, 1998).

5. See John Kasson, *Rudeness and Civility: Manners in Nineteenth-Century Urban America* (New York: Hill & Wang, 1990).

6. This publishing boom only accelerated after the Civil War, as economic growth and vast improvements in transportation in the last quarter of the nineteenth century coincided with a revolution in printing technologies, so that books could be produced in unprecedented quantities and distributed widely. Ibid., 37–43.

7. For example, Smith describes how some Northern soldiers eagerly ate care packages of moldy food. Smith, *Starving the South*, 152.

8. For example, Mary Cornelius observed casually, "Sandwich Island arrow-root is as good as the Bermuda for such purposes, and costs a third less." Mary Hooker Cornelius, *The Young Housekeeper's Friend* (Boston: Taggard & Thompson, 1863), 95. For more on the international provenance of American ingredients, see Kristin Hoganson, *Consumers' Imperium: The Global Production of American Domesticity, 1865–1920* (Chapel Hill: University of North Carolina Press, 2007).

9. For more on the standardization of American culinary measurements, see Laura Shapiro, "The Mother of Level Measurements," in *Perfection Salad: Women and Cooking at the Turn of the Century*, 2nd ed. (New York: Random House, 2001), 100–119.

Mary Hooker Cornelius,
The Young Housekeeper's Friend

1. Amelia Simmons, *American Cookery: or the art of dressing viands, fish, poultry, and vegetables, and the best modes of making pastes, puffs, pies, tarts, puddings, custards, and preserves, and all kinds of cakes, from the imperial plum to plain cake: Adapted to this country, and all grades of life* (Hartford: Printed for Simeon Butler, Northampton, 1798), Michigan State University Special Collections.

2. A beer quart almost certainly referred to a standard quart measure today, meaning four cups or 32 liquid ounces.

3. The phrase "a plenty of cold water" is original.

4. To try lard meant to render it, as by melting.

5. "Spinage" was a common way of spelling "spinach" in the nineteenth century.

6. The author originally categorized all of the following recipes for pickled items under "On Cooking Vegetables."

7. Mango was a generic pickling term, not a reference to the fruit known as mango today. In the nineteenth century, "mango" could refer to any fruit that had been pickled whole with spices.

8. Muskmelons refers to a category of melons with aromatic orange flesh and netted rinds, of which cantaloupes are only one example. Her spelling of "cantelopes" is original.

9. Hartshorn referred to carbonate of ammonia, also used in smelling salts.

Mrs. S. G. Knight, Tit-Bits; Or, How to Prepare a Nice Dish at a Moderate Expense

1. The phrase "a fresh water" is original.

2. The author originally wrote "the long bone," rather than "the long bones."

3. Nineteenth-century authors sometimes spelled nasturtiums as "nasturtions."

4. "Cold slaw" was a common alternative spelling to "coleslaw."

5. The editor inserted "that" for clarity in this sentence.

6. Maizena is a brand name of cornstarch.

7. Today, it seems strange that the author categorized "Pancakes" under "Puddings." But it seems less strange when we think that most nineteenth-century puddings were not creamy dairy desserts but heavier dishes made from a batter of flour and eggs, very similar to the ingredients in pancake batter. In fact, people at the time could—and apparently did—think of pancakes as another way of cooking the same kind of batter that was used in puddings. In this case, the recipe would have produced something closer to fried apples than hot cakes.

8. By "moss," the author was referring to Irish Moss, a common thickening agent made from red algae.

9. A demijohn was a large bottle or vessel with a narrow neck, usually with the capacity to hold between three and ten gallons of liquid.

10. "Summer complaints" was a euphemism to describe intense—and dangerously dehydrating—summer diarrhea, caused in many cases by contaminated water.

P. K. S., What to Do with the Cold Mutton: A Book of Réchauffés, Together with Many Other Approved Receipts for the Kitchen of a Gentleman of Moderate Income

1. The author used "maccaroni" instead of "macaroni" in the first reference to the pasta in the sentence. Since the author otherwise uses "macaroni," the editor changed it here for consistency.

2. A salamander was a round sheet of metal that was placed in the fire until very hot and then held above a dish to brown it. Nineteenth-century cooks sometimes used a heated shovel for the same purpose.

3. The author originally wrote "sippers of toast." "Sippets" was commonly used in nineteenth-century cookbooks, including later in this one, to describe thin slices of toasted bread.

Ann Howe, The American Kitchen Directory and Housewife

1. Andrew F. Smith, *Starving the South: How the North Won the Civil War* (New York: St. Martin's Press, 2011), 145–162.

2. For more on the transitions between home baking and industrial baking, see Aaron Bobrow-Strain, *White Bread: A Social History of the Store-Bought Loaf* (Boston: Beacon Press,

2012). See also Ruth Schwartz Cowan, *More Work for Mother: The Ironies of Household Technology from the Open Hearth to the Microwave* (New York: Basic Books, 1983), 59–63.

3. The spelling of "cardamums" and "cummin" is original.

4. A "sound" is the air bladder of a fish, a gas-filled sac that helps fish remain at desired depths in water. Air bladders can also be used to produce or receive sounds, hence the name. A cod "tongue" is not the fish's tongue but rather a small, succulent muscle found on the fish's neck.

5. "Scollops" was a common alternative spelling of scallops.

6. "Ochra" was a common alternative spelling of okra.

7. "Maccaroni" was a common alternative spelling of macaroni.

8. Nineteenth-century authors often used "nasturtion" to spell the flower that would be called "nasturtiums" by the twentieth century. When pickled, nasturtium buds have a taste similar to capers.

9. The author originally wrote "peal," but the editor corrected the spelling because Howe otherwise uses "peel" in her text.

10. The spelling of "carraway" is original.

11. Nineteenth-century authors sometimes referred to egg "yelks" instead of egg "yolks."

12. The phrase "the whole in well" is original.

13. The spelling and phrasing is original.

14. A junk bottle was a heavy bottle made of dark glass.

15. Spermaceti was a waxy substance extracted from the heads of sperm whales, which was often used in home remedies or domestic products in the nineteenth century.

What Shall We Eat? A Manual for Housekeepers, Comprising a Bill of Fare for Breakfast, Dinner, and Tea, for Every Day in the Year

1. See John Kasson, *Rudeness and Civility: Manners in Nineteenth-Century Urban America* (New York:, Hill & Wang, 1990).

2. The author originally wrote "sifted flower" instead of "sifted flour."

3. The spelling of "majoram" is original.

4. Unbolted means unsifted.

5. Bannock (as it is usually spelled) is a biscuit made with oatmeal or barley meal, or, especially in New England, corn bread baked on a griddle. The qualifier "Indian" suggests the latter.

6. A miroton is a thick, seasoned sauce poured over sliced meat or fish.

7. Like the East India Pickle suggested in Ann Howe's cookbook, India Pickle would have referred to a mix of vegetables pickled in vinegar, cloves, and other spices.

8. Savoy biscuits were small sponge cakes, also called ladyfingers.

9. A tammy was a rough piece of cloth used to strain foods.

GLOSSARY OF NINETEENTH-CENTURY COOKING TERMS

This glossary contains terms that appeared multiple times in the cookbooks, which the editor judged likely to be unfamiliar to modern readers. If an obscure term appeared only once, its meaning is indicated in a note rather than in the glossary.

arrowroot	The starch from the tropical arrowroot plant, used as a thickener in cooking.
blancmange	A gelled custard.
bushel	A unit of measure equivalent to thirty-two quarts, or eight gallons.
do	An abbreviation of ditto.
firkin	A small barrel or vessel, or a unit of measure roughly equivalent to eleven gallons.
flummery	A thick custard.
gill	A half-cup, or four fluid ounces.
indian meal	Corn meal. "Indian" was used in recipe titles like Indian pudding or Indian cake to indicate that they were made with corn meal.
isinglass	A collagen made from fish bladders that served roughly the same role as gelatin.
lights	The lungs of an animal.
made mustard	Prepared fluid mustard, as opposed to dry or powdered mustard.
Maizena	A brand of corn starch.
peck	A unit of measure equivalent to eight quarts, or two gallons.
pounded	Crushed to a fine powder.
rennet	A substance made from the lining of animal stomachs, used to curdle milk for cheese-making and other purposes.
rusty	Rancid, when referring to meat.

sago	A kind of starch derived from tropical palm stems, usually available as a flour or in pearls, similar to tapioca.
saleratus	A form of bicarbonate of potash, roughly equivalent to modern baking soda.
saltpetre	Potassium nitrate, used in curing meat.
samp	Coarsely ground cornmeal, or a cornmeal porridge.
sour	Stale or spoiled, often used to refer to old bread.
souse	A dish in which meat was boiled and then soused, or soaked, in vinegar and spices.
spider	A long-handled frying pan with legs.
vol-au-vent	Saucy meat or fish surrounded by a pastry shell. Sometimes used to refer to the dish as a whole and sometimes to the pastry alone.

INDEX

A

African Americans, 11, 16, 23–24. *See also* slavery

alcohol, 15–16, 27, 77, 157. *See also* beer; beverages; mead; rum; syllabub; wine

almond dishes: cake, 161; custard, 163; pudding, 170

American cuisine, 28, 32

anchovy sauce, 83

apple dishes: baked, 52; crab-apple preserves, 56; dumplings, 143, 168; fritters, 169; jam, 97; pie, 47, 92, 163; pomme mange, 167; pudding, 50; puffs, 162; sauce, 99; soufflé, 180

arrowroot dishes: blanc-mange, 53; ice cream, 139; pudding, 159

asparagus, 68–69; soup, 175–76

Aunt Chloe's biscuits, 87

B

bakeries, 113

Baltimore pie, 93

barley dishes: broth, 159; water, 72

bass, 64

Beacon Street sauce, 98

bean soup, 167, 168

beans: string, 68, 127; baked, 127–28

Beecher, Catharine, 14–15, 17

beef, 78; alamode, 58, 79, 171; au gratin, 108; brisket, 58; corned, 79, 118; curing, 66; frizzled smoked, 60; hashed, 108; heart, 79; patties, 158; potted, 109; ragout, 161; savory, 79; smothered in onions, 118; soup, 158–59; spiced, 78–79; stew, 79; tea, 72, 148–49; tongue, 79

beer, 15, 73, 101, 147

beets, 126

Berwick pie, 92

beverages, 73, 147–48. *See also* invalid cookery

bird's nest pudding, 50, 90, 142

biscuits: Aunt Chloe's, 87; brown, 163; buttermilk, 44; drop, 133; hard, 133; soda, 86; sour milk, 86; Tessie's wheaten, 23–24, 102

blackberry pudding, 179

blancmange, 98, 166; arrowroot, 53; calf's foot, 53; isinglass, 53; moss, 97

blockade of South, 19, 31

bohemian cream, 172

Borden, Gail, 20

Boston crackers, 170

brains. *See* calf: brains; calf: head; lamb dishes: head; mock turtle soup; *ris de veau*; sweetbreads

brand names, 30–31, 42, 88, 144, 182